MOSTLY MAINE

MOSTLY MAINE

Short Stories
and Other Writings

by Edward M. Holmes

Illustrated by Arline K. Thomson

University of Maine at Orono Press
Orono, Maine

FIRST EDITION

Copyright © 1977 by the University of Maine at Orono Press. All rights reserved. No part of this publication may be reproduced by any means whatsoever, whether mechanical, electronic, photographic, or otherwise, without the prior permission in writing from the publisher.

Manufactured in the United States of America.

ISBN 0–89101–035–1

Library of Congress Card Catalog Number: 77–085638

9 8 7 6 5 4 3 2 1

CONTENTS

ACKNOWLEDGMENTS

"Across Decades" is reprinted with permission from *Maine Life* (March 1974), Liberty, Maine.

"Catabasis" is reprinted from *Bachy* 7 (Summer 1976), Papa Bach Paperbacks, Los Angeles, California.

"The Clam Clique of Carmody Bay" is reprinted with permission from *The National Fisherman* (January 1973), Camden, Maine.

The epigraph at the head of "Evading the Dumbbell Life" is reprinted with permission from "The Last Days of Cowboy Capitalism," by 'Adam Smith,' *The Atlantic Monthly,* CCXXX (September 1972), 49, copyright 1972 by The Atlantic Monthly Company, Boston, Mass.

"Hadwell Versus Otis" is reprinted from *Marshroots,* II (May 1973), 2, The University of Maine, Orono, Maine.

"Jail Ain't What It Was" is reprinted from *Down East Magazine* (January 1961), Camden, Maine.

"A Memory for Mother's Day" is reprinted from *Marshroots,* III (Fall 1973), University of Maine, Orono, Maine.

"Lost and Found" is reprinted with permission from *Maine Life* (July 1974), Liberty, Maine.

"Please Don't Lean on the Counters" is reprinted with permission from the December, 1973 issue of *Yankee Magazine* published by Yankee, Inc., Dublin, N.H., copyright 1973.

MOSTLY   MAINE

INTRODUCTION:
EVADING THE DUMBBELL LIFE

> "They don't want to have what one of them called a
> dumbbell life, which is to say a blob of work at one end, a
> blob of home life at the other, and a conduit between, a
> railroad or a freeway. There's a lot of stuff about walking
> on the beach, that the worthy cause is themselves, and that
> work should fit life, not the other way around, and they
> talk a lot about intimate relationships, wives, children,
> and so on. . . ."
>
> Former Dean of Admissions
The Harvard Business School

And it's taken all these decades for enough of them to come to that
conclusion to make even a dent on the Harvard Business School!
Something I could have told them, tried sometimes to tell everyone,
and especially my mother, almost forty years ago when the NRA was
on its way.

Not that I hadn't tried the work ethic: selling bathrobes at R.H.
Macy's for instance, from which spot I was fired for coming to work
without a hat, or numbly existing between the nice-nice stuffiness of
Montclair at one end of the D.L. & W. and the dollar-obsessed
stuffiness of Wall Street at the other until this angel with a flaming
sword in one hand and *liberté* burned into his forehead met me on

the Hoboken ferry and offered me ten-dollars-a-week-and-found to be stage carpenter and seaman on a floating theatre. Already I had discovered that some money came at too high a price and that the only things worth doing for money were things you would do whether you were paid or not.

But in three months the floating theatre became, of course, a financial flop, and there I was again one of the one-out-of-twelve unemployed, with nothing but one unemployed showgirl to show for my brief flier in the living market. Discouraging, but not frightening. No worse than waking up in a small town on the banks of the Weser as I had one July, to find myself in on the opening scene of the German Republic's bank holiday with exactly three marks negotiable currency in my pocket, or going broke in Paris with four days between me and my job on the *M.S. Lafayette* at Le Havre, or going through customs and stepping out into West End Avenue without a nickel for carfare or a telephone booth. So I went up to the old-home attic and dug out a canvas backpack, which I filled with cold-weather gear, foul-weather gear, *Walden,* and *Moby Dick,* and hit the highway for towns north, then west, then south, in search of newspaper or perhaps other employment: Waterbury, Concord, St. Albans, Syracuse, Oswego, Superior, Hibbing, Fort Wayne, Oil City, Wheeling, and then Ashland, where I fell afoul of Lyman trying to sober up at the intersection of a dirt road and the tarmac, now and then signalling one of the rare cars that rattled south. He wore a black suit, a black tie, and a grayish shirt that he'd been sleeping in for three days, and he started talking at me before I could even hear his voice, let alone understand much of it once I could hear it. But if him and me was to walk down this road together, soon as some of his friends come by they would give us a ride and we would get to Paintsville right smart. He had not been drunk but three days. Some of the boys said, "Come on, have a drink with us," and here he was. He had tried to ride home last night on the freight train, but the trainman had pushed him off with an open palm: *Too* goddam drunk to ride on freight train! So he was walking, afraid he might get arrested again, like the time in St. Louis when the judge says: "Lyman, when that little girl comes out of the institution, you are going to marry her." "Oh, no I'm not, Judge." "Why not, Lyman?" "Well, Judge, I'd just as leave go to the penitentiary for one thing as another: I'm married already."

"And what about your wife?" I asked.

"Oh, she's in Kansas City. I only lived with her ten days."

"How do you get out of troubles anyway?"

"My father — having sufficient currency. . . ." He made a vague palm-like motion with one hand as if he were polishing the top of a newall post, a motion which implied that, decorously, it explained all things.

The Kentucky sun, at mid-May Day, baked our backs. Near a country school, supervised children, singing, danced around a be-ribboned pole, and watching them, I pondered what it could be that drove me off prowling cross-country in the company of something like Lyman, when any sensible suburban youth would gracefully be seeking comfortable contacts along the Manhattan-Essex County axis, or perhaps courting a millionairess.

Trust your deepest psychic needs, some knowledgeable bloke once said, and doing that, I had found myself roaming suburban streets nights and gravitating to the poorest sections I could find: no lawns, no landscaping, no formidable, if not forbidding, front entrances.

"Wallio! Hey, boy!" "Frankee! Goddam, lend me half a buck." "Ah-h, stingotz!"

"Who's that a picture of, Miss Dawson?" "That's my boy, Marie."
"Your boy?" "Sure, my boy." "But my God, Miss Dawson, he's white!"
"Harr-arrh yes. But he's my boy, Marie."
Music of a kind.

A horn blast and exhaust roar jolted me back into Kentucky. I jumped into the bushes to let him pass, tires churning road dust into our nostrils.

"Well, damn that Archie," Lyman said. "I ain't never going to buy him another drink."

Lyman's friends — they all had something in common, I noticed: they would slow down just enough to get a good look at him and me, then soar past faster than ever. We sweated, and toiled up hill toward an oasis — Schlitz, Blue Ribbon, Red Cap. "Er-r, how much currency do you have on your person?" Lyman inquired sedately.

"Oh, about eighty cents," I lied.

"Well, if you will stake me to a beer when we come to this tavern we are approaching, once we reach my home in Paintsville, I shall re-imburse you to the extent of one dollah to he'p you on your way."

"Now that is right nice of you," I told him, and when we reached the bar I did indeed buy him a beer, and one for myself, and sat quietly at one side, belching in a contented way, and staring, fasci-

nated, at the outrageously attractive blond-haired, blue-eyed lad
who sat cross-legged on the bar, one hand clutching a bare foot, and
the other, with Schlitz by the neck, gesticulating, as he described in
minute detail the dimensions and quality of the valley's young
women — shape of breasts, the texture of bellies, the softness of lips.

It could not last, of course, and when Lyman and I finally
returned to our lonesome road, we were just in time to catch two
heavy-laden trucks toiling up the highway and over the mountain.
Lyman jumped onto the tailgate of the first and beckoned to me to
follow, but I pretended I could not make it, and instead chose a
precarious spot atop the load of cord wood that followed, not much
caring about where I was going or who was driving, or how he was
going to feel about an uninvited guest — not, that is, until, for no
reason I could discern, he drew up alongside the road and came to a
stop where there were no buildings, no homes, no sheds, no cross-
roads, or even fences, nothing but woods, woods and our mountain
highway. Worse, I heard him open the cab door and dismount.
Trembling, I peeped over the edge of the truck: he was circling it,
looking for something. Me perhaps? I flattened myself on the logs,
barely breathing, and waited, muscles tensed, pulse high, even after
he apparently climbed back into the cab and slammed the door. Was
he the kindly mountaineer, or the suspicious, violent variety? I
waited, and waited, and waited. No movement. No sound. Nothing.
I concluded he must be asleep, and lay as if paralyzed, not daring to
risk the sound of a motion. Only when the engine at last started
again and the truck began to roll slightly, did I dare climb aft, lower
myself to the road, and dash instantly into the shelter of the woods,
where I rested until the highway was silent.

Once more I walked, my feet scuffing the gutter dust, the back
of my neck gently baked in the soft, windless sun. It could have been
worse — I knew that — as I walked, waited, and walked. And then
along came Donnie, gliding his "Amy Dear" to a gentle stop on a
slight upgrade — the only way, I later discovered, that Donnie's
truck could gently do anything.

Donnie was stringy, gentle voiced, and casual of speech, and he
was job-hunting with his truck, hauling anything anywhere for
anybody. His T-shirt was splotched; his jeans, torn and worn at the
knee; but he was bound home to Darling Amy and wanted someone
to talk to while he did it. By God he loved Amy: there wasn't another
wife like her in all Kentucky, and if he thought she ever would find
out about his laying other women, he'd never touch one again.

I told him that was a noble sentiment, and he agreed, wondering if I liked to drink whiskey, which I said I did, so we came to a gradual pause at the next general store (desolated — all fields and woods — who were the customers? crows and rabbits?), where Donnie laid out seventy cents, half mine, half his, for a half-pint of something brown and alcoholic, which, while he shifted gears and swung the wheel at mountain turns, we passed back and forth, drinking from the bottle.

And then suddenly, without warning, there was Sugah, a highway hazard if I ever saw one, gray trousers pulled tight over saucy buttocks, and jettish hair provocatively flung shoulder length, lifting one thumb overhead and casually pointing down the road. She never even turned her head, which shows how much she knew: for Donnie she didn't have to.

He brought both bare feet down on the brake and clutch pedals, and with a somewhat delayed reaction "Amy Dear" slowed, drifted, and eased into a gentle glide. While we were still in motion, Donnie swung open the cab door, leaned out, and craning his neck, shouted words of joyous encouragement: "Come on, Sugah! Hurry! Run!"

Sugah did not run. Why should she? She walked to the nearest entrance and took her place between the two of us as if she owned it, which, for the time being at least, I guess she did. Her neck was grimy and some of the dirt had come off on her once-white blouse. Her fingernails were in mourning, but the lipstick was still bright, and the eyebrows dark. And just after Donnie had got us rolling again — before we had really had a chance to say anything one way or another — along comes this bright red pick-up truck and roars alongside to pass.

"Blow your horn! Blow your horn!" Sugah screamed, reaching over to the center of the wheel and doing it herself. "I want that boy to know I got a ride!"

"What boy?" Donnie asked.

"That boy. I been out with him three days. But I told him, 'I don't have to have you to go home with. I got a thumb!' "

"Ah. What was wrong?" Donnie shifted into second on an upgrade.

"He wanted me to go into this restaurant, but I told him I wasn't going into no such a goddamn hole. Last time I was there they insulted me, wouldn't give me no place to sit."

"Well, I'll be damned."

"So I said, 'Go ahead in there if you want to. I don't need you anyways!' And I don't."

"You sure don't, Sugah," Donnie said. "Ain't you from Pikeville?"

"Yeah."

"Thought I'd seen you around. You in that gray house on the other side of town?"

"And a hell of a pigpen, too — if it is my goddamn sister-in-law's."

"Yeah, I remember. Seen you there once or twice."

"That place," she says. "The other night I come into the front room and there they was, all setting at tables with their drinks and girls, and the music had just gone off, and I clapped my hands right loud: 'Clap, clap, clap, everybody!' I shouted. 'I've got the clap!' "

"Did you?" Donnie asked.

"They all looked at me and then started talking, and pretty soon this great big fellow about seven feet tall gets up from the table where he was setting with two of the girls and staggers over to me. He stands there, swaying back and forth. 'Are you the little girl says you got the clap?' 'Mebbe I am and mebbe I ain't, mister,' I said. 'Why don't you take a chance?' "

We heard no more from Sugah: a rear tire exploded; Donnie swore mellifluously and brought "Amy Dear" to a ragged, bumbling halt. We all got down on the highway where Sugah, after one glance at the crumpled rubber, turned gracefully to the road, hailed a Buick sedan and almost instantly rode off toward the deep South. Donnie seemed not to miss her, just stared gloomily at the flat tire.

I looked under the body of the truck. "No spare?"

Donnie shook his head.

"Maybe we can patch it."

"No tools neither," Donnie said.

So I stood out in the road beside my back-pack for half an hour until some reckless soul stopped to take me to Pikeville and a garage where I told them about Donnie and "Amy Dear" stranded up there in the valley. Then I beat my way along Route 119, and somewhere or other walked through a town, across a thing they called Big Fork, and into Mingo County, West Virginia.

West Virginia . . .

In Germany, earlier, I had fallen among friends finally, despite having the wrong language and only a scrap of paper with Dr.

Schroeder's name, no street address, and the name of a town that did not even exist. Yet the state railroad, a tall young German in the Bremen station who had once worked in Brooklyn and was homesick to hear somebody speak United States, two taxi drivers, and *drei-und-zwanzig* – all these got me, about two a.m., to the doctor's apartment, where he and his wife pressed upon this strange young American salami, liverwurst, salad, warmed milk, cake, and at last schnaps, under the influence of which, the doctor, V.M.D., discovered that he (the young man) could speak a kind of eccentric schoolboy French, and thereafter communicated the changing facts of life of July 1931, when suddenly no one in Germany could cash a check — no, not even American Express — nor change foreign money, nor draw his pay from the government, nor leave the country, if he were a citizen, without official permission. So next day the doctor translated the four-inch headlines for him into French, explained the mass meetings in the park across the street — first Communists, then Nazis, then Communists again — translated the paint-splashed signs on walls and buildings (*Arbeit und Brot;* Follow Hitler — He is Going Places!) — no one had to translate the swastika or the hammer and sickle — and after his bilingual friend, the Doctor's nephew, Joachim, joined them, exposed both youths to the best beer and food and whiskey in Wesermunde-Lehe, on the Island of Wamrooge, and in Helgoland (tax-free caviar, tax-free Egyptian tobacco, tax-free champagne — open the bottle with the purser's corkscrew on the gangplank when you board the return boat). And everywhere on the streets, the girls —

"*Gehen-Sie tanzen zum* Haus Vaterland?"

"*Ja, aber nicht mit euch, Frauleins.*" And no wonder. The doctor, after all, was picking up the tabs, was not rich, did not own a car, yet here he was spending, in time of depression, almost lavishly. The young American expressed concern, and was told, in translation: "Had you been through a war, a revolution, and an inflation, this would be nothing." The Doctor took a deep swallow of beer, then ordered steinhagers all around. "We are dancing on a keg of powder," he said.

It seemed like that, for the morning paper daily told of street fights, of stabbings, deaths of the police, or others, or both. And the young American could remember when he was sixteen, a tourist in France, reading in the press of the mobs angry over the execution of Sacco and Vanzetti, throwing bricks through restaurant windows at Americans. It sounded like great sport, but he had not seen it, nor felt it, nor did he see now, nor feel, the violence.

Berlin was different, but not much, really; it was just that the girls were almost ubiquitous, and that the Doctor was no longer with them (the young American had been allowed finally to cash a check). Beutel now was the guide, but Beutel was almost penniless, and it was up to Joachim and him to pick up the tabs. They looked, these young men, as if they might have money, and so at the tables in Berlin's lesser bars, five or six girls that no one would want to kick out of bed, girls needing food — or clothing — or rent-money almost instantly flashed under the trio's faces their license cards that showed the date of the latest medical examination.

He feared them. What had happened since that latest examination? But Beutel, who worked in an insurance office, tutored someone in English, and gave boxing lessons, could afford less than a third of an apartment and one meal (for one mark) a day (crackers and milk for the other two) — Beutel, depression beaten, had given up hope, and two years later died in a Berlin hospital of syphilis.

To Austria, hospitality from Joachim's people among the Alps; on the Paris Express, friendliness from the Czech tourists and an innocent Jewish shopkeeper; and in Paris, kind assistance to the Jew and him both from a quiet French traveller, a cab driver, and a hotel clerk, although the bunch of them could barely communicate at all in speech. Repeatedly in a café on the Rue Magenta they bowed, smiled, sipped their beer, and tipped their hats.

And now, in Mingo County . . .

I had not walked fifty feet into the state before somebody offered me a lift. His voice was kindly and easy, though his appearance was almost as disreputable as mine. Both of us wore scrubby beards and crummy clothes, and were mostly unwashed. His loaded, open-bodied truck, bearing a Kentucky license, was pulled up at the side of the road, and his twin, or something akin to it, was down at the edge of Big Fork, filling a bucket with water which, presently, he carried up the bank and schlurped carelessly into the mouth of the truck's radiator.

I thanked him kindly for the ride and slung my backpack over the high tailgate that helped contain an apparently heavy load of cartonned freight, then started to hoist myself in after it.

"You ride in the cab with us," my host said.

"Oh, that's all right," I told him graciously. "I don't want to crowd you; I'll get along all right in back."

He stared at me curiously for a moment. Then, firmly: "Mister, you are a-going to ride in front."

"Just as you say," I said, and went up and took my place in the middle of the cab.

When all were aboard, and the truck under way, it was a tight fit, but I appreciated the ride and spectacular valley ahead: steep cliffs on the left, spotted with green life, and soaring toward mountain tops; and to the right more steep cliffs dropping away to the ever-lowering Big Fork. And no fence, nothing but rock-edge between us and a sheer, lethal drop . . .

About then the driver shifted into low gear, whereat my host on the right opened the glove compartment and produced a forty-five calibre automatic which he dangled nonchalantly across his lap, its muzzle casually pointed toward my legs. Then with his left hand he opened the cab door and stared back down the valley. "Hit's all right, Joe. They ain't nobody coming."

I held my breath, but how long can a person hold it? When I exhaled, it was with some hint of nervousness.

"Don't you worry, my friend," gun-holder said. "Last week we was hijacked. We lost fifteen hundred dollars' worth of liquor. It ain't going to happen this trip."

Fervently I prayed that it would not, and hastily tried to estimate what my chances were of taking shelter below the dashboard to avoid flying lead. But no hostile forces drove past us in black limousines, or mis-used hearse, or a truck, to bring us to a halt. No shotgun-equipped bandits ambushed us — at least not yet — and meanwhile I was left to wonder why these bootleggers (importers from a low-tax to a high-tax state) had given me a ride. After all, I had not even asked for the lift. Did I look ferocious enough to intimidate a hostile force?

Later, another car driver, black, enlightened me about highway life: "If they was stopped, they was a-going to shoot it out, and after someone was killed, they would throw the gun to the gutter and put *you* out on the highway. You are a vagrant, and you are a damned Yankee, and the State Police would pick *you* up."

But there was no shoot-out, and before we were into the next town, Joe brought the truck to a halt. Gun-holder opened the door and got down. "Mister, you are a-going to get off here."

"Yes sir!" I said, jumping, and then, under his scrutiny, extracted my knapsack from the load in back. Contentedly I stood there, watching them drive ahead, then shouldered the pack and happily walked the two miles into town to a restaurant.

Night fell quickly over that village that crouched in a valley, and I walked a mile, and then rode six in somebody's car to a mountain pass, where the road forked, and my driver left me, because I felt I should head for home through Bluefield and he was going farther south.

A dismal and crumblike lunch room huddled next to a bedraggled gas station close to the forks. I shunned it, for I was not hungry, and for an hour and a half stood, sentrylike, watching bats soar in and out of the forest, awaiting nearly non-existent traffic. Finally, drained of strength and ready for sleep, I moved a hundred feet up the highway and started to climb a gentle rise into the woods. At once I was assailed by a harsh voice from just outside the door of the restaurant: "Where do you think you're going, mister?" I stopped.

The man stood, with his companion, just a few feet from the restaurant door, a double-barrelled shotgun slung gracefully in one hand, the stock hugged gently between elbow and ribs.

"I was just going up here to find six feet of ground to lie down on."

"You go in there, and you'll find six feet to lay in permanently," he said.

"Just as you say." I returned to the road and put down my knapsack.

In a way, I was tempted to go up there and talk to him, to find out, if possible, what harm he thought I'd do, even what made him like that. A still, perhaps? But to face an extra conversation at that end of the day, half way through the night — I was too tired for that. So I stood, and when standing was too much, I walked a little up the road, farther into the shadows. Twice when I did that, shotgun-toter and his mate came promptly out to the highway, waving that double-barrelled menace left and right as they searched. "Where's he at now? Where's he at?"

Each time I replied: "I'm right here, Mac."

This statement was good for another twenty-minute truce.

Then at last, unbelievably, a tractor and trailer the length of a freight car at least, drew up abreast of me and stopped. Cincinnati Red Cap Beer. The driver called to me: "Come around this side. I want to talk to you, mister."

I did as he asked.

"What's your name?" "Where you from?" "Where you going?" "Why?"

I answered all these questions as humanly, as casually as I could.

He looked me over carefully. "Well, I *guess* you're all right. Come around the other side and get in."

Which I did, reaching far above my head, it seemed, to grasp the handle to the cab door, and then to lift myself up, pack and all, to the level of the seat, where I was confronted by a sharp-pointed, eight-inch knife, firmly in the driver's grasp, and aimed, with no uncertainty, at my heart. I paused: he froze: and there we balanced for a few seconds, like living statues, waiting for exactly what? Then slowly he lowered the blade and sheathed it in the leather case at his belt. "That's all right, my friend. This was just in case. We fought the Hatfield-McCoy feud in this valley, and we don't trust nobody!"

I was beginning to understand his feeling, and the next day (after a night's rest in the Bluefield switchyard, a small spot of weedy earth between two of the six or eight switchyard tracks) Arnie, in a different way, taught me to understand more of it. He was driving his coupé east, and had picked me up because he was lonely.

"Mister, it is getting along toward noontime; you and I ought to have a bit of refreshment. Now if you open that glove compartment right there, you'll find a pint of mint gin. I hope you like it.

"No. No! You take the first drink. He'p yourself. . . . There. That's fine, Yes, now I'll have one. . . . Good, ain't it?

"You see, I am not used to drinking with anyone else. In my place of business — I operate a poolroom in Hopkinton up there in the mountains — in my place of business I cannot afford to drink with customers because they get disorderly. I can't have that. And so when one of them gets like that — even if he is a friend of mine (we all grew up together in the same place) — I just do what I have to do: I hit him over the head with a billiard cue and knock him out.

"Now there was Jerry, came to see me last night: 'Arnie,' he says, 'Arnie, you done just right. And you do it again. Any time I am drunk and disorderly, you just reach for the nearest billiard cue and hit me over the head with it.'

"So now, when I want to drink, I buy me a pint and take it up to my room and drink. But they ain't really no pleasure in it."

"No, I should think not."

"Now if you will just pass that bottle again, I will have me another swallow, and then we will stop at a restaurant here and eat dinner. I want to take you to dinner."

"Oh, now, there's no need of your doing that. I have —"

"Mister, I would be proud to take you to dinner. It will be a pleasure for me."

Later, Arnie told me about his throat and about tobacco. There were times his throat just closed up on him, and the only thing to do then was to chew tobacco. "I got a job once being a waiter in a Cincinnati restaurant," Arnie said. "And after I was hired, I went to my employer and I said, 'Mister, there is something I've got to tell you: I chew. And if I disappear for a few minutes out back it is because my throat has closed up tight and I have gone out there to chew just to open it up.' "

"Did he understand?"

"He didn't seem to mind any. But you know, I think I would be better if I had my tonsils out. It is a little too cold nights now, here in May: I might catch cold with that surgery just fresh. But when it warms up a bit — say in July — I'll go to my doctor and have him put me in the hospital and take out those tonsils. Then maybe I won't have to chew."

I advised Arnie to do just that, and an hour later we parted company at a Virginia crossroad, both of us feeling, apparently, as if we had known each other a couple of months.

There was always another car coming on that highway, but only at twenty minute intervals, more or less, and after six of them had ignored me for reasons all doubtless sound and understandable, I succumbed to impatience, beginning to yearn for a few days of a New Jersey suburb, which by now would be lushly flowering, which had my girl in it, and home-cooked food, and a bed with a mattress. I sank even to considering, in a vague way, a spot of job-hunting. And just as my emotions were beginning to steam a bit, along came this shiftless young vagabond, who didn't even carry a backpack, and took up a position on the highway a hundred yards up-traffic from my post. Now in the unwritten and unspoken rules-of-the-road-for-hitch-hikers, such a move is similar to piracy on the high seas. My resentment, powered by both righteousness and self-interest, soared when I was faced with his flagrantly immoral act. I glared at the wretch, who looked away. A car ground tediously up the highway and passed him and me both.

Without caution, without consideration, without thought of the consequences, I shouldered my pack and stalked up to within five feet of him.

"Mister," I said, trying to control my heat, "I was standing here a long time before you were. I am in a hurry. I intend to get the first ride, and I want *you* to walk down the road there at least three hundred feet."

I pointed, and stared at his expressionless face, and after perhaps four seconds, he shifted his gaze and rather hastily did exactly what I had said he should.

Only when the moment was over, when he was really gone, did I suddenly taste the dryness in my mouth, feel the accelerated heart-beat. I was not used to being the source of even tacit threat, nor to being victorious either, and sensed a slight twinge of guilt. So when a somewhat decrepit truck came to a stop beside me and a kindly farmer and his wife offered me a lift almost to Richmond, I asked if they would take the other hitch-hiker too.

"Why certainly, sir, plenty of room."

I waved to the man to come back.

"Only thing is," the farmer was saying as he took a hammer out of his tool chest, "I got no lock, no catch on them doors even. I just drive two three nails in them to hold them shut." With the claw-end he withdrew two ten-penny nails and opened the doors for us.

I climbed aboard; the other hesitated. Then: "No sir! I ain't going to be nailed up in no truck with that goddamned Yankee feller!"

Alone then, nailed-in, tomblike (I thought of Queequeg's life-saving coffin), I was jolted through sixty miles of Virginia landscape in almost utter blackness, and for twenty hours thereafter, sleepless, nerve-taut, dully, mulishly begged my way north toward the megalopolis, toward Jersey City where Mayor ("I-am-the-law") Hague's police seized me, frisked me, and rushed me out of town as if I were a leper, toward much that I knew not was coming (and just as well perhaps): toward the chaos of job-getting and job-losing in a newspaper office, toward consumer co-ops, toward business-managing the health co-op of utopia (Greenbelt, Maryland), toward putting all belongings in a truck and trekking to Maine, toward clam-digging and lobster trucking, toward fishing craft and coastal schooners, toward carpentering in shipyards and a turn at the almost-desert-island stuff; and also toward some of those things the boys at the Harvard Business School were telling the dean about: closeness with wife and children, the worthy cause (ours on a lean budget), walking on the beach (you should see our beach; rocks is more like it), toward mountains, and schools, and involvement with human beings. It led to no vice-presidencies, to no bundles of stock options, to no memberships in country clubs, but just possibly, finally, it was to be worth more than all that.

THE CLAM-CLIQUE OF CARMODY BAY

Twice lately I have read articles about machines designed for clam-digging, and have perused pictures of such moderately outlandish rigs. Since but yesterday it was the conventional wisdom — at least in my neighborhood — that clam-digging called for a strong back and a weak mind, I suppose such devices should be welcomed. But I am not at all sure of it. What, I ask myself, will they do to the clam-cliques, if they still exist, like the one at Carmody Bay that sought out and encompassed me and my wife during the winter of the Phoney War?

Jobless, incomeless, but not hopeless, Jane and I had bought a ton-and-a-half enclosed truck and moved from Maryland to Maine, planning to wedge our way into the lobster-shipping business, living the while far from cities, suburbs, and cirrhossis of the liver. We rented a house near the center of the village of Carmody Bay, and as winter came discovered, by trials which were mostly errors, that although assuredly there were lobsters to be bought, transported, and sold along the east coast of the United States, the best any small operator could do at it that year was to lose money slowly. Discouraged, often I would let the truck stand idle in our driveway while in desultory fashion I walked a tenth of a mile east to the post office, two-tenths of a mile west to the village grocery, and then back, wondering what I ought to do next to make, just possibly, ten cents.

Opportunity in its modest way, however, approached neither from east nor west, but from across the street, where stood the village pool room and barber shop. Its messenger, Harley Benton, was one of several footloose young men — Myricks, Whittens, Beals, Jensons — who spent a considerable number of hours around the barbershop stove and, when they had them, spent an even more considerable number of dimes and quarters, winning and losing at cowboy pool.

Harley came to our woodshed door and asked if I would do some clam-hauling for them. It seemed they had had a fellow with a truck who called for the clams twice a week, took them to the factory and brought back the money, but for reasons unknown to any of them, and without warning, he had quit. "Them clams ain't getting younger," Harley said. "Some of them already growing pretty ripe."

I agreed to his proposal, and at seven the next morning, with Harley to pilot me, I made the rounds of ten or twelve Carmody Bay homes, dwellings, camps — whatever one should call that rural, depression housing where the cheap paint scaled as soon as it dried, the chimneys were porous, the cracked windows were patched with friction tape, and the yards, front, side, and back, looked like the spot where industrial society had reaped the whirlwind. At each stop one of the clam diggers brought out jars, pints, quarts, once in a while a gallon jug filled with clam meats, and I put down in my notebook his name and the number of containers. I remember one man who had a milkcan more than half full of meats which he sniffed and then casually emptied onto the snow-encrusted earth. Later, from experience, I judged that those meats must have cost him, and perhaps his wife also, between twenty-five and thirty hours of severe human effort.

I soon grew used to the semi-weekly trips, even enjoyed them, for putting my foot gingerly into the clam business like this quickly led to a more thorough immersion. Within a day or two, Harley insisted I join him and his friends on the flats. Alton Myrick lent me his second-best clam hoe; Ben Whitten provided a creel; and Orville Jenson a croker sack. When they found that Jane too would dig and help steam out the meats, they supplied her with surplus tools and unofficially made us members of the club.

It meant we went with them as the tide ebbed, trying to learn to dig efficiently, grabbing quickly anything that was a clam or even looked like it, feeling our shirts and sweaters slide up and away from our belts in back, exposing bare flesh to the winter winds, and knowing the harsh pain of stiffened legs, of bent backs.

After four hours of digging down, across, and up the flats, each of us put his take in a burlap sack and deposited it in a tidal pool to prevent freezing. For retrieval, we stretched a rope from the neck of each sack to some rock or tree well above tide level.

The next step was strictly a group effort: all joined in gathering dry wood, and somewhere along shore building a fire under a twenty-gallon galvanized iron tub, in which we steamed each digger's clams — one batch at a time to keep them separate — and working together plucked out the meats and put them into his glass containers. When, after two or more hours, the last man's clams had been picked out, each of us repaired to his home kitchen, enjoyed a brief lunch, and then got out the shears. We would pick up the clams one by one and snip off the black "neck," for although the "necks" were perfectly good, healthy food, consumers recoiled at their appearance, and the canning factory would not accept them. Jane and I usually gave ours to our two long-furred cats.

Including us was a friendly act on the clam-diggers' part, but it was also advantageous for them. They had lost one clam-trucker without notice, an expensive mishap, and if they got this one to dig some clams for himself, he would gain more cash each trip and be less likely to quit. Besides, we used the truck to bring distant wood — driftwood or dead spruce — to stoke the fire for the steaming out.

To Jane and me it made considerable difference: not only could we now work at something that clearly made a dollar, but we had neighbors — Alton and Orville and Ben and Joe — on a first-name basis, and were less isolated, less foreign in what was still, for us, a strange community.

But there was more to clam digging and trucking than what I have said here, and it led to more yet. It was sixty miles to the canning plant, up one peninsula and down the next, and week after week, Harley and sometimes Alvin rode with me, enjoying the ritual, exchanging stories, jokes, singing the day's popular lyrics — "South of the Border," "Ricky Ticky Tin," "Scatterbrain" — and when they forgot the words or grew tired of them, making up others less decent but much more sprightly. We coasted down hills to save fuel, bought cut-rate gas and oil, and ate a sandwich lunch we had brought from home. We kept a careful watch of the scales at the canning factory — seventeen cents a pound for meats — figured the tare down to a half an ounce, and my two-cents-a-pound deduction for freight, then wrote it all down in my little black book.

Coming back, as we passed near the joining of the peninsulas at the county seat, we stopped at the Green Front, and once more consulted the little black book; Orville Jenson — pint of New England rum, $1.20; Alton Myrick — quart of muscatel, $.90; Ben Whitten — pint of gin $1.15; Joe Teele — pint of drinking whiskey, $1.00. And so it went. With the liquor aboard, we drove her for home port.

Back at the house, I put each man's bottle out on our kitchen table, under it a slip of paper accounting for his income and expense, and beside it his remaining cash. While Jane and I, city folks that we were, sat in the dining room to eat, the boys, by ones and twos, would come quietly and without speaking into the kitchen, in the dim half-light collect their money and other loot, and just as quietly go outside and, often with other villagers, climb into the back of our truck, which I had swept, and which I had furnished with a couple of old car seats.

After supper, Jane and I would close the rear doors to the truck, climb into the cab, and with raucous roars behind us, drive everyone about fifteen miles to a neighboring town to the picture show and a dance. Each rider paid me twenty-five cents. The picture was always a serial that usually left the heroine in danger of imminent and catastrophic death, and the dance was sufficiently well-oiled to seem short and sweet — though often it wasn't. Half the county was there, or at least it felt like that: fishermen, clam-diggers, factory workers our landlord, the deputy sheriff, mothers and uncles, fathers and aunts, many of them offering their own and then sampling the other fellow's bottle. Coming home after midnight, the roars and screeches, the songs and shouts from the back of the truck were even more raucous.

And so it went for many Saturday nights, until in April Jane and I packed up and left, not to escape from Carmody Bay, but to go to the fairly remote island from which we had planned to conduct our lobstering business, an island we had delayed moving to, for quite practical reasons, until after the winter.

In one way, it was the wrong time to make a move like that: that spring the Phoney War was phoney no longer; Hitler's men were moving into Norway and Denmark, and people of the Maine coast — the eastern corner of the United States — felt a certain not-too-rational distress. Our friends the clam diggers were silent, but others talked:

"Why would anybody want to move off to a spot like that?"

"I know. No telephone, no store, nothing!"

"Now, son, you don't want to go out there; that is, not unless somebody's paying you $25,000 to do it."

How could I explain to them what a secluded island meant after Washington, after Boston, after New York? I could not, of course, and so I lapsed into silence. But those questions, and the suspicions hiding behind them ("He wouldn't be out there if he wasn't a spy of some sort.") — these followed us along the coast for miles and for months, for years even, with at times unpleasant and even dramatic results. A few of them — the suspicions — are not dead yet. But they were a thing in which the clam-clique — Harley and Myron, Alton and Orville, Ben and Joe — in which none of them ever put any stock. Together we had dug the flats, had turned our fingers blue with the cold, then singed them picking the hot clam meats; we had hauled the freight and sold the meats and swilled the liquor and spent the cash. And there was a bright residue left: we knew, all eight of us, whom to count on for loyalty, whom to trust.

ACROSS DECADES

The day Jim asked me to cross the fields with him to meet Clara Holbrook, Nature was putting on a forecast of coming attractions: fall weather in the midst of summer. A chill northwest wind bent the hay in the meadow and clipped the wave tops in the bay. Almost rhythmically the spruces nodded their heads before it; my hair streamed, and I turned up the collar of my jacket.

As we approached her house, Clara came from the shed door en route to the nearby well, but she stopped and put down her bucket to be introduced to me, the wife Jim Archer had brought with him to Medric Island. Clara was a short woman, not fat, but in no way frail; you could see muscle strength in her hands, her wrists, and feel a not harsh, but certainly trenchant perception in her blue eyes. She smiled, shaking hands firmly, then asked: "How do you like the wind?"

"Oh, I love it," I said without thinking.

She turned to look at Jim, solemnly nodding her head. "She'll do," she said.

I felt that I had, without warning, passed an examination. While Jim dipped the well-sweep, filled her water bucket, and carried it to the shed door, Clara told me how glad she was we were going to be there in the fall. Blaine, the son with whom she lived ashore at Oak Harbor during that half of the year that was unfit for a lone woman, or perhaps anyone else, on Medric Island, would now permit her to stay after the summer people went. Would I please keep an eye on her for his sake — this with a self-deprecating, quizzical smile, as who should say, "One must humor a son some way even if it's silly." There was of course Lew Medric, our only year-around neighbor and an islander of life-long standing, but he was just a man. Obviously Blaine felt a woman, even a young woman, was more likely to tend out on this sort of matter. So would I, please, when I glanced through a window, notice her goings and comings, just to make sure that she did both? She was sorry to be a trouble to me, but Blaine —

If I could not watch her, Blaine would not permit her to stay on into October here in what had been her home, her house, where she could "watch the storms come up and the storms go down." Later, when she went berrying, she promised, she would tell me always which field she was going to. Someday soon she would come to our house to make a formal call.

She never did make the formal call, nor did she ever forget she was planning to make it.

Jim and I found her a difficult neighbor to keep up with: she was merciless about doing favors. If we bailed the rain water out of the pea pod that she still kept at the beach — although it was two or three years since she had rowed the three miles ashore in it — she would bring to our shed door a basket of currants and an ancient magazine, relic of an age well before even the previous Roosevelt. If, grateful for these, we invited her to share a supper, she would soon be back with blueberries and bunches of homegrown carrots. A ten-minute repair job on a door or window brought an avalanche of apples and highland cranberries. In the effort to keep up with favors, we simply lost the race.

Nor could I even fulfill properly her son's request that I know where she was when she went berrying. Conscientiously she would stop at the door to tell me she would be gathering cranberries in the north meadow, yet six hours later, a full bag over her shoulder, she would approach her house directly from the south. It was not that she meant to deceive me; she had simply, as the sun moved, followed the best of the fruit north to south.

Sometimes nights when Jim or I walked past the old open-doored barn attached to her house, we would hear her sawing wood in the dark: no lantern, no moonlight. We knew, too, by experience, that in the morning, with those slim sticks of half-dozy wood, she would build a cautious fire under exactly one of the kitchen stove's potlids. And Lew Medric told us how — in former years when there had still been a year-round village on the island and Clara Holbrook still kept a cow — how she would often milk the same way, in total darkness. Once, he said, she fell asleep there with her head against the critter's side and the milking only half finished.

She saved. She saved everything: bits of string, marling, lobster warp, wood chips, boxes, leaking cans, rusted chisels, lengths of snarled wire, defective lamps. Nearly always, old things that could be patched up and put to use were for her more exciting than shiny new ones. On a nail in her woodshed hung a clean new clothesline, the two-year-old Christmas tag and ribbon still on it: "A Merry Xmas to Mother from Blaine and Ephie." She had never uncoiled it, for the old clothesline was not worn out yet, and to her the new one was, I suppose, much more reassuring than money in the bank.

And she understood herself, was amused at herself in a wry way, and in despairing amusement could forgive herself. She picked up a bucket once from her barn floor and proferred it for my examination. The bottom was half rust, half non-existent; I could have dropped a hen's egg through it in three different places. "Now to most people," she said, "that thing is worthless. But to me it's a good bucket."

I nodded, knowing what she meant, knowing she would fit a false bottom into it — cardboard perhaps — then save it for the carrying of dry produce, as if it were a basket. She might, of course, never have occasion to use it, but that was beside the point — there it hung, usable for someone, some time: stored wealth.

Weeks later she was hunting in her woodshed — something for me it was, I forget what — and turned over an old jacket, five or six weathered clapboards, a time-stained catalogue from Sears Roebuck, a bag of clothes pins, and a rotted dip net, all without success. "The trouble with me is I keep things *too* handy," she said.

And because, in a detached way, she understood herself, she also understood us. We could see it in the wrinkles around her eyes, in the brief shrug of her shoulders, in the slight lift of the arms that sometimes said, "After all, from mere human beings, what do you expect?" For if Jim, and I, and Lew Medric were not as strange in our way as she was in hers, would we be out there, in mid-Depression, on an isolated island, preparing to spend a winter against all practical reason, safety, comfort, and common sense? Recognizing fellow eccentrics, she appreciated us.

I was in her kitchen one morning to borrow — what? Eggs? Baking soda? Yeast? ("We used to frig around with a potato," she said once, "and make yeast.") And while she was at the cupboards, I noticed empty envelopes she had dropped to the floor between the table and the sink. Stooping, I picked them up.

"Now, my dear," she said, accepting the envelopes, "I thank you for your kindness, for you had no way of knowing — *this* one is to remind me to write cousin Sarah a note; this one" — she dropped them one by one — "is to make me put the old jelly jars up attic; and this one is for — well, something I don't want to forget." And she grinned, blinking, permitting us to laugh quietly together about herself.

"Aunt Clara's crazier than a coot," Lew Medric said, sounding exactly like Clara Holbrook talking about Blaine, or Lew, or perhaps — I daresay — us, but he didn't mean it, not really, any more than she would, and Jim and I knew that. Oh, she was odd all right. She was simply, like the rest of us, imprisoned and shackled by her past, only her past was different, different even from that of other Medric Islanders who had known boats and critters and gardens and wood-lots in the days before gas engines, radios, and films in the wooden picture palace off to Oak Harbor helped lure folks ashore.

Even in the late nineteenth century Clara Holbrook's life had been almost like one in the late eighteenth. Little more than a child, orphaned on one coastal island, she had become a bound-out girl, indentured servant to Phil and Dora Holbrook who, with their son, were farming Great Moose Island and fishing the seas around it for subsistence.

Great Moose, a remote two miles of wilderness, lies like some unaimed pancake batter, spotting the northwest border of the griddle of the Gulf of Maine. Every wind takes miles of uninterrupted sweep before bludgeoning it, and seas from the North Atlantic can roll a hundred miles before assaulting this, their first obstruction. It is a grim spot, except sometimes in summer perhaps, but whether the Holbrooks thrived or not, they lived on it, struggling four-foot logs into the fireplace; storing, for food, seabirds and dried fish; raising the mutton, pork, and beef when they could; plowing the sodded soil to plant; saving and re-using everything as long as they could; and storing feathers, wool, and salted fish to barter, at rare intervals, for other and different riches of the earth.

They were alone, neighborless, and so it was little wonder that Clara, when she was sixteen, married Erwin Holbrook. After all, who else? Little wonder too, when you begin to think about the house and its chimney of clay and rocks, that finally one zero night, fire flattened it, forcing the two couples to take shelter in the sheepshed over night, and in the morning row themselves and what little they had left the six miles to the nearest mainland port.

But before a year was out, Erwin Holbrook had had more than he could take of living on a continent. Any island the size of a hemisphere was for him no island whatever. He had to be where he felt surrounded by water, where he could hear, smell, be aware of it at any point of the compass day or night, else he could not sleep. And so Erwin and Clara Holbrook moved to Medric Island where there was a village, a church, a cemetery, a post office; to an island which was a little less remote, a little less inaccessible, a little less rugged and forbidding than Great Moose. There they acquired a house, raised their sons, and farmed the land and fished the water. There, in the third decade of the twentieth century, Erwin Holbrook died and was buried; and there, in the fourth decade, Clara Holbrook returned whenever she could where Lew Medric, and Jim, and I, in a way, could look out for her; and she, in a way, could look out for us.

It was in October of our second year that the clothesline broke, the old clothesline, of course, which Clara had not discarded yet because she assumed it wasn't quite worn out. She gave it a tug to take up slack, and at once it parted, plummeting her to the turf, except that the ground was not all turf: part of it was the well curb's sharp, pointed edge, so that with a damaged spine she lay there, hours perhaps, unable to get up.

Lew Medric, walking home from the woods, came near finally, but it was Clara, lying quite conscious and doubtless in pain, half-hidden in the tall grass, who spoke first. "Sonny" — white-haired Lew Medric was *Sonny* to no one but Clara Holbrook — "Sonny, come here a minute and help me up."

Lew, not versed in the caution of first aid, promptly did. Then, discovering that she could neither stand nor walk, he carried her to a bed in her house and came to commandeer our help. Jim and I, at first together, and then by turns, sat with her through the long hours while Lew Medric rowed ashore, and until Blaine Holbrook arrived with his powerboat, with a stretcher, with other assistance.

Clara never cried out, and made no complaints except about herself: "There, you see," she said, "just because I was too saving about that clothesline, I've made a heap of trouble for everyone else.

Nobody on an island ought to do that." We tried to comfort her, to assuage guilt, but it was no use; as an old resident, she knew common-sense, island truth when she saw it.

Neither Lew nor Jim nor I went ashore to the funeral the next February, for it had been, and still was, an agonizing, cold winter. But we, and Blaine Holbrook, and the minister stood at the Medric Island graveside sharing those ultimate rites of man. It was a sub-zero day, calm, the sea slate gray under a gun-metal sky, and as I listened to the minister gently and calmly reading the words, visions of things I could remember, and visions of things I could not remember but had only heard about, passed through my head.

Blaine Holbrook suggested we take the flowers the short distance from the cemetery to our house, where they would survive a little longer and at least be looked at. And I made a pot of tea, and the men sat in straight-backed chairs, or stood near the stove, talking quietly, easily, soaking up wood-fire warmth and steaming tea before starting their homeward and frigid journey.

Then while the weeks passed and the spring approached, as one nearly always does with the newly dead, I saw her each time I looked through a window or went out of the house: Clara Holbrook crossing the field, leaving her home for the north meadow or approaching it from the south, carrying a bucket of water from the well, or fastening wind-whipped towels to a taut clothes-rope. And then one day without even thinking about it ahead, I saw myself seize three opened letters from our mail rack and drop them to the floor, one by one, between stove and sink.

PLEASE DON'T LEAN ON THE COUNTERS

Some of us felt in a way sort of relieved when word got around that Milton Teel was about to sell his store and retire. It wasn't that we were especially mean or didn't like him; it was just that we were growing almighty tired of his whine. To hear him tell it, he had to pay more for canned goods wholesale than he would, retail, from a supermarket up to Bangor; he had thousands of dollars owed to him from customers right here in Oak Harbor and mistrusted he might ever collect; and he had to work such long hours to sell 50¢ worth of stuff that he might as well live in slavery.

Well, maybe so, we thought; or maybe half-so anyway. But it was a strange thing that Milt's Buick sedan never got to be more than two years old before it was turned in on a new one, and that if one of us did pay up his account with a check, Milt was a likely as not to tuck it in the hip pocket of an old pair of trousers and never miss it for three, four months.

So we more or less looked forward to Cliff Randall's buying the business and taking over. Cliff had been a 20-year man in the Coast Guard, and during his years at the base over to Burnt Harbor had married Alec Benton's youngest girl, Margaret. Cliff was from away, of course — Pennsylvania or some such — but he had been around a few years and we all knew him to be reliable and honest. We also soon found he liked to see things in good order and run right. First off, he held a quick discount sale to get rid of as much stock as he could. What was left he moved over to his garage in a pick-up truck, and then he tore into that store building.

Mister, I want you to know it was something to watch. He took out them counters with the taped cracks across the glass; he heaved out the half-mended chairs; he made 16 trips to the town dump with rubbish and cultch, and he had such a smudge from cartons and half-rotten wood burning down on the beach that some of us set out to wonder about the fire hazard. He shovelled and swept and scrubbed; he washed the windows; he scraped and sanded; he painted and varnished. He built new counters and brought in new stock with white-and-black lettered cards everywhere so there was no doubt about the price of nothing. Then he went up to Bangor and had a painter make him a 20-foot sign which he fastened up over the door: RANDALL'S CASH MARKET.

That give us kind of a jolt, specially the middle of it, because from the way Cliff was going at things, we run of an idea that perhaps he meant it. But that wasn't the worst: first morning the store opened we found there wasn't no chairs in it, not even at the desk where he kept his records — he had built it four feet high and stood up to it, like he was afraid if he set down he might relax.

Wellsir, we stood around shuffling our feet, buying some to-bacco or candy, and leaned against the counters. And the next day there was a couple, three signs up (Cliff was getting sign-crazy) reading PLEASE DON'T LEAN AGAINST COUNTERS. Well, say, that almost finished us. It left a post in the middle and two door jambs. Almighty uncomfortable, I called it. And then if we did stay there any time, Cliff was always asking was there anything he could do for us. That drove us right out onto the highway.

And things went from bad to worse fast: Aaron Abram and Phil Dexter and I, and I don't know but a half dozen like us, would walk from home past the cemetery and the church, down to Phipp Schuyler's boat shop, then on to the fish wharf, up over the hill to the post office, and then back again. Aaron begun smoking so much a man could tell where he'd walked by the road-count of cigar butts. Phil Dexter's wife went home to visit her mother, said she couldn't stand his fidgeting and pacing another minute. And Ollie Young liked to killed himself baiting and setting trawls just to give him an occupation.

Finally I got that desperate I waylaid Doc Wheatley and told him about it. "Yes, I heard," Doc said. "But there ain't nothing I can do."

"Health's your business," I said. "You want a epidemic of nervous breakdowns, this is the right way to get it."

"You might open the schoolhouse nights for a talk-it-over club, or start going to prayer meeting."

"Are you out of your goddamned mind, Doc?" I asked.

But the truth of it was, Doc did do something: he come around casual to Cliff Randall's house and tried to change his way of seeing it. "You don't have to extend credit," Doc told him. "That don't matter. If you'd just give them some place to set. . . ."

Cliff wasn't mad; he was serious. He just shook his head. "I can't do it, Doc. I'm running a business. I'm doing something. And I can't stand them loitering all over the place."

"Maybe they need some place to loiter."

"Not around me they don't."

So that was that.

But of course trade dropped off to zero or thereabouts, and soon it became clear to everyone that Cliff was just in the wrong place. I think it was Doc Wheatley finally singled out Joe Ramsey, got two, three others to co-sign a fistful of his notes up to the bank, and give him the word when he figured it was the right time for Cliff to sell out, which Cliff did (at a loss, no doubt) and moved himself and his family and his belongings to a part of the world that better suited his nature.

Joe was a good choice. He is not very ambitious or energetic. He likes to talk and knows the history of everyone, and some over. He is quite a liar, and not beyond cheating a little when he thinks he can get by with it, but we all know that and watch him for it. Anyway, first thing Joe does is put in two benches and three chairs around the stove. Then he lowers that desk and gets him a swivel chair from out of his mother's attic. It didn't take no time for the windows to grime up and the paint to reach a respectable dullness. I took up a collection and got us a checker board, a cribbage board, and a fresh deck. Doc talked Joe Ramsey into painting out Cliff's sign and got him to do a kind of home-made one, not too neat and not too big neither, that says RAMSEY'S INFORMATION CENTER.

Which is accurate, I guess, even if some of the information is a mite warped. Anyway, it sure suits us. We have quit walking the roads; Joe is exchanging enough goods and credit to keep almost one comfortable leap ahead of the bank; and it seems like all Oak Harbor has breathed a deep sigh of relief — only this time with no mistake.

JAIL AIN'T WHAT IT WAS

Say what you've a mind to, Doc, jail ain't what it used to be. You take it eight, ten years back: suppose I was up before old Judge Ellis. He'd look over the charge against me, hear my not-guilty plea — which he'd know better than to believe in the first place — flick his tongue in and out of his mouth same as a snake, and say, "Guilty: ninety days." Then because he'd know I had traps down, he'd give me 'til December to get them on the bank, and I would serve my term in winter when a man can't fish to no benefit or get no work anyways.

The way it was then, I'd be up to the jail with four, five other fellows. Come a snowstorm, we'd shovel the walks around the courthouse, and every few days, if one of us had the money, we'd slip down to the state store and get us a pint. So long as we come back within ten, fifteen minutes, Paul Myrick was satisfied, but he said if we was longer than that, he'd lock us out — ten below and a howling blizzard — no matter what. He didn't give a damn. So generally we poured him a drink and had him set in on the draw poker. It was more like a club than anything else. Why, last time two of my old friends was there. Spider Johnson had shot one of the grand jurymen between terms of court, which I claimed was all foolishness, and Spider admitted it. Just a flesh wound, you know, and Lawyer King had proved it was accidental when Spider gets up and tells it right out how he'd been Sunday-hunting after a rugged Saturday night over to Poker Point and mistook that juryman for a game warden.

Well, mister, I give you to understand, Judge Ellis didn't think but a damned little of that answer. Spider tells him that down east, where he come from, they always took a shot at a game warden.

"Kill them?" asks the Judge, staring at Spider like he was drilling a hole right through him.

"No, Your Honor," says Spider, "just pepper'em a bit. I wouldn't waste nothing bigger'n birdshot on a warden," he says.

And he was in there for six months.

Then there was Nancy Nickerson: up until she come, the grub was terrible. The mashed potato should have been squeezed out of a tube like paste — I don't know but it had been — and the meat was red as a sun jelly. Even Paul Myrick couldn't sleep.

"For the love of a just God, Paul," I says, "where is this stuff coming from?"

"Sheriff Ames sends it here in a taxi," he says.

"You know as well as I do," I says, "he has one of his extra women on pay cooking it for us — that is, if you could call it cooked."

"Extra women?" says Paul.

"You ever know him to have less than two since he was fourteen?" I asks.

"Well, what will you do about it?" Paul says.

"I'll do something if I can once get close enough, providing he ain't lost his hearing altogether," I says.

So one day Paul unlocks the cell door and tells me Ames is coming across from the courthouse. I tackled him there in the hallway before he could get past. "Sheriff," I says, "I can tell you how to save the county a pile of money."

"Is that so?" he says, like he felt doubtful about it.

"Yes sir," I says, "you can get some woman that knows how to cook decent grub throwed in jail for the winter."

"Oh, the grub's not so bad," he tells me.

"Maybe you think it ain't," I said, "but just come in here and try it. Christ man, if we eat this stuff one more week, every prisoner in the place, and Paul Myrick too, will be up to the Eastern Maine General with ulcers, appendicitis, colitis, boils, blood poisoning, and I don't know but some diseases man ain't yet put a name to. It will run up quite a bill for the county. Now if you was to tip off your deputies and pull in Nancy Nickerson —"

"Being a cook ain't no crime," Ames says. "I can't have her arrested on general principles."

"You've come close to it before now, Sheriff," I told him.

Well, say, it wasn't above ten days before Nancy was in trouble. Seems she run of an idea that Crow — that's her husband — that Crow was over to Leo the Liar's, chasing Leo's daughter. 'Course she never had hitched up very well with Leo anyway, a man who had the state championship, you might say, for sowing false reports. Anyways, when Leo wouldn't let her into the house, she stands out there in the moonlight with Crow's twelve-gauge and lets fly at Leo where she see him through one of the upstairs windows. Skinned his knuckles a bit with the flying glass.

Shooting with intent to kill was the charge, though God knows if she'd took better aim, the town would have give her a medal for community service. Judge Ellis sets $2,000 bail. Not that that made any difference; Nancy nor nobody related to her had more than twenty cents. So there she was, cook, and the rest of the winter we eat pretty good.

But the way it is now, Doc, this new fellow, Judge what's-his-name, he's got all this foolishness about pay-role, probations, or whatever. First thing, he sends me to you, like because I hit Marie harder than usual I must be sick. Shows you how much he knows; he'd hit her himself was he to live with her for over three, four days. And you asks me questions I wouldn't ask my own brother — no offense, Doc, but that's the way it looks to me — and when you can't think of no more, you looks some up in a book.

Now here I am, cutting my own firewood all winter, where the selectmen won't allow me a damned stick, and coming thirty miles up from the coast once a month, wearing out shoe leather up to the knees, to tell you I ain't broke no laws — at least not so anyone would notice — taking your time and costing the county money, or so they tell me. So if you ain't got no more questions, I'll be on my way. Might get home before dark. Besides, I see you got a waiting room here chock-a-block full of patients, and I don't aim to stand in the way of the public health. See you next month, Doc.

HADWELL VERSUS OTIS

Tommy T. Hadwell? Do I know him? Meanest man to Mapoisett Island, next to my brother Otis. Otis has got the first dollar he ever earned, framed and hung up on the setting room wall, same as "God Bless Our Home," or such a matter. And since he put it there he's had a prejudice against spending more than ten cents to a time, unless of course it belonged to somebody else. Otis would save his old lobster bait to feed to the cat. He used to set down on the wharf sneaking candies one by one into his mouth as if he was picking his teeth or something so's we wouldn't notice and make it public he was too mean to offer us any. I guess he is the only man in the state that pays his poll tax in quarterly installments to get a mite more interest on his savings account.

And Tommy T. Hadwell — a man would steal the Lord's Supper and next day go back for the tablecloth — is almost down to his level. I've seen Tommy T. stuffing the children's mattress with lawn cuttings; I've seen him steal fish heads from the gulls and take them home to make soup. One day he borrowed a pocket knife from Herb Sniper, cut him a chew of tobacco — never offered Herb none whatever — shoved the tobacco into his pocket and handed back the knife. Herb never so much as moved a muscle. "Take the knife and to hell with it," he says. "I wouldn't touch it now no more than if you'd cut a rotten clam with it." Didn't jar Tommy T. a mite. He just looked puzzled.

Him and Otis made a pair all right, and I give you to understand, mister, we set up and took notice when we found them tangling on a trade. One March when there wasn't nobody else running for office, Tommy T. got himself voted second selectman, kind of an oversight, you might say, on the part of the electorate. Well sir, setting right there in the selectman's office, he struck a bargain that didn't come up for none of the rest of us. Murray Colbath had just turned over the page to a listing of tax delinquent property that nobody in three years had offered to pay so much as a nickel for. About half of it was alder swamp. "Tommy," Murray says, "how much will you give for the old Andersen lot?"

"Twenty-five dollars," says Tommy, never thinking anyone would seriously consider such a price.

"Sold," says Murray, right off quick, and him and Herb Sniper, who was third selectman, out-voted Tommy T. and held him to his offer, though it like to killed Tommy T. to take the twenty-five dollars out of the savings account. The annual taxes on the Andersen lot come to more than that.

When Otis heard about that deal he said if Tommy T. paid fifty cents for the place, he was beat out of twenty-five. But down to the store we could see that Otis was bothered. The idea that Tommy T. should get so much for just a little almost keeled Otis over. We could see the muscles twitching about his mouth, and before long he begun growling about how he would have the selectmen up in court for trading land within the town office, no public sale, and this and that, but nothing ever come of it. And about the time we figured he had cooled off, we heard he had been up to Tommy T.'s and offered to trade his cow for the lot, even.

"I don't want your cow nor nobody else's," Tommy T. said.

"I'll trade you my cow and give you money to boot!" Otis said, like that was something unheard of, which it was almost.

"No sir. I don't want no cow with nothing to boot."

"You are a hard man to trade with."

"Maybe I am and maybe I ain't," Tommy T. said. And a few nights later, while he was setting on the stoop straightening rusty nails, he see Otis coming up the path to his house. Otis kind of kicked one foot in the dust, nervous.

"Mister, I am going to offer you a goddamn good dicker this evening."

"I doubt that," Tommy T. said. "But what is it?"

"I will trade you my powerboat, even, for that Andersen lot."

Neither one of them said nothing for several minutes. We all knew perfectly well Tommy T. wanted that boat. And Otis must have knowed it when he'd tried to swap the cow for the lot, and when he tried to swap the cow with something to boot, but anyone that knew him at all would know Tommy T. had to say No at least twice before he could say Yes. Otis knew the Andersen place wasn't much of a lot, but then he knew his boat wasn't much of a boat neither, a made-over pleasure craft that was too long, too slim, and unwieldy for lobster fishing, not to mention that if anyone had made application, the state more than likely would have give it an old-age pension. So he waited.

"How long does that offer last?" Tommy T. asked him.

"About ten minutes," Otis said. So they went into the parlor where Otis signed over the boat to Tommy T., and Tommy T. dug the quit-claim deed out of his strong box, throwing away the lawyer's letter that was clipped to it, and Otis took the blank form for a new deed he had brought along with him out of his pocket, and they copied one onto the other, and got Cash Hymer in from across the road to witness the signing. The same night, Otis mailed that deed out to the registry at the county seat. And the next morning Tommy T. went down to the harbor to examine his new property; he found it all right, fast to the mooring, and laying on bottom in two fathoms of water even when the tide was ebbed.

Up to the store we braced ourselves and waited for the tornado, kind of looked forward to it to liven things up, only it never struck. Tommy T. said nothing and done nothing about the boat, and we never see why until two months later, after Otis had paid his tax and built him a camp where he could work on gear down by the shore on the Andersen lot. Clem Andersen, up in Portland, sent Otis a bill for land rent. The year the town thought it seized that property, Cash Hymer, who was clerk, filed the lien one day too late. Not only that: he had recorded the selectman's oaths wrong in the book, and every modicum of business they done that year was null and invalid. And so their quit-claim deed to Tommy T., and Tommy T.'s to Otis wasn't worth even the ink, let alone the price of the stationery.

All that was two years ago. Tommy T. and Otis don't fight, but they don't speak to one another yet. I suppose neither one of them's got the brass to look the other right in the eye. And come to think of it, I can't say that I really blame them for that.

LOST AND FOUND

After they lost the *Ellen Jay* on Outer Litchfield Ledge off Fishhawk Point, Ev Miller and Hank Torey did the best they could not to speak to Hal Gustavsen, or — what amounted to the same thing — come face-to-face with him anywhere here in Rockhaven. And they had to work at it: neither one of them, of course, could come down to my wharf just after daybreak when most of the men was going aboard their crafts, or if it was one of them halfway bad days when a man didn't know whether it was fit to go out and haul or not, standing around the bait shed talking about going out, and needling each other the way they do. Nor, sometimes, did the two of them even dare go to the post office at mail time nor to the movies nights. Hank Torey see Hal coming toward him one day on the road that passes the fish factory, but before Hal got anywhere near him, Hank slipped off between two buildings somewhere and went right out of sight. I know because Hal told me about it himself.

I got to admit there was no reason at first Ev or Hank either should be down to my wharf any time, since neither one of them had a boat to go fishing in any more, and both of them knew enough to think twice before coming to me for credit to buy one. Still, it must have been trying for them in a place this size to keep from meeting a man.

They had been setting trawls in the *Ellen Jay* two three months before they lost her. Hal Gustavsen had gone out of his way to get them to fish in her on shares. I don't know what the deal was exactly, but I dare-say it was twenty-five percent for the boat, twenty-five percent to the owner, and twenty-five percent to each man — something like that. Anyway, Ev and Hank had nothing to lose out of it except their labor, if you've a mind to count that.

None of us ever asked why Hal Gustavsen didn't fish in the *Ellen Jay* himself any more because the reason was obvious. He had fished in her for years — even before his wife died — and then in June in the year I am speaking of he went out to make a set and took some visitor from away — name of Redford — and his son Ben (Hal's son, I mean) with him. Ben was about twenty, a fisherman in his own right — hauled summer and winter in a twenty-eight foot lobster boat and was pressing the high-liners. He went with Hal and Redford that day only for the fun of it, kind of a start-the-summer celebration. Trouble with Ben was he had a bad heart, or so Dr. Norwood tells me, and along with that, high spirits and plenty of energy. Way Hal and Redford told it later, they was three miles off shore, and Ben was standing on the after deck, one hand on the mast that supports the *Ellen Jay*'s riding sail. Everything was going fine — some swells, but no rough seas nor high winds nor nothing — until Hal glances aft for a second and sees that the stern deck is empty. Well sir, he pulled back on the *Ellen Jay*'s throttle, swung her around as fast as he could, and retraced her wake a short time to what he thought was the right place — though how he could guess one spot was more right than another I don't pretend to know. Then he puts the *Ellen Jay* in neutral, kicks off his boots and dives overside, dives deep, like he thought he could make it to the bottom even in all them fathoms, or get a-holt of Ben before he was clean out of sight — which of course he couldn't.

Not only that: he had the devil's own time getting back to the surface without drowning himself, and even staying on the surface long enough for Redford to pull up alongside and drag him aboard. Lucky for him that Redford knew enough to handle the *Ellen Jay* even a little bit.

Reason he was in such hard plight was he was wearing quite heavy trousers, and a wool sweater, and jacket, and though he had kicked off his boots — something hard for any man to forget to do if he knows he is going overside and has any chance — still, with his whole heart and soul suddenly right up there in his mouth, he never thought to take off anything else.

Worst of it was, he blamed himself for Ben's death, claiming if he (Hal) had stayed cool for a minute, him and Redford might have sighted Ben when he surfaced. Hal couldn't believe Ben hadn't surfaced at least once. But the way it was, Redford put all his attention on saving the man he could see, and it took him five or six minutes to do that. So Hal blamed himself, took the whole load on himself. Set right here in my office, in that chair you're setting in, shaking his head and telling me, then putting his head down in his hands, and the tears rolling off his face in a freshet.

It wasn't just me he told; it was everyone, anyone who would listen and I guess there wasn't no one but felt he had to listen so long as Hal wanted to talk. This thing had left him all alone in the world, so to speak, and we felt mighty bad for him, deep-down bad where there wasn't really no way to say it. But there wasn't one of us, not a single one, nor any of us together, could get him to see that it wasn't his fault, that he shouldn't go around day and night thinking, "I drowned my son. If I hadn't done what I did, diving overside, we could have saved him." We tried, and tried, and tried, with no results. So it was no wonder to us he did not want to step foot aboard the *Ellen Jay*. We all understood that.

So what he did was dig up Ev Miller and Hank Torey to take the *Ellen Jay* on shares and go trawling. They weren't the best men for the work, as he knew quite well, or any of us could have told him. They was not too responsible, nor ambitious, nor energetic, and perhaps not too smart neither. But the best men for such work was already busy on their own. Hal didn't really have much choice. Meanwhile, Hal went lobsterfishing, using his son's boat. It didn't bother him any to do that; maybe it even made him feel better, just a mite. And afternoons when the *Ellen Jay* was due in from a trip he would be down here to the fishwharf to watch the count and then divide with Ev and Hank whatever it was the trip had stocked.

And that was how things went until that September Ev and Hank rowed in here in a skiff in the dark and told us the *Ellen Jay* was lost. They never reported to Hal, never dared to. I picked up the phone here myself and called him, but at first he was out or the party line was busy or something, and by the time I could reach him, Ev and Hank had talked it all over with them that was here on the wharf, and by the time Hal got here, Ev and Hank had gone off into the darkness, and home I guess. Hal could have followed them up, of course. I asked why he didn't.

He was silent for a minute, and his eyes had that kind of distant look. Then he said: "What difference would it make?"

The way Ev and Hank told it, and the way I and no doubt several others told it to Hal, was about like this: toward dark, just as they was coming in, the *Ellen Jay*'s engine conked out. Neither one of them ever seemed too certain what was wrong with it. First Ev said it was the condenser, and Hank said no, it was the coil; then Ev thought perhaps it was the timer, and Hank said well, it could have been worn points or a corroded battery terminal. Other times they talked about the gas filter, the fuel pump, and the air-intake. In other words, they didn't know what it was, and when the engine failed, with the ebb tide setting toward Litchfield Ledge not too far to port like a black sea beast groaning as the waves flushed over it, they was so jeezily scared they didn't know where to turn. They didn't try anchoring nor kedging, and whether either one could have saved the *Ellen Jay* we'll never know.

First off, Ev jumps into the big skiff they was towing and has Hank pass him the *Ellen Jay*'s bow line; then rowing against tide and swells both, he tried to tow her clear of the ledge. Time he got her bow swung around, he was about wore out; so then he comes back alongside, Hank gets into the skiff with him, and with two pair of oars they give it another try. They get her started away from the ledges all right, but it isn't enough. When the tide picks up, most they can do while they have their strength is hold their own, and soon as they begin to wear down, the current takes them. Last of it, they have to cast off the *Ellen Jay* or go on the rocks with her, and with the end of their breath, they row away, hearing the splintering crash of the *Ellen Jay*'s transom against the ledge. She was a complete loss all right; here and there some of us picked up a few bits and pieces.

Four, maybe five weeks after that, Hal Gustavsen come down to see me on the wharf in one of them slack times when nobody else was around. Not that I hadn't been seeing him two three times a week anyway when he come up to the wharf to buy gas or bait, or perhaps more or less as a favor or because he needed cash, to sell me a catch instead of carring it. But this time he comes on foot.

"Carl," he says finally, "how long do I have to put up with it?"

"With what?" I said.

"Them fellows dodging away from me."

"Oh. Well —"

"Like I was cursed or something."

"I wouldn't go so far as to say that," I told him. "You know why they're dodging away from you."

"Yeah." He sounded tired.

"Because they blame themselves," I said, "the same as —"

"All right, all right. Yeah, I know. But I don't like it. I don't know that I can go on standing it."

"Go see them. Go to their house one at a time," I said. "They'll listen. They got to listen."

Hal leaned back against the counter and scratched his head. "I don't want it to be like that. I want them and me to be together sometime when neither one of us can help it."

"Well, stick around here," I said.

"Why? They ain't been down here."

"Not til yesterday," I said. "But they'll be back."

"What for?"

"They got hold of a boat," I said, "Hank's father's boat. It ain't much."

"So?"

"But it still floats. It goes, even."

"Yeah?"

"And they figure to go lobsterfishing in it, that is if they can get credit for gear."

"And you're going to extend it to them?"

"Not by a damned site I ain't. I been stung on that kind of fisherman before this."

Hal nodded. "I see. Not even if I was to co-sign their note?"

"Well, that might make a difference."

"When do you think they'll be here?" he said.

"Not today," I told him. "It's late now, and more boats will be in before you know it. Tomorrow maybe, middle of the morning, after they figure everyone's gone out, you included."

"Thanks," said Hal. "What am I supposed to do? Hide my boat somewhere so they won't see it to the mooring."

"I don't believe you have got to go quite so far as that," I said.

And he didn't. But he was down here, perhaps an hour after the last of the boats had gone out, not here in my office, you understand, where I was, but out there where the counter is and the coils of potwarp and the paint and hardware and whatnot, just hanging around. And about ten-thirty Ev and Hank wanders in, and there they was right in front of Hal, and no way to back out without seeming silly. So they looks at each other, and there is a little shuffling of feet, and then Hal says, "Hi, fellows," and they said, "Hi," and "How is everything?" back.

"Not too good," said Hal.

"No?" Ev says.

"How's that?" says Hank.

"Some of my friends ain't speaking," said Hal. "They don't even want to meet me on the street."

"Yeah, that's us, Hal," Ev said. "And you know why, don't you?"

"Do I?" said Hal.

"Because we lost you a boat. We lost you the *Ellen Jay* and you know we can't make it up to you, not if we work the rest of our goddamned life."

"That's right," Ev said.

I heard Hal take a step or two, like he was coming toward them, but instead of lifting his voice, it was like he whispered: "You think I care about that? You think I care about a goddamned boat?"

"Thousands of dollars," one of them said. "Thousands . . . We know that."

"Yeah. And I'd give it up, that and three times over, ten times over if I had it — for something." For a few seconds there was silence. Then again I heard him: "Don't you fellows know that I know what can happen when something terrible comes to you on the water, when a man is afraid and can't hardly draw a breath, or see, or think straight, and loses his head? For Christ's sake, you think I don't know about *that?*"

There was more shuffling of feet. I heard a board squeak, and some breathing, and someone open a cooler lid. Then Hank says, "Which is it you'd rather have, Hal, a root-beer or a Seven-Up?"

Hal said something, and Ev said something, and there was a little laughter, and I heard the coins ring on the counter top.

Ordinarily I would have left my desk and gone into the store part at that, but I didn't. I stared out the window at Hal's boat at the mooring, and felt my muscles relax. When, finally, I did go out, there was the change, with a few cents over, on the counter top, and through the window I could see all three of them sauntering up the road, drinks in one hand, and talking together like they was right in the middle of summer, or something like that.

TWO OF A KIND

Frank Townsend has always been a wild man ready to take chances — big chances I call them — at catching fish. Years back, he was as poor as any of us, poorer than most no doubt, but he had a boat (one he'd built himself — he was talented like that) and he got in on the beginning of the dragging business, going out on days when it wasn't fit for no one to be offshore, nor even inshore maybe, yet bringing in catch after catch, hundreds, then thousands of pounds of ground fish to the head of the wharf where Bert Clinton, our fish buyer, was damned glad to see them.

Luckier than a backhouse mouse I called him: had any of the rest of us tried that, we would have been listed as overdue and presumed dead before a year was up. But Frank was also a driver: for him, every day was a fishing day. And he wasn't afraid of expense. He run up some giant-sized bills for gas and repairs and gear (I heard all about that from Oscar over to the machine shop), but he also run up giant-sized catches to match them. None of us pretends it was ever easy. Running chances like he did takes toll of a man, and we wasn't really too startled when on his time ashore, and sometimes on the water, he commenced to take aboard quite a cargo of liquid bait. Frank always talked too much, too loud, too wide, even when he was sober, and of course once he got several slugs of that giggle juice seeping out through his pores he was louder than ever.

47

Anyone could hear him from one end of the harbor to the other. At the same time, after two three years we come to see (and got used to the idea) that Frank was a big fisherman in Oak Harbor, even if he did talk and drink too much — items that sort of separated him, you might say, from the quiet, hard-working residents of Christian Ridge who lead a steady, respectable life.

There were other things too. No one ever quite openly accused him of doing malicious damage to his competitors, but it was easy to think he did. The day one of the other draggers was broke down and had found water in his gas tank and all through the cylinders, Frank coasts by in his boat and yells, "Yeah-h-h! I guess you won't be going out dragging again for a few tides, will you?" That kind of thing don't set too good, especially where he was the man had been in a little sea-going traffic dispute with Frank twenty-four hours earlier.

Yet the next week Frank was a likely as not to stop in at some cove, or island, or whatever, pick up a mooring and then sound the horn until fellows come out in skiffs and dories and punts to see what is the matter. Then he, and his helper with him, would start cleaning and giving away fish as fast as anybody would take them — cod, hake, mackerel, cat, anything — and like as not deer meat too, for Frank couldn't keep the sights of his rifle off an island deer once every few months, legal or illegal, and mostly illegal of course.

Whatever he done, he wanted it slam-bang-whoosh and a big sweep of the paint brush. Most of the other fellows, when they was driving on the highway, would not pick up hitch-hikers, would not look them in the eye; just stare past them, pretend they didn't exist, and drive by. But Frank picked them up, and then he would make them pay for the ride in answering questions: where did they live? where were they going? where had they been? what did they do for a living? why did they do that? did they carry knives? what did their parents think of them? what was the idea of bumming around the country in the first place? and I don't know what else. Then he would like as not go five, six miles out of his way to get them on the best road to where they was going and hand them a dollar or two just for the hell of it. There was nobody else like him to Oak Harbor.

So in a way I suppose I should not have been surprised over what happened here a year ago September. Frank had had a new engine put in his boat — he had to have a new one every four five years, the rate he drove one — and he was trying it out in the harbor, testing it for speed, for acceleration, for throttling down — points, timer, spark, choke, everything. Well sir, while he was at it, in slides this thirty-six foot sailing yacht, shiny black hull, stainless steel rigging, and milk-white dacron, and rounds up to the mooring the owner had rented for the season. I was standing right out there to the end of my wharf, watching, and I could see he wasn't going to make it the first try. The sails begun to luff (as they should) and while the hull was sliding ahead, he runs forward (a big man, but fast just the same), grabbing a gaff as he goes, to reach down with and snag that buoy. But already wind and current was sliding his craft off to leeward, and he couldn't do it.

Most yachtsmen take in sail before they're even inside the harbor, and come up to a mooring or anchorage under power; and nine-tenths of those that don't would switch on the power after they'd once failed to pick up a mooring under sail. But not this man: he puts down the gaff, runs aft, twirls the wheel to leeward until the sails fill, and comes around to do it again. Again he misses! I recognized him that time, and thought, "No wonder he don't quit."

Just then, of course, as luck would have it, along comes Frank Townsend, motor idling dead slow, and yells to him, "What you need aboard there is a seaman, mister!"

The man never replied, nor even turned his head, for which you can't blame him. I wouldn't have either.

For the next forty-five minutes, or maybe an hour, I was busy down on the float, taking care of two or three of my lobster catchers, one after another, that come in to sell what they'd stocked, gas up, maybe buy oil or something else, and put bait aboard for the next morning. And the last of them had just pulled away from the float when I heard the god-awful smash of a collision, wood splintering and engine roar and thump-thump-thump-bump! I looked up the harbor and see Frank's big, broad-beamed craft really afoul of that sailing yacht, which it must have hit, damned near full throttle, almost amidships. Frank was scrambling out of the hatchway, and I figured at once that he had been below fussing with that new engine when she hit. He was already idling now, and he hung there alongside that yacht only a minute or two before he eased up forward, cast off the yacht's mooring, lashed the two craft together for and aft, and kicked ahead at moderate speed toward his own wharf. The tide was just about past the peak, which was lucky for him, because it meant he could ground the yacht out alongside his wharf and make her fast so she would not cant over, nor take in very much water through that raw, jagged hole in the side of her, no matter how tide and wind worked. Then he put his boat off on the mooring, rowed in here to my float, come up to the office and asked could he use the telephone.

Which I told him he could. He was breathing hard and there was blood running down around his neck from a cut on the back of his head. I asked him about that, and he said the sudden stop of the crash had knocked him flat down in the cabin where he cracked his head on a tool box or something. He had been too excited to care or notice. And what in hell was the name of the fellow that owned that yacht and where did he live?

"Name's Paul Blake," I said.

"You know him?"

"I know him enough to talk with. I've listened to him enough."

"Where does he live?"

"Up to the county seat."

"Look up his number for me, will you, so I can call him?"

I dug out the phone book from under a stack of receipts and spun the pages to the right section: B for Blake.

Yes, I'd heard quite a number of things about Paul Blake, and from Paul Blake too. I had heard them at the Lodge, at the town office, at Blake's office, and from a lawyer acquaintance I talked with one day up to a Route 1 restaurant just this side of Belfast.

Paul went into business quite a lot the way Frank went at the ocean. He had started with nothing and built up his general contracting firm by taking chances and then learning to cover future chances. But the truth was he enjoyed gambling. He would walk into the office of some outfit where he owed one or two thousand for equipment and offer to match coins with the boss for it — double or nothing. Sometimes he found a taker, and sometimes he won, but it didn't discourage him any when he didn't. Midway through one long, lost weekend at somebody's hunting camp, Paul had a hot pair of dice in one hand and fifteen hundred dollars of winnings clutched in the other, but coming home Sunday night he had to borrow fifteen cents for a cup of coffee. That tickled Paul; he told everybody and got quite a laugh out of it. And if you were in a poker game with him and he said, "Five," you were wise to check whether he meant five dollars or five hundred. I've seen him in a restaurant pull thirty-five hundred-dollar bills out of his pocket to pay out less than twenty.

He sang the same tune when it came to trading. Once when somebody tried to buy a house from him for less than he'd asked, his voice boomed into the telephone: "I will *refuse* fourteen thousand, nine hundred and ninety-nine dollars and ninety-nine cents!" He would have, too.

Often, I think, it was the roaring voice with the determination behind it that got things his way, like his dispute with the local bank president, again over the telephone, and Paul, in high dudgeon listing his assets — shovels, bull-dozers, back-hoes, trailers, tractors, garages — "and," shouts Paul, "I got four or five thousand dollars in a safe-deposit box in your bank — that is, if you haven't had your fingers into it."

"You can't talk to me like that!"

"Well, you better hang up then, because I'm going to go right on talking like that —"

End of discussion.

Deer hunting too, and sometimes poaching, though he kind of put the damper on that after he began to get powerful enough to have to seem part-way respectable and somebody nominated him for county commissioner. What really calmed him down a bit, I think, was the time he killed a yearling out of season, and with the same shot put a hole through his Buick's right-rear fender. He couldn't see taking it to the body shop in a state like that, nor parking it around down town neither, so he puts the deer in the trunk, picks out a rugged oak, and backs into it two or three times *kawhango* until that fender was mashed and the bullet-hole unrecognizable. I never heard it from others, and he never told me himself until years later. Then he says to me: "Pour yourself another: it ain't going to do you no goddamned good there in the bottle." We had already had four or five ninety-proof Scotch.

So you can understand how I was kind of interested when Frank picks up the phone to talk to Paul, a man he has just insulted, and tell him he has drove the bow of his powerboat slam into Paul's yacht. When Frank gets an answer at the other end of the line, he says who it is calling, and there was a moment of silence just long enough for Paul to be saying, "Frank *who*, for godsakes?"

And Frank says, "Townsend. I'm the guy that yelled at you when you was trying to pick up your mooring under sail like a damned fool about an hour ago." . . . "Just shut up a minute and hear the rest: after you'd left I rammed your craft with my power-boat and put a hole in the side big enough for you to crawl through." . . . "Yes, that's what I said."

Frank held the phone off to one side about sixteen inches, and even at the other end of my office I could hear the outrage, though not too plain really.

"I was below decks to release a jammed accelerator," Frank said. "You think I do that kind of thing for the fun of it?"

More roaring, long distance.

"All right all *right!* Now calm down, will you? . . . "Well, don't then. But I heard you the first time." . . . "Are you going to come down here and have a look at it or ain't you?" . . . "You do, goddamn you, and I'll punch you right back." . . . "You better get down here and look it over." . . . "No, she ain't about to sink. She's at my wharf and grounded out by this time." . . . "Sure I moved it. I couldn't be any more liable than I was already." . . . "How long?" . . . "All right, I'll wait."

Frank hung up and turned to me. "He says about twenty minutes."

"That's possible," I said. "He cruises around eighty."

"There ain't no goddamned hurry," Frank said.

"What do you think of him?"

"Sounds natural enough," he said.

I told Frank I was curious, wanted to go look at the damage, and he said he didn't care whether I did or not, so I went over with him and found it was more or less what he'd said. "How much ruin to yours?" I asked.

"About what you'd expect. I got some work for me up there on the bow," he told me.

Paul Blake didn't take even twenty minutes; he was there in eighteen. We heard his big sedan roar to a quick stop on the dirt road beyond Frank's building, and the next minute he was down on the wharf like he was on his way to a fire. I stepped back, not knowing quite what to expect, and Paul came to a stop about six feet from Frank, who hadn't budged, and the two of of them stood there as much as a minute and stared at each other. I held my breath. Later I thought they was reading each other's minds, but now I think it wasn't minds so much as it was blood, flesh, nerves, and the kind of life the other fellow probably lived, or maybe how he lived it. Whatever it was, it come to a place where Frank said, "Your boat's right here," and jerked his head to port.

"I see it is."

The masts were looming up there above the wharf, above the gear, the shed, and everything, like a couple of monuments.

Twenty minutes later they had looked over the damage from outside and inside, above and below, right and left, and I don't know but two or three other ways. They knew just how many strakes of that beautiful, clear-grained cedar was shattered and where they butted, and what to do about the cracked oak frame. Then they set there in the cockpit, and Paul stares across at Frank and says, "This one is going to cost you a bundle, mister."

"That's my business," Frank said.

"It sure as hell is going to be your business, time my insurance company gets through with you."

"I don't give a damn for no insurance company," says Frank.

"No?" Paul glares at him.

"I'll repair it myself."

"You?"

"Why not? I built *my* boat." He nodded in its direction off at the mooring. "I can rebuild yours if I've a mind to."

"Not unless I say so by God!"

"Well, why don't you say so? What have you got to lose? I can put her in a cradle right here on the railway, haul her out and work on her same as I do my own boat. If the weather turns bad, I'll dismast her and haul her into the building. You won't even have to pay no storage for winter."

Paul snorted. "It'll cost you more in lost hours of fishing than sending it to a yard."

Frank looked him right in the eye. "I said that was my business."

And again the two of them stared at each other as if by looking and breathing they could learn something. Finally Paul turned his head away to look at me — silent, but he was asking a question.

I nodded. "He can do it. He's a good builder."

"All right," Paul said. "When are you going to start?"

"Tomorrow."

And he did. He hauled Blake's outfit up on his railway where it so happened I could see it from my office window and from the head of the wharf too. He worked on the yacht one day and went dragging the next. First it was all tear out the damaged planks and clean up. Then Frank got to work with some oak he had on hand and brought in new cedar planking and a supply of copper fastenings.

About every third session, especially Saturday or Sunday, Paul Blake would drive up in that big bus of his, skid to a quick stop near the wharf, and set down there on a crate or a sawhorse and watch Frank work. I went over there once or twice and it struck me like a grim kind of business: neither one of them had so much as a word to say to the other. Then a week later it begun to be different. Frank was getting out planking, marking the stations, sawing the stock to fit, and then planing the caulking seams, squinting down the length of the plank to see had he got it just right. And suddenly it struck me the way Paul was watching him (and the way I was watching him too, for that matter) was more like the way some people will watch a painter at work after he has set up his canvas and easel, or whatever, along the shore somewhere.

And the next time I see the two of them over there, Paul was holding the after end of the plank while Frank drilled, counter-sunk, and fastened the fore end. When it come to putting the clamps on, I never see anybody so careful: it was like he was putting cotton-batting or velvet under them clamps to make sure they didn't leave no rosettes on that high-priced plank stock.

That was the afternoon they talked over which day Paul could come down there to help, and Frank adjusted his dragging calendar to fit Paul's schedule. Next thing I knew, a few days later, they sent some kid over to tell me to come quick as I could, and I got there just in time to watch them finish putting in the shutter plank and help them celebrate with three six-packs.

"You fellows are nuts," I told them. "What's so particular about putting in a shutter plank on a repair job? Anybody would think you'd built the whole boat from the keel up."

"Well, goddam it, we could," Frank said.

"You don't want any ale, you don't have to drink it," Paul said. So I drank it.

After that came the sanding — a tiresome disagreeable job if I ever met one — and I don't mean just the new planking either: they sanded the whole port side of the hull, one with a belt, and the other with a disc-sander, and then repainted it. Time the two of them finished, that craft looked like she was new out of the shop and had never touched water.

Then there was an argument: Paul wanted to launch his boat, sail it a day or two, and then take it to the yacht yard for the winter. Frank tells him he is crazier than a coot to go sailing for sport halfway through the fall. He offered to take the masts out and stow them, haul the boat into his building, and not charge Paul a cent. They yelled and swore at each other, getting louder and louder til I could have heard it all the way to the office, had I been that far away to begin with. Then all to once, Frank changes his mind, says he is tired of the damned craft, don't want to see it again, and wouldn't think of storing it — that is, unless Paul would agree to go hunting with him up near the Allagash or such a matter.

"Well, I'll leave it here then," says Paul, "just so I'm sure it'll be a trouble to you. But I got to see my agent about doubling the fire insurance."

That give Frank a chance to growl back at him for being a fussy landlubber, and in the end, of course, they went hunting together, and Frank come back with a big buck on the fender of his car and a god-awful headache.

Oak Harbor has not been quite the same place since, at least not on weekends from May to October, for if Frank and Paul don't zoom out of here hell-bent for damnation in one craft, they do it in the other. Days there is not much wind they go in Frank's powerboat, all loaded with bait, beer, and sometimes beauties — whether their wives like it or not — throttle wide open, and horn blasting at the least hint of somebody to sound it at. But when there's a blow , they sail out in Paul's yawl, never a reef even when they'd go better for it, her sleek hull laying over until you expect to see her go flat, and them skin-taut, dollar-a-stitch sails just barely skimming the wave tops. Then likely as not, Paul comes about and scuds back through the harbor, cutting in close to the wharves, his crew shouting and toasting the mainland with a bottle; then out again, sailing on edge, and off to where I know not and care less — just back before Monday.

I stand there on the wharf sometimes, mister, watching and hearing, and I can't help feeling a grin spread over my face. If I was placing bets, I wouldn't give neither Paul nor Frank much chance for a long life: if they don't drown or crack up on the highway, they will someday stop a bullet or something. But meanwhile, mister, by God they intend to enjoy things, and it gives me a kind of broad, deep pleasure just to hear them and watch them doing it.

THE PANHANDLE PORTRAIT

All of us that congregate down to Joe Ramsey's now and then knew about the Morrison fellow's plan to buy Uncle Merle Hanscom's Panhandle nearly as soon as Uncle Merle did. I don't know but sooner. Not that the Morrison man is any great talker, but he has a wife and two three young ones and dinner-table talk the same as anyone else. So if his son, who seems to spend no less than two-thirds of his time with Phipp Schuyler's daughter, who raises no serious objections to that — if his son, as I say, was to mention it to her, and back at her house she told Phipp, who would talk about it to Aaron Abram (who works in Phipp's boat shop), and on his way home from work Aaron give it to Phil Dexter, who is almost always the first one after supper down to Joe Ramsey's Information Center — if a string of things like that happened, which seldom fails, you can see how we might know about it before Carl Morrison ever stopped in at Uncle Merle's to suggest it.

Not, you understand, that it was any great news. Uncle Merle's property kind of nestles inside the Morrison place like a kitten against a soft sofa-cushion, except for a strip about seventy-five by thirty with a tall, lean, grayboarded antique of an out-house standing up there at the end of it like it was on guard duty. Nobody has used that out-house, not even to stash any fishing or farming gear in, since before Pearl Harbor. Even for Uncle Merle, who is more ornery and contrary minded than most, it was not too handy.

57

So a few nights later, when Uncle Merle dropped in at Joe
Ramsey's to buy him a loaf of that fog-like bread, a half-pound of
cheese, a dozen eggs, and some chewing tobacco, Phil Dexter took
his eyes off the game on the checkerboard long enough to say to
Uncle Merle he understood Merle was about to sell his Panhandle to
that Morrison fellow.

"And why not?" Uncle Merle said. "It don't do me no good, and
I can look at it just the same whether I own it or not."

"There ain't no doubt of that," Phil said.

"His money is just as good as anyone else's," Uncle Merle said,
like somebody was going to contradict him. Uncle Merle is living on
his Social Security checks plus what he still can dig out of the clam
flats when he feels like it; we can't see that he is suffering any, but
obviously a little extra cash would taste good, like icing on the cake.

"It sure better be," Phil said. "Thing you want to watch out for,
Uncle Merle, is next thing you know he will be buying the whole
property out from under you, house and all."

"I guess there ain't much danger of that, not while I got half a
brain left."

"Keep a sharp lookout, Uncle Merle," Phil said.

And that might have been the end of the whole business, except
that the next evening when Aaron Abram was walking down the
road past the Morrison place, he stopped to pass the time of day with
Carl Morrison who was out there clearing bottles, cans, and candy
wrappers out of that bushy hedge he has which fences off his yard
from the rest of us trekking up and down the highway to no particular purpose. When anyone talks with Aaron, one thing leads to
another quite fast, and before he even knew it perhaps, the Morrison fellow let slip that the reason he was buying the Panhandle was to
get rid of that goddamned out-house which soared up across his
view of the sunset like a cigar butt stuck in an icecream sundae.

If Morrison had known what Joe Ramsey's was like perhaps he
would never have said it, but obviously he didn't. He has not lived
here over a year or two now (come here from the city, like some
others, trying to find a place fit to live in, I guess), and it takes time
for a man to get all his bearings. Fact is, Aaron told us that one day
when Morrison and him had been talking (Aaron will talk to anybody that will listen) and Aaron said he had to be on his way, Carl
Morrison asked where he was bound, and Aaron said "Prayer meeting."

"Prayer meeting! On Tuesday night?" Carl asks him.

"Every night," Aaron says.

"Who does the preaching?"

"All hands," says Aaron, and even then, it seems, Morrison didn't catch on to what he was talking about.

So of course word about Carl Morrison's wanting to buy that land so he could tear down the out-house and get it out of his view of the sunset filtered through all tongues at Joe Ramsey's in about ten minutes, and an hour or two later had reached nearly every corner of Oak Harbor, north, east, south, and west. Nor was it long, of course, before it got back to Uncle Merle Hanscom, and once it did, mister, I want you do know he was some goddamned put-out. He wasn't going to have no newcomer barge into town and and buy up land just so he could tear down Merle Hanscom's out-house. Be goddamned if he was! So he goes up to Morrison's and tells him he's changed his mind about selling that parcel and the deal is off.

Morrison, polite as can be, says he's sorry to hear that, but maybe he had not figured the value just right and would Uncle Merle feel better if he was to get about half again as much?

Uncle Merle says no, he would not.

So Morrison says how about twice the price, which was going it real steep since the land wasn't worth more than about a fourth of what he had offered in the first place.

And Uncle Merle says no, it is not for sale, and goes off like he was mad, which I daresay he was, at that.

Which left Carl Morrison puzzled, of course, and after a few weeks (late in April, I'd say) he started dropping in at Joe Ramsey's Information Center himself, evenings, buying a little of this or that, leaning against a post and watching the checker game, and getting a word in now and then about nothing in particular, until we got used to his being there. Naturally somebody asked him, the second or third night he was there, about the land deal, and he said it was off (which we all knew anyway), and that he didn't even have the beginning of a notion why. Nobody was going to come right out in the open and tell all they knew, but one or two did allow that Carl should understand Uncle Merle was a strange character, contrary as a hog on ice, and if anyone wanted to get him to do something, he would have to approach Uncle Merle when the phase of the moon was just right, or such a matter.

None of that was really much help, of course, but some time the next week Aaron Abram walked home from Ramsey's the same time Carl Morrison did and told Carl that Uncle Merle had got wind of the idea Carl wanted to tear down that ramshackle old out-house, and being odd anyway, had taken offense and would be damned if he'd sell. "So that's it," Carl Morrison said.

"Yessir, that's it."

"The money ain't going to make no difference."

"I should judge not," Aaron told him.

"Well, now at least, I've got something to think about," Carl said.

For a time nothing happened. Then one day in May, Carl Morrison's wife brought one of them folding chairs out to her side yard, put an easel and a framed canvas in front of it, and set there with brushes and tubes of paint, and a small piece of plywood to smear things on, and painted herself a picture of the view to the westward — or so we took it. The day after that she was out there again, but that wasn't all: Carl was there too with the same equipment (except no chair: he stood up to do *his* painting) about thirty feet away from where she was and looking at things from a little different angle. Day after that, their son was out there with them, and more of the same equipment. It was like they were forming a kind of painters' semi-circle all concentrated on Merle Hanscom's Panhandle.

Strange thing was, though Merle Hanscom see his neighbors there suddenly all turned into artists, he didn't seem to give much of a cuss: it was their place, and if they wanted to act like lunatics on it, that was up to them.

But not so with the rest of us. I want you to understand, mister, the bunch down to Ramsey's was some damned curious trying to figure out, first, what that Morrison fellow thought he was up to, and next, what them pictures, if they really was pictures, looked like. Trouble was, Carl Morrison had quit coming in to Joe Ramsey's altogether and didn't even walk the town roads neither; if he had to go fifty feet, he did it in that car of his with the throttle two-thirds open if not more so, so even Aaron got no chance to talk to him. And if his son was saying anything more to Phipp Schuyler's girl, we never learned of it. Aaron wouldn't go up to the house and ask them outright, or just look over their shoulders neither, though there was plenty down to the store tried to get him to do it. Aaron felt friendly with Carl, but not so friendly that he could do a thing like that and feel comfortable about it.

Then the next week they had company, a man and a woman from away somewhere—Pennsylvania, to judge by the license plate—and every day it wasn't rainy *they* were out there doing the painting, and one or two of the Morrisons besides. It began to puzzle us what on earth they could ever do with so many pictures of one place; it wasn't after all, like they was in the postcard business. And then, in a way, we found out.

Up the road a piece from Joe Ramsey's is a thing called The Country Store, which it isn't, of course. There is nothing country about it. It opens only from late May to October, and for the most part takes in tourists — or that is, usually only tourists offer to go in there. It is filled with a mixture of all kinds of culch that they call "crafts," for some reason or other, plus a few beat-up lobster buoys. Charlie Ramsdell's daughter and son-in-law started it about the time they got through going to college and couldn't think of nothing better to do. It is a harmless enough outfit, I guess; brings in a certain amount of income for that couple to pay their taxes with, and maybe some over, or so they tell me.

Well, Phil Dexter was walking past it one day, which he has to do anyhow to go aboard his boat or just to join the group down to Ramsey's and he see that Philadelphia car outside The Country Store, and Carl Morrison and them guests of his carrying armloads of framed pictures into the place. Now that news roused us up quite a bit, and after we had talked it over for a time, and stirred it up, and looked at it this way and that, three or four of us went along to that crafts outfit to see what was going on. The car wasn't there any more, and Charlie Ramsdell's girl looked kind of tickled to see us come in, and then asked what she could do for us.

I told her I didn't rightly know, and she said perhaps what we would be most interested in was the new Oak Harbor art exhibit. I stared at her for a few seconds. "I guess that's right," I said.

She pointed over across the store. "Well, it's right in there, in that room," she said.

And it was, a separate room, a kind of shed off the main building, and not a thing in it to speak of except all them pictures, framed and hung up on the wall, and every last one of them, of course, featuring Merle Hanscom's out-house like it was the Eiffel Tower or something. Some of them was done in deep, heavy, thick paints you could almost bite into, and others was in light colors, airy and fancy, as if the sun was shining right through them the whole time. And one or two was just black and white. They come in all sizes, and all prices, mostly expensive, according to the little sticker of paper down under the frame of each one. Also the artists seemed to have a lot of different notions about just what Merle Hanscom's antique out-house looked like.

We glanced them all over, with a number of comments not too

complimentary, and went out without buying nothing, which didn't seem to bother Charlie Ramsdell's girl in the least. Back at the store the news of the exhibit begun to spread quite fast, but Phil Dexter couldn't wait: he had to trot right up to Merle Hanscom's and fetch him back to The Country Store to see how famous his out-house had got. He wouldn't tell Merle what it was all about, just made him come with him and kept him curious enough so he would.

Wellsir, Merle looked them pictures over, and those of us that was watching him was hard put to it to tell how he felt. He done a little quiet growling, like a dog that isn't angry yet but just ain't friendly, yet it seemed to me, the more he looked the redder his face got. He didn't ignite though, and when he set off for home he was only muttering a bit.

What set him off, finally, was what he found when he got abreast of Morrison's. What he saw there was no less than eight people all setting behind easels and all painting pictures of Merle Hanscom's out-house. Some of them was holding a paintbrush up straight, eyeing the building with it across the top of their thumb like they was measuring it with a ruler. And there was one fellow going from picture to picture, apparently pointing out to the artist what he, or she, was doing that was, or wasn't just right.

Time he got to the house, Uncle Merle was almost running. He stopped long enough in his shed to fill a one-quart can with kerosene, strode out there to the end of the Panhandle, opened the door, doused the inside of the building in good shape, and with one stroke lighted a match and threw it inside. Then he stepped back to watch.

Now I want you to know that place made quite a goodlooking torch for a few minutes. There was some wails and shouts from over in Carl Morrison's lot, but Uncle Merle never even turned his head to look, and most of the crowd kept right on painting. They were an art school, we found out later, one that Carl Morrison knew the teacher of, and Carl had persuaded them to come over from Knox County and do some landscape scenes from his property. One or two of them run to the house to get to a telephone and call the fire department, but Morrison suggested (so Aaron told it after he talked with him later) that perhaps they should wait long enough to see if the fire was going to spread. It didn't. The place blazed up and fell over on its side. Then Uncle Merle walked slowly back to his house, returned with two buckets of water, and wet down the grass around what was left of the boards still burning. He never so much as looked over to where that art school was hard at work.

That was all near the beginning of the summer, which by now is almost over. The grass has growed up and covered the burned embers where Uncle Merle had his fire, and he acts like he was quite satisfied still to be owning that Panhandle. Down to Joe Ramsey's we are sure Carl Morrison is satisfied. And Aaron Abram, who has been up there to find out, says that couple that runs The Country Store ain't complaining, even if there is an eighth-of-an-inch of dust over all them paintings. They even sold one of them, he said, though they didn't recall who it was bought it, and Aaron told them if the fellow paid so much as a dollar, he was beat out of fifty cents, an idea that down to Joe Ramsey's Prayer Meeting nobody disputes.

LAWRIE

For a long time afterwards he could see the looks on the faces of the members of the board — that was what everybody called them, these samples of the outside world that sat around a table apparently to judge him again — could see the wide-eyed looks almost of shock, as if, having asked him a straightforward question, they felt there was something improper, something indecent about his stating, quite simply, the truth.

Then there was the scuffle of George Fitch's feet beside him under the table, and Fitch's nervous shuffling of the legal papers he had brought as he hustled them back into that black case, and the gray-haired man at the other end was saying something about "withdraw while we consider." So when Lawyer Fitch rose on one side of him and Art on the other, he got up too and walked out with them to the corridor where the windows were not gray things up over head, as they had been in the room, but were sensibly on the side, giving a wide view of bright foliage, the yellows, reds, browns, purples in the afternoon sunlight. And the two of them stopped and stared at him while he stared only at the sun-struck leaves even now fluttering to the earth. Then George Fitch shook his head and began muttering, "My God, Ben, how could you do it?"

Do what? What have I done now? he wondered, while Fitch who already knew better than to wait for an answer, went on growling, swearing: "My *God*, I never thought it, never *dreamt* it, that you would blow it like that. What in hell were you thinking about?"

"Laytenville. What do you suppose I ever think about?" Ben asked.

But no one, not even Art, answered, and after a minute, Art took his elbow gently and led him out to the car. Fitch was quietly whispering with someone at a side door but he followed, too, at last, and then they drove, mostly in silence, the forty miles back to the stone walls and the tower, where Art took him in and turned him over to Jeff who led him back to the few cubic feet he was used to, where he climbed into the bunk, and about half closed his eyes the way he had been doing for years, until the grayness of the wall changed texture, and the light changed too, and now for the eighthundredth or perhaps the thousandth time he saw Lawrie staring at him, felt the soft texture of her hair as he touched her head, gently crumpled her ears, or smoothed the silky softness of her flanks; felt the cool slap of her tongue against his palm, and watched her brownish tail comically swishing the dust of the cabin floor, Lawrie the while cocking her head saucily to one side so that he knew she was saying, "What next?" "What do we do now, you old bone-in-the-earth?" or whatever it was she thought he was when he just sat there, half-looking at her and trying to calm her with the touch of a hand.

What he was thinking of sometimes was the week Lawrie had not come home at all, when he and Beth had scoured the woods and highways, or so they thought, and put up signs at the store and the Laytenville post office and offered a reward, and still no sign of the dog, until on the eighth day, a big-boned, giant-sized, out-of-state hunter came to their door to say he had found a bitch about twenty feet off the road, who snarled and growled when he offered to touch her, but obviously could not get up on her legs.

So a few minutes later Lawrie happily let Beth pick her up and carry her to the hunter's car in which he took the three of them to the nearest veterinary surgeon. The dog had a broken pelvis that had already begun to knit, only a trifle out of place, and a few days later Lawrie was, miraculously, restored to her home and was beginning to walk again, anxious now never to be more than a few yards from master and mistress, as if closeness of the three could ward off the death she had stared so long in the face. But it could not, for within a month Beth died.

The physician explained to Ben why this had happened without warning. Ben, however, not only failed to remember what the man said but scarcely listened when he said it. What difference did it make?

Oddly, then, it became as if Ben were closer once again to his wife when he could stare into the dog's eyes, something Lawrie, like many dogs, was reluctant to have him do unless there were action she wanted from him, something Ben too was often reluctant to do because of the pain of returning at last to reality. But at times of course, they would stare into one another, deep, deep, and in the midst of her dark pupils somewhere the world turned back and there was Beth again in the cabin, stoking the wood firebox, or washing her hair at the kitchen sink, or cuddling puppy Lawrie, or holding both arms out to him, Ben, smiling, as she sometimes did — and for Ben the grandeur and delight, and then, by contrast, the pain, were so great that the tide would flood in his eyes, and he would blink, twist his mouth, flex his muscles, and standing up, reach at once for the shotgun on the wall.

Lawrie would prance then, playfully crouching, shifting position, crouching again, and together they would leave the cabin and make for the woods and whatever game was in season, or, at times, that was not in season, though it mattered little to Ben whether he brought home meat or not. It was the going that counted, and for Lawrie the circling through the woods, the exciting odors, the thrilling sounds, and the movement of a twig or branch or clump of grass that would freeze her, nose rigid, front paw lifted, ears alert, and tail taut, waiting for Ben too to sight the quarry.

Finally, of course, mercifully, he slept, and then, somewhat less mercifully, awoke once more to the gray world of confinement, to the dull round of physical functions, of washing, shaving, eating (who cared what?), of going to the woodwork-shop and turning out the smooth, sanded, hairjoint surfaces he had learned to make so well without thinking about them, certainly without ever caring about them. Then back again, at last, to the bunk, to the coarse-grained, colorless wall, and withdrawal to Laytenville.

Except that this time, a day or two following his return from that strange visit to the board, Jeff came for him and escorted him to Mr. Duren's office, where Duren himself sat beyond his desk and in a chair at one side was Lawyer George Fitch again, and they greeted Ben kindly and had him sit in the other one of the three chairs, while Mr. Duren explained to him that the petition Mr. Fitch had filed on his behalf had been denied, and that he and Mr. Fitch both were extremely sorry, because so far as they were concerned, since his conviction Ben had been a calm and productive inmate, who would not, presumably, be different if he were outside.

Ben looked at both of them calmly, showing nothing, and trying to think of the words to explain to men like these that the Laytenville he longed for was not just outside there to go back to but was fifteen if not more years in the past and therefore a man was just as well off one place as another, and it really did not matter. But he could not find the phrases, so he was silent, turned his head a trifle, and shifted his feet.

George Fitch cleared his throat and leaned forward: "What we want to know, Ben, what we are just curious about is what on earth ever brought you to say a thing like that. To begin with, neither of us believes it for a minute."

"Why not?" Ben said. "It happened, didn't it — once?"

"Yes, once," Fitch said.

A Saturday it was, and he and Lawrie had walked the half-mile to the cemetery, Lawrie chasing scents in circles around him, boundingly happy because this was one of the days Ben did not go off to the wood mill to work, leaving her tied on the run or in the pen, in dejection, in sombre despair, until the distant hour of his return, or until she could gnaw the rope or dig under the fence and escape (as she sometimes did) to the real business of life, in the woods. But so long as she was with him, she would not make off anywhere else, as they both knew; and so while Ben sat calmly, stolidly, for a time near that stone that held Beth's name and dates carved irrevocably into it, the reddish-brown dog surveyed the lots in quick-step march, nose, ears, and even eyes alert to every insect, bird, or odor; and only when, having exhausted the possibilities of the place, she stood once more before the man, inquiringly, almost patiently staring at him, did he get up and start their return trip.

Then when they reached home, there was Jake Braden's car in the yard, and Jake himself, standing near the cabin, awaiting their return, his warden's visored cap pulled down somewhat over his eyes because of the sharp sunlight. And the three of them stood there, the men talking, Jake reminding Ben he had warned him twice before about Lawrie-on-the-loose, and saying that early Friday morning he had spotted three dogs snarling and yapping over the carcass of a downed doe in a clearing, slashing bloodily at the fresh-killed flesh — and a doe carrying young, at that. Jake had got one of them with a rifle shot, as was his duty, but the others had made off, and of the two, one clearly was the reddish-brown, silky haired Lawrie. And·it was his, Jake's job now, whether anyone (Jake included) liked it or not, to kill her.

"You kill Lawrie," Ben said, "and I'll kill you."

But before Ben even realized what Jake was doing, perhaps even before Jake had absorbed the words Ben said, Jake had drawn his revolver and held it out for Lawrie to sniff, which she did in a gingerly fashion, and at that moment Jake squeezed the trigger and shattered the dog's mouth, face, and brain.

Ben moved at once to his cabin, entered, re-appeared at the door with a thirty-thirty, and taking quick but careful aim, shot Jake Braden through the heart as he walked away toward his parked car.

"And what they said was, 'If it came up like that again, if you was standing there with your dog and a warden stepped up to you and killed it, what would you do? And I told them (you heard me): 'I'd do the same damn thing I done last time, and don't you forget it!' "

"But it couldn't *be* the same dog!" Fitch was half out of his chair, his voice louder.

"Nobody never said that," Ben told him. "They said 'your dog,' and Lawrie was the only dog I ever had, I ever will have —" He stopped.

Fitch leaned back in his chair and covered his face with his hands. "Oh, Jesus, Jesus Christ!" It was no more than a murmur really.

Then Mr. Duren said quietly: "Ben, do you want to work in the shop today?"

"No," Ben said.

And so Mr. Duren signalled for Jeff, and Jeff held the door for Ben and went with him, silently, back as far as the entrance to his cell, where Ben, alone now, rolled back into the bunk, turning his face to the rough, kindly gray of the wall, and waited for the accustomed change, for the shift to the other world, with Lawrie's warm, silky fur beneath his touch, with her tongue at his wrist, and the limitless, dark depth of her eyes drawing him back into a quivering, vibrant life when there was still Beth.

But at last, of course, he slept, and when he awoke, could only ask himself, again, how many years yet he would have to live.

A TIME TO GATHER STONES TOGETHER

Mark Robbins had been going on the water as long as almost any of us could remember, even as long as Abner Lawton could remember, and Abner's vision of things went a few years farther into the past than any of ours did.

Abner remembered Mark from the days when Mark was a middle-aged, vigorous fisherman setting and hauling as many lobster traps as anyone on this part of the coast, and that may have had something to do with why Abner still gave Mark space on the wharf to stash his gear, and room in the big work shed to repair it, even for years after Mark Robbins' catch in lobsters was not worth much of anything to Abner, or any other lobster buyer either, for that matter.

Mark would come down to the wharf slowly each morning, even in those last years when the rest of the fishermen his age either were dead or were sensibly staying on the bank. And he would stand around with the rest of us, fall mornings, if it was blowing, talking about whether to haul or not, and finally going out if the rest did, or not if they didn't, just like anyone else.

But as the years passed we caught on that he was not really doing even so much as he used to: he would haul one, two traps, bait them and set one of them at least, and then set there, resting his weight on the cheese-rind and perhaps leaning against the hauling davit. After a while it got so one of us was holding back, trying to think up some excuse to stay near him just to make sure he kept going. But doing it made us resentful, one or another of us, to feel we had to lay back like that to watch over him and lose that much time from hauling our own string.

Finally, when I figured I had about all of that business I could take, I stopped Doc Wheatley one day up near the post office and put it right to him: if Mark Robbins was his patient (and he was) why didn't Doc lay down the law on him, tell him to stay off the water and go up there to his house on the hill where his wife Edith could look after him?

Doc stared at me several seconds until I begun to feel nervous. "There's no law says a patient's got to do what the physician tells him, Myron."

"Not even for his own good?"

"Not even for that," Wheatley said. "Besides, who is sure what's for his own good?"

"You fellows are supposed to," I said.

"*Supposed* to is right," Wheatley said. "I gave him some pills to ease the pain when it strikes. What more can I do?"

"When what strikes?" I asked.

"I'm not aiming to discuss my patients' troubles with you, Myron, or with anyone else, except perhaps another physician," Wheatley said, and that was the end of that.

So the next day, down by the wharf, when Mark wasn't with us, I told the others about what Doc Wheatley said, and after they had growled this way and that over it, Abner Lawton said: "All right, if you fellows have to complain about watching him, don't do it."

"What do you expect us to do," Charlie Boyd asked, "leave a half-helpless man to hisself?"

"That's right," Abner said. "Leave him to himself. He ain't never asked you to haul in company with him, has he?"

"No, he sure as hell ain't done that," Al Morrison said.

"Doc Wheatley give him some pain-killing pills when he is out on the water," I said.

"What for?"

"To kill pain," I said.

"Look," Abner told us, "he ain't asked no favors of none of you, has he?"

No one spoke.

"Well, then, I know damned well he don't want none of you

doing none for him now." And Abner walked out the door, crossed the wharf, and went back into his office.

So we stopped. We stopped slowing down, and hangin back, and hovering over Mark Robbins like we was a sheep dog looking after the flock, or whatever. And then one bright, October-sharp afternoon, I come in past Fishhawk Point and see Mark's boat drifting right up against the rocks this side of the Clam Cove. I eased up in there until I could hook a tag-end line with my gaff and hauled Mark's craft clear of the boulders far enough so I could make fast a line to tow his boat into port. And while I was doing it, I see Mark was laying on the floorboards just aft of the controls, and to me he looked deader'n a froze mackerel.

So I brought Mark's boat in to Abner's wharf, made his and mine both fast there and shouted to Abner for godsakes to telephone Doc Wheatley quick. Abner comes down to the float, goes aboard Mark's boat for a minute to check for a pulse or breath or something similar, and then says: "Yes, I will. But I guess there ain't no particular rush about it."

I went up to the office with him, where he calls Wheatley all right, and then hangs up the phone and looks at me like he had not even noticed me yet. "Now," he says, "who's going up there to tell Edith Robbins about this?"

"You got the telephone right there," I said.

"No-sir, I ain't going to do no such a thing." Abner leaned back on the edge of his desk. "Not with a piece of news like that."

I waited.

"One of us has got to go up there to tell her," Abner said.

"Well, why don't you do it?" I asked.

"All right, I will. But you was the one found him and his boat. You was the one towed them in here to the float —"

I took a deep breath. "Yeah. It's more like Doc Wheatley's business though."

"True enough. And the Doc will do it if you've a mind to set here and wait."

"I guess I ain't going to do that," I told him, and I walked out and up the road then the path a quarter of a mile to the Robbins house. But I found myself walking slower and slower, stopping now and then to pick up a stone a heave it off into the bushes, and yet after a time, of course, there I was at the kitchen door where there was nothing for me to do but to knock.

Edith opened the door and held it for me to come in, which I
did, nodding at her like a damned idiot instead of speaking. She
closed the door, and the two of us stood there looking at each other. I
couldn't speak. But she could, standing there straight and spare, her
gray hair pulled back tight over her head. "It's about Mark, ain't it,
Myron?"

I nodded.

"Well, what is it?"

"He's —" I stopped.

"You mean he's dead. Is that it?"

"That's right," I said.

"Was he aboard his boat?"

"Yes."

"You're sure: he was aboard his boat. You wouldn't lie to me?"

"So help me, God, he was, Edith," I said. "I was the one found
her adrift, just nudging against the rocks near Fishhawk Point. I
towed it and — and him — in to Abner's float. Doc Wheatley is down
there now, I guess."

She turned away and looked out the window. She didn't set
down. She didn't cover her face with her hands. There was no tears,
no sobs, nothing. I begun to feel uneasy, and took off my cap.
"Edith," I said, "the most of us been fishing out of here alongside
Mark all our life. It's going to seem mighty — We all feel —"

"Don't bother to say it, Myron. It was what he wanted."

"But — But —"

"Would it have been better if he died in a hospital, or some
nursing home, or even here in the house?"

"What I was saying was —"

She interrupted. It was like she was not listening, like she
couldn't hear me even. "The one thing Mark wanted was to die
aboard of his boat out there on the water. Well, he got his wish, a
man over eighty; and neither you, nor I, nor anyone has to feel sorry
about that, or pretend about it."

She turned from the window and faced me, her eyes wide and
excited, kind of. "On the water, day after day, year after year, all his
life, and he never quit. I'm proud of him, proud of him for that," she
said, standing tall and straight.

"Yeah, you're right, Edith. Of course you're right."

And he ain't the only one around here to be proud of, neither, I thought.

ANYTHING UNUSUAL HAPPEN?

PROLOGUE: Good evening, ladies and gentlemen. I am that old-fashioned device, a prologue, and I shall appear again at the end of the play in the role of Doris, a not too important character but a necessary one, I believe, to help wind things up.

Our drama takes place shortly after the midpoint of the twentieth century. It was not exactly the best of times. Many rather apathetic and doubtless some bored Americans, having lived — many of them quite painlessly — through the years of a hot war, and having been taught by *Newsweek* and *Time* that there was now a cold war, voluntarily, and more or less dutifully, stood watches to warn of supposedly impending attack from the Union of Soviet Socialist Republics, a nation that had recently, in defending itself, sustained the loss of more than twenty million citizens, and therefore was obviously about to conquer the earth.

The watchers performed this noble duty from Ground Observation Corps posts, wooden towers built on public land, or perched atop factories or other buildings. The one you and I visit this spring night stands at the summit of a town hall overlooking a valley community of 4,000 or so New Englanders.

(PROLOGUE waves a hand, and thanks to lighting or a withdrawing curtain, three walls of an hexagonal room are revealed. In spaces between the dark windows right, left, and center, charts of airplane silhouettes and typed lists of names stare from the walls. A table, center, five or six feet long, is strewn with magazines and supports a telephone. A door left leads to a balcony outside, but the true entrance is through a trap door in the floor.

(A young man sits beside the table in a wooden chair, its hind feet firmly on that trap door. A desk lamp sheds dim, yellow light on the thin book he is reading. A medium-strength spotlight comes up on the PRO-LOGUE stage left.)

PROLOGUE: I shall not tell you the name of that intense young man beside the telephone but let it become apparent later. Nor shall I reveal the title of the book he is reading. If I told you that, you would know something! But listen carefully: you will find he mumbles aloud some few nuggets of wisdom he culls from the text.
   (PROLOGUE fades slowly into darkness.)
MAN: *"Was ist gut? Tapfer sein ist gut.* All that increases the feeling of power, . . . power itself, in man. *Was ist schlecht?* All that comes from weakness." (He turns a page) ". . . was fond of all such as like not to live without danger."

(He looks up idly, thinking he hears the motor of a plane. Slowly he lays down the book, gets up and turns off the desk lamp. Starlight beyond the windows shows the slim summit of a church tower and the branches of an elm. He crosses to window and stares at the sky, first right, then left. He opens the door to the balcony outside, listening to the night. Nothing but wind. He closes the door and returns to his chair, the desk lamp, and his book.)

MAN: (reading) "shopkeepers, Christians, cows, women, English-men, and other democrats belong together . . ." (Pause. The church clock strikes one.) "the worship of mediocrity, the hatred excellence . . . . What is hated by the people . . . is the free spirit, the enemy of all fetters, the not-adorer . . ."

(He stares into space, thinking it all over. There is a noise of someone on the stairs below. He looks unhappily at the floor, displeased. Someone knocks on the under side of the trap door. The MAN lowers the front feet of his chair to the floor so that his weight is squarely on the door. More knocking.)

MAN: Stop that.

VOICE: (A woman's voice, insistent.) Let me up.

MAN: Go away. You are not supposed to be here.

VOICE: I *am*. I am supposed to be here, and you're not.

MAN: Leave me alone. How do you expect me to hear planes over all that racket?

VOICE: It is *my* watch.

MAN: No.

VOICE: Al Littlepage sent me. He said it was my watch. If you don't believe me, call up and ask him.

MAN: I never call up.

VOICE: Then I will.

MAN: You will do nothing of the kind.

VOICE: Don't be too sure about that. I shall scream and cry down here unless you let me up. (A pause.) Well? (Pause. She screams.)

MAN: Oh, God almighty!

> (He rises and moves the chair. At once the trap door opens and the woman who has been speaking climbs to the floor of the post and stares at the man in some perplexity, trying to decide who he is and what makes him like this. She is a self-confident, vigorous woman, a year or two older than he. He finds her presence even more alarming than he had imagined, and backs away left.)

WOMAN: Whatever made you think this was your watch?

MAN: (remote and superior) The list.

> (He points to a typewritten list on the wall, but when she crosses to examine it, he moves away.)

WOMAN: (reading) "Twelve to four: Mal Tower." Are you Mr. Tower?

MAN: What else?

WOMAN: (reading the list) And I'm on from four to eight. You know that's amazing: you were right!

TOWER: Of course.

WOMAN: But I was certain my watch, and Doris's, was at three. Mr. Littlepage said —

TOWER: Mr. Littlepage is a fool.

WOMAN: And then when no one answered the telephone — Where were you, anyway?

TOWER: Here.

WOMAN: And you didn't answer —

TOWER: I never answer the —
WOMAN: You never call up and you never answer?
TOWER: (remotely) Why should anyone who has ten cents be permitted to invade my privacy with trivialities, with nonsense, with attempts to sell something, with messages of ill omen?
WOMAN: But if you had answered, I wouldn't have come here.
TOWER: (avoiding her eyes) There are exceptions to every principle: this time perhaps answering would have been worthwhile.
WOMAN: (smiling with amusement) And you never call others, I suppose, out of respect for their privacy?
TOWER: Other?! They have none to respect. They live under glass in spotlights if possible. They flaunt their coming and going, their buying and selling, their eating and drinking, their courting and marrying, their births and deaths.
WOMAN: That leaves a little.
TOWER: But not much. Besides, I have nothing to say to them.
WOMAN: So-o-o!
TOWER: They have no thoughts, and their instincts are weakened to fretful impulse.
WOMAN: They are beneath you.
TOWER: (a gesture toward the windows) Indeed, are they not?
WOMAN: You know, you are a rather interesting specimen. Where do you live?
TOWER: (looking away) On the tragic plane.
WOMAN: (musing) Oh yes, of course. (Pause.) But even on the tragic plane, do not practical matters sometimes intrude? I mean . . . you're clothed and shaved — somewhat; you apparently wash, and eat, and — Well, for instance, suppose the filter center should telephone here, something important, or suppose a plane flew overhead.
TOWER: It is impossible for me to take seriously the avowed purpose of this happy cupola.
WOMAN: I might have known. So you take advantage of it?
TOWER: As I do of all things, as a wise man should.
WOMAN: That you may be alone?
TOWER: (loftily) I am alone in any event. Even when I am down there in their sweat and stench, pawed at by their clichés and luncheon clubs, half-suffocated in the mutual throat-slitting of what they call "working together" — even there I am beyond them; I am alone.
WOMAN: (with a gesture around her) Then why — this?

TOWER: Here it is easier. Here I rest, take surcease from the strife of keeping mankind in his place.
WOMAN: And womankind?
TOWER: Her too, until tonight.
Here I am literally as well as truly above them all, apart from them. Look out here at their sheds and ornaments:
> (Warming to his speech, he goes to the window, and when she moves beside him, he neglects to draw away. Scornfully:)

The county courthouse: thin marble pilasters disguising shoddy brick, like the veneer that is the law itself, keeping a pretty polish on the petty haggling of lawyers who jockey within its walls to determine who cheats whom and who will pay for whose uncovered indiscretions.

Beside it the jail sprouts like a perennial skunk cabbage, its dank cells smelling of social vengeance as wholesome as an unwashed latrine, its inmates the weak and the foolish who have been caught breaking laws the strong made to contain the weak. On the top floor, over the jail, resides the sheriff. A scrawny vulture hovering over society's refuse, he collects food money for the prisoners and spends half of it to clothe his wife and other more expensive women.

Look. The library: a dusty repository of moldy superstitions, of pedantic misinformation, and meeching falsehood, smothering here and there a few grains of wheat that no one in Homeville — least of all its encrusted, thin-brained librarians — knows how to winnow.
WOMAN: Not even you?
TOWER: Perhaps. (Turning to another window.) Over there is the school, where fools are taught by the half-ignorant to be bigger fools than before, where on selected evenings, adults — those with such meager maturity as Homeville boasts — gather in sweaty crowds to watch schoolboys throw a ball here and there and schoolgirls strut about in thinly disguised sexual ritual — all, young and old alike, screaming, wagering, and disputing with one another over the results, as if putting a ball in a particular place secreted somehow the very meaning of life.

Down here lies that glittering mart, the drug store, filled with packaged pain-killers, Its panaceac pharmacopoeia offers to prevent everything from blues to babies. It sells rattles for children, indigestible colored-glucose for callow youth, and cliché culture in paper-backs for the older innocents, who buy here the same books they could borrow for nothing at the library their town grudgingly supports.

Beyond are the cocktail lounge and the theatre, cesspools of the community, where the wretched escape from tawdriness into further tawdriness, to the accompaniment of canned cacophony.

That curious structure is a lodge. In it, men dressed up like children at play call one another by odd, childish names and solemnly perform meaningless rituals in the delusion that they are doing something significant. (He points to the church tower:) Every seventh day most of these and other idiots wander into yonder temple because they fear what their neighbors may think of them if they don't. There they listen to teachings which each of them seriously believes keep everyone else from being altogether evil. For himself, of course, each holds a rather relaxed ethic, but nearly always he lacks the courage, the strength, or the intelligence to take advantage of it.

At the hospital, doctors when not engaged elsewhere treating the illusory symptoms of those who think they are sick and are not, or the genuine symptoms of those who are sick but will get well anyway — doctors blindly following a sadistic tradition here stretch out the days of those who are sick and would be better off dead. Between doctors' calls ghoulish visitors come to this abbatoir to gloat over the ill luck and weakness of the sick, silently congratulating themselves on *their* superior good sense which keeps them less unhealthy.

And the undertaker (He turns to another window.) — mortician he prefers to call himself — high priest of the inner temple of true materialism, the worship of the corpse. This skilled, unctuous, sanitary collector of garbage has surrounded his necessary disposal of rubbish with a colossal quantity of mumbo-jumbo and hush-voiced garnish, calculated to mute at excessive expense the fact of death and pretend it is something else.

Then, the bank! Oh, the conservative, the respectable, the rock-bottomed and copper-sheathed institution that condescends to borrow a thousand dollars from you, to lend five thousand of it to me — providing I don't need it — and then prates selfrighteously to both of us about honesty and trust! This one is the most glorious and delectable hoodwink of simpletons in the bunch, for it hoodwinks even the simpletons in the bank who piously suppose themselves honest and ethical and upright —

WOMAN: Mr. Littlepage
TOWER: Yes.
WOMAN: Who is a fool.
TOWER: Precisely. His secretary knows more about running the bank than he does.
WOMAN: Then she should be president.
TOWER: No need of it. She has the power. What does she care for the title? Besides, she is his mistress.
WOMAN: You seem to know a good deal about the People's Trust.
TOWER: As well I might. It is there I work.
WOMAN: Where President Littlepage takes you into his confidence?
TOWER: I would not accept his confidences if they were offered. But one sees certain things.
    (There is a flash of lightning.)
WOMAN: You make a fascinating purveyor of gossip. You have such a comprehensive, beatific view of our old, rock-founded New England community.
TOWER: (apparently bored) I am, I regret to state, a teller, and meet a large number of citizens.
WOMAN: You are new here.
TOWER: I have been here a month.
WOMAN: Otherwise I should have known you. Where did you live before?
    (Faint thunder.)
TOWER: On the tragic plane.
WOMAN: I mean, where did you live on the, uh — on the trivial plane?
TOWER: Another state, another town, another bank — all dismally alike, depressingly myopic, bigotted, and gregarious.
WOMAN: I am surprised you work.
TOWER: It is the price you pay for insisting on living.
WOMAN: But it must gall you so.
TOWER: True.
    (Lightning.)
WOMAN: If you could just promote something and get away from all those people . . .
TOWER: For instance?
WOMAN: Oh, I don't know, but you should think of something, a teller with your brain and your opportunities.
TOWER: Do you take me for a warped fool? In other words for a criminal?

WOMAN: Ah, you have moral scruples.

    (Thunder a little nearer.)

TOWER: Do not take me for a child with a brain-washed slave morality either. I would not hesitate to make off with half the bank if I could do so safely — and providing I wanted it. Do you think for a minute that Littlepage does not do the same? Do you think he hesitates to vote himself a bonus, or an increased dividend, or a higher salary? He just happens to have his hands legally near the till; I don't.

    (Lightning.)

WOMAN: (From now until the light goes out temporarily, her tone changes. She may be arch, but never ironical.) Is there nothing you want?

TOWER: (Staring at her.) Such as?

WOMAN: What does any man want? One like you with brain, with clear insight into character and situations, with superior courage — one like you could take all that a man might want.

    (Thunder. The starlight dims out.)

TOWER: (Hesitantly looking her up and down:) Money?

WOMAN: If that's the way to what you want. You would never let the repulsive, small-minded people of some narrow community stand in your path. I know you wouldn't. You are too big a person for that. And what are the things a man wants money for? For power, for luxuries, for women —

    (She stands right, obviously posing, the primary stimulus be-
    fore Pavlov's dog.)

TOWER: (Quietly:) What's your name?

WOMAN: (Slowly:) Ev-e-lyn.

TOWER: Evelyn.

WOMAN: (smiling) Eve perhaps.

    (Lightning.)

TOWER: Do not lie.

EVELYN: Who would stoop to lie?

    (Thunder.)

TOWER: Don't.

EVELYN: I shan't.

TOWER: I do not want money.

EVELYN: No?

TOWER: Nor luxuries, except the luxuries of thought and freedom.

    (Lightning. He takes a step toward her.)

EVELYN: And women?

TOWER: Not women, but woman.

> (He crosses, starts to embrace her. Loud thunder. She laughs, sliding away from him. She moves quickly center and sits on the table facing him. He follows her and she holds out one hand, for a moment making him hesitate.)

Do not tease.

EVELYN: I am not teasing.

TOWER: It is ridiculous to tease.

> (He tries to kiss her. she turns her head sideways.)

EVELYN: (laughing) You talk too much.

> (Thunder and lightning, which last apparently shuts off the electricity, for the desk lamp goes out. In the light of the second flash of lightning it is clear that she is permitting him to kiss her neck, her lips. The lightning ceases. The thunder rolls on, gradually growing fainter. A jet plane roars low overhead, then only receding thunder, then silence. When the desk lamp comes on again, EVELYN stands right, adjusting her hair and skirt as if TOWER were not even present. He is seated on the chair, leaning forward, his arms on the table, watching her intently, devouringly. Count of five.)

TOWER: (almost tenderly) My name is Mal.

EVELYN: (unconcernedly) Is it?

TOWER: Short for Malcolm.

EVELYN: Oh.

TOWER: (gently) Did you live here, in Homeville, when you were a child?

EVELYN: Of course.

TOWER: (eagerly) What was it like?

EVELYN: You have already told me what Homeville is like.

TOWER: But what was it like for you? What were your parents like? your brothers and sisters? your friends? What things now half-forgotten brought you fear, pain, anguish, joys?

EVELYN: What can it possibly matter to you?

TOWER: I want to know. I want to know everything about you! And you won't even tell me your name!

EVELYN: I told you.

TOWER: Yes, Evelyn. But your last name?

> (She sits at the table staring through the window right, at the returned starlight.)

EVELYN: It is no concern of yours. Anyway, it is my husband's name.
TOWER: (standing) To hell with your husband!
EVELYN: Really?
TOWER: Yes, really. (He comes part way toward her around the table.) The Biminis, Honduras, Madagascar? Naples? Zurich? You name the place and we're off to it —
EVELYN: (laughing) The bank teller's fantasy!
TOWER: Don't laugh! What I told you I meant. Money? The lack of it won't stand in my way. I can take money, safely, quickly, and be out of the country — like that.
EVELYN: Do, by all means. I assure you I'll never say a word.
TOWER: You'll go with me.
EVELYN: (amused) You think so? Why?
TOWER: Because everything is different now —
EVELYN: Oh, is it?
TOWER: You I shall have, and possess, and love, and keep —
EVELYN: On the tragic plane?
TOWER: Where else?
EVELYN: But suppose I am on the trivial plane?
TOWER: You were not, moments ago, here in the darkness — and the light.
EVELYN: Very exhausting thing, that tragic plane. As a steady diet I would never endure it.
TOWER: (intensely) You do not know yourself.
EVELYN: No? And do you?
TOWER: I do. I know you —
EVELYN: So soon?
TOWER: Quickly, instantly, in a flash of lightning, I know you to the center of your soul and possess you.
EVELYN: And yourself?
TOWER: Myself I have known for many years, perhaps always . . .
EVELYN: The cosmic consciousness . . .
TOWER: Yes, cosmic, mine, and yours . . .
EVELYN: You, who were alone, exalted, keeping mankind in his place and womankind in hers!
TOWER: I told you all had changed. Before, I had not reached the new level of understanding, had not discovered the mate —
EVELYN: Mate?
TOWER: who will bear my children.
EVELYN: Your children? What, contribute to the miserable human race?

TOWER: No. The super-race.
>   (She stares at him in unbelief. He interprets her look as
>   surrender and comes closer to her.)
By noon tomorrow I shall have the money. I will call for you and you
shall go with me.
EVELYN: (pleasantly) In the noonday sun.
TOWER: In the noonday sun. And why not? What care you and I
for their petty morality, their sniveling laws? Where shall I come?
(Count of three.) Where?
>   (When she does not reply he comes close to her, touches
>   her hair with his hands, starts to embrace her. With a
>   sudden angry motion she pushes him away, catching him
>   off balance so that he half falls against the table.)
EVELYN: Ignorant fool! You think I would bear you a child. As if
you were a god, the condescending Jove? Where now is your aloof
superiority that looked down on the pettiness, the cowardice, the
hypocrisy of the strong and respectable, and the even more degrad-
ing hypocrisy of the weak? Where is the hard ivory of your mind
now, Mr. Tower, that so delightedly spotted the unlovely truths of
life and pointed them out for my benefit. I had known them all a
decade ago, more than a decade, but I never felt surprise at the
discovery. You did.

You, the strong, the independent, the philosophic, the reserved, the alone — within ten minutes of coming here I had egged
you on to butter your own ego — it was ridiculously easy — to the
point where you had no choice whatever. You thought you had
made a conquest. You! How entertaining!

There was a conquest all right. I led you on to prove that I could,
that I could drive you where I wanted, and even change your mind.
(TOWER keeps his head down, eyes lowered.) Now the lone
philosopher aspires to the role of lover, of mate, of father. Now he
would steal for the sake of these banal joys, foolishly risk the clutches
of hypocritical law, risk his magnificent freedom — not just risk it,
but throw it away!
TOWER: Evelyn, do you know what cruelty is?
EVELYN: And why not? Are not the strong cruel to the weak?
TOWER: (pleading) Please, listen to me —
EVELYN: I have listened. I listened a long time while you told part
of the truth about Homeville. You were not far wrong, for all you
left out. They are not much, weak, cowardly, self-deceiving fools,
but they are more than you, the lofty talker! You are not even up to
my husband.

TOWER: (softly and sadly) You love him.

EVELYN: Who said anything about love? He begot children better than any of yours would be. He supports them and me better than you could —

TOWER: (hopefully approaching) And if you don't love him?

EVELYN: Oh, can't you understand? I am tired of you! I am bored with you! The moment of my amusement is over and I want you out of the way. (She opens the trap door.) Now get out before I start screaming like a lunatic or wring your scrawny neck —

TOWER: Evelyn. Evelyn, darling —

EVELYN: No! Get out, get out, get out! Go to hell if you're not in it already. GO!

> (Beaten, TOWER slowly descends. EVELYN slams the trap door over his head, stands a moment staring at the door, and then, apparently dismissing him entirely from her mind, goes the long way around the table to the telephone. She dials a number, waits.)

EVELYN: Daylight blue calling. . . . . . I wish to report a jet plane. . . . Passed here six minutes ago. . . . In the storm I couldn't tell . . . probably northeast. . . . Not high at all, low in fact. . . . You're welcome.

> (She hangs up and straightens the magazines. She is looking through one of the windows when DORIS opens the trap door and enters.)

EVELYN: You're late, aren't you, Doris?

DORIS: Evelyn Littlepage! What are you doing here?

EVELYN: Country club parties bore me. Besides, I could see Al was about to get drunk. I came down here to escape.

DORIS: Escape Al?

EVELYN: Al and everyone else. Sometimes I wonder how you can stand being his secretary. My God, it's bad enough being his wife.

DORIS: (looking away) Who was on?

EVELYN: That new teller from the bank.

DORIS: (not interested) Oh. Anything unusual happen?

EVELYN: Unusual? What do you mean?

DORIS: Just what I say. Did anything out of the ordinary happen?

EVELYN: (thinks it over, then deliberately) No, nothing out of the ordinary at all, really).

> (She stares seriously at DORIS as slowly the lights fade.)

CATABASIS

Because Cathy had sent a strongly worded telegram (COMING TOMORROW NOON   I ACHE   I SUFFER   WHAT MUST I DO) I went down to the boat to meet her. Dim, sombre drums were throbbing within me too as I drove slowly down to the wharf, pulling off at the side into the ragweed and pebbles and dust, where I hoped no one would see me and speak. And after the *Governor Silsby* had caromed into the slip, and a beer truck, a camper, two bugs, and one Oldsmobile had growled and zoomed their way up the ramp and off toward town, I got out and waited.

She was the last of those on foot, tall, strong as always, her hair pulled back sharply from her face, not fluffed out as it had been a few years earlier; her eyes still sharp, piercing, yet ever on the verge of compassion.

I held out my arms, but she did not accept the invitation. She dropped her suitcase, grasped my hands, and squeezed them tight.

"Charlie." She looked in my eyes, beyond them. "Thank you."

"For what?" I said.

"Just for being here."

"Lunch?"

"No. I have eaten." She turned and looked away, across the harbor. "Pardon me: I lie. I mean, I can't eat."

"Come on. Get in the car," I said. And I broke free from her and reached for the suitcase.

87

At the house, after she had talked polite nothingness with
Mother, had left her suitcase in her room and run briefly the waters
of purity in the bath, she came back to the study where I waited. She
talked at first, her eyes scouring the walls, the watercolors, the ship
models, the sculpture, though it was clear to me she did not really see
them. There was someone between us, between her and the watercolors — watercolors of lobster boats, of skiffs, of dories, or rocks
and buoys — or perhaps I am wrong; perhaps it was merely I who
could not expunge his presence, Hal's presence, though I do not
believe it.

He had come to Rockhaven years before I did — Hjalmar
Gustavsen, the youth, the immigrant, learning to speak a Yankee
English, to chip bricks in the granite quarry, to struggle toward
making more than just a living in the world, in the land of liberty and
equality. And by the time I set up practice here (if you could call it
practice: no one came to the office at all the first few months), Hal
had what you might consider a full life already behind him: by
degrees he had left the quarries and become a lobsterfisherman, first
in a skiff, later in a small powerboat, then a larger one; he had
married, had had a son, and for some years had deserted lobster
fishing for trawling, and gave other Rockhaven fishermen a jolt
when he delivered his catch by sea direct to the Boston wharves
where he auctioned it off as if he'd just come in from the Grand
Banks — except that his catch was fresher and brought a higher
price. Not that he grew rich, but he got by, and then some. In the
days when ground-fish at Rockhaven brought three-fourths of a
cent a pound and lobsters scraped bottom at twelve cents, nobody
did more than that.
    If there was a cataclysmic turning point in Hal's life, and I claim
there were two or three of them, one was his son's death. Quickly, in
his teens, the boy had become a man. With a powerboat, a substantial
string of traps, and his father's almost tireless drive, he set traps in
the most dangerous waters, where he lost many but gained even
more in the catch. "No gain without some risk" would have been
inscribed on his gravestone, had he had one.
    Worst of all, he did not lose himself at sea; he fell, plunged,
dropped (no one knew which because no one saw it) from his father's
craft while it was under his father's command, and so far as Hal or
anyone else knew, he never surfaced, nor did anyone ever find his
body, though his father nearly drowned too in an attempt to do so.

Hal, already a widower, struggled then not just with bereavement, but with a despair compounded by profound loneliness. There were his in-laws, and there were his fellow fishermen, who were kind and sympathetic, but they scarcely filled a life. There was the sea and his work upon it. And yet —

"Charlie, for God's sakes! I am speaking to you: what was she like?"

Cathy had grabbed my shoulder and swung me sharply back to the present, to my own study. "What was who like?" I asked.

"Margaret. Margaret Gustavsen. Did she fail him too? Did we both fail him?" Cathy stood before me, high over me because I was still slumped in that deep leather chair of mine, a device calculated to move one to another time and place.

I stared at her. "You think *you* failed him?"

"God damn it, you know I did, Charlie! Don't act like this, as if you didn't remember anything."

"I didn't know her — Margaret, I mean. She was before my time. It was all right — her marriage, I guess. I never heard anything else, not from Hal, not from anyone. She was what she was, a Rockhaven kind of wife —"

"Don't be nasty."

"I'm not. It's a compliment as such things go. All right?"

"All right, but why then did she have to go and die on him?"

"You ask that? Ask *me* that? You, who've lived more than four decades now on the crust of our cruddy earth?"

"But he loved her, Charlie. I know he did."

"He loved you too, when you came along."

"Oh Jesus-Jesus-Jesus!" She turned away to the mantlepiece, put an arm along it and bent her head down into her arm.

Silence.

In a way, I wanted to hold her close, to talk of a great many things, but they were all things she knew already, had known for years. Instead I stepped up behind her and turned her toward me. She buried her face against my chest, and clung fiercely, her hands clutching at the taut flesh of my back.

The change — the first change — started when Hal became an activist. The price of lobsters was down, badly down, with little three-quarter pounders (chicken lobsters, they called them) flooding the market. Men continued fishing from habit — inertia at work — and it was then that Hal read something, in *The Readers Digest* perhaps, about fishermen's co-operatives on the Nova Scotia coast. Someway, one way or another, he followed this up and, after writing a letter or two or three, acquired as house guest an organizer of co-operatives who, despite youngness and inexperience, learned first to listen to lobsterfishermen and later to talk to them. The result was, in fact, a fishermen's co-operative that lasted several years and perhaps sowed the seed that later produced others along the coast.

But that was not the crucial change for Hal, though he may have thought so. It was that the organizer, Jim Archer, talked with him almost endlessly: first it was fishing and economics, of course; then politics, then sociology of a kind. And within a week, as a means of promoting the co-op, Archer was conducting group discussions with a handful of fishermen in Hal Gustavsen's kitchen. The friendly arguments ranged wide, even if never deep, and persisted between Hal and Jim often late into the night after the other men had left. It was not that Jim Archer brought any new ideas (Hal knew about socialism, co-operatives, anarchism, communal living, and passive resistance) so much as it was that he provided a speaker and hearer, not just an audience but a suddenly very exciting idea-echo-chamber, into which the two of them now and then lured a few others.

When Jim went away, he left some books, and Hal discovered, or perhaps rediscovered, for all I know, the satisfaction, or the pleasure, or the escape of immersing himself in reading. With Jim gone, he could hold his discussions with the authors of books. And there he might have stopped, or his interest withered, or stagnated, had it not been for Rockhaven's summer populace. Hal came to know some of them, to see the world their way, perhaps an academic way, and with the greatest enthusiasm, graduated, you might say, cum laude.

"Who did it to him? Who did it first?" Cathy asked.
"Did what?"
"Changed him, took him away from what he'd been before?"
"A lot of people, a lot of us."
"Yes, *us*," she said.
"What are you trying to do, flagellate yourself?"
"No! Damn it, no, Charlie." She buried her head again, some-where near the lapels of my coat. Then, muffled: "But I've got to settle certain things with myself. Don't you see? Can't you under-stand that?"

The truth was, I *could* understand it. I stroked her hair. "All right," I said. "There were a lot of us did it. That Archer kid who came here organizing everyone to the hilt, or trying to, him with his Ivy League degree and a head full of concepts —"

"And you, I suppose, had no concepts?"

"Oh, don't worry, I had them too, and I too was an influence. I don't deny it; I accept it. Why can't you do the same?"

She shuddered. "But you didn't marry him."

Slowly I took a deep breath, then let it out. "We weren't alone, Archer and I," I said. "After us came the Friends."

"I wasn't a Friend."

"No, but you were a friend of the Friends. And you know, from there on, how it went — Quaker meetings, concerns, discussion groups, books in soft, gracious livingrooms with open fireplaces —"

"But how — how did he run afoul of them, him in his sensible fisherman's house down there on the creek and them in their Edwardian summer villas along the north shore, all built on Nineteenth Century, dollar-a-day, Yankee-coolie labor?"

"Your prejudice is showing, Cathy," I said.

"I don't give a damn if it is!" She sounded like tears.

"How do I know? I can't remember everything. I may have introduced him to them myself, or then again, perhaps he was doing some caretaking —"

"Oh, God, don't bring that up."

I was silent.

After he came to know them, the engrossing people from Germantown, from Sewickley — after he had talked and talked with them and thrown himself into the realm of ideas, of books, with the same energy he always directed at fishing — he called in a carpenter and a mason, and had them merge the parlor and downstairs bedroom into a livingroom with a fieldstone fireplace and heatilater at one end, wood panelling, and bookshelves from floor to ceiling. He installed a new rug, two easy chairs, and a couch, and bought enough books to fill all the shelves right and left. It took months because he had to drive at the fishing to earn the money to do it — but no matter; he would have driven himself in any case. Nor was that all: he read the books, all of them, not dutifully but from curiosity, for pleasure: *The American Dilemma* and *A Study of History*, *Hiroshima* and *The Naked and the Dead*, *The Adventures of the Black Girl in Her Search for God* and *Cry, the Beloved Country*, *Native Son* and *Invisible Man*, *The*

Lonely Crowd and *Dark Legend,* and *The Young Lions* and *Mr. Roberts.*
His list went on and on, seemingly endless with excitement.

To go to Hal's house and talk, evenings, became a pleasure for
me, and sometimes one or two others. It was a place where we could
argue — whether we knew what we were talking about or not — stare
at the phantoms in the open-fire, and roar and laugh at each other
without anger, without bitterness. There were the weeks when Hal
saw everybody as other-directed:
    "You're about as other-directed as a wildcat," I told him.
    "But how do you know a wildcat is not other-directed?"
    "What, with his little psychological radar bouncing messages off
all the other wildcats. . . ."
    "Sure, why not?"
    "You're out of your mind, Gustavsen. Out there on the water
how much do you think about any other fisherman, or how much do
you think about what he thinks of you? He's not helping you catch so
much as a crab even —"
    "But back here in port we do, we are, Charlie, thinking of each
other, I mean. We form a co-operative!"
    "Self-interest."
    "Sure, self-interest, but broadened self-interest."
    "Inner-directed," I said.
    Hal bounced up in his chair and then down again. "All right,
what about you?"
    "I'm inner-directed too," I said. "The more I hear about other-
the better I like inner-."
    "You — who come out to an island to practice medicine, when
you could have gone anywhere, made six times the money!"
    "I am out here," I shouted, "to try to keep some of you triple-
distilled idiots from digging your graves with your teeth, and suc-
cumbing to epidemics, and asphyxiating each other with tobacco
smoke, and —"
    Suddenly Hal was laughing, and then we were both laughing,
and anyone else if he happened to be present. Later it was Theodore
Reik's warmed-over Freud, *Listening With the Third Ear,* and then
Frederic Wertham's catathymic crisis: "You and your mother-
murderers!" I told him. "You — a squarehead — don't even know
your *Hamlet.* Hamlet never murdered his mother."
    "No, but he wanted to! Don't you see? He took it all out on
Polonius behind the curtain — he discharged the impulse."

"Dead, dead for a ducat."

"Exactly."

"I don't accept that. The case is unproved —"

"You know what you remind me of? The 'perfessor' in *Raintree County*. You are just as cussed, as odd —"

"That book again!" I said, grinning.

And that was the way it went, many nights, among several of us around Hal, lounging in front of Hal's fireplace.

But I was not back there now; I was in town in my own living-room with my friend Hal's widow, who was also my friend, and had been before she became his wife, seeking comfort in my arms, but more comfort than just arms could ever give. And I was not quite sure what to say next.

"Look, Charlie, I didn't marry him just to show off, or prove something about the human spirit, or out of pity, or even for fun —"

"It wasn't fun?"

"Yes — idiot — of course it was. But that wasn't why —" She pulled away from me and walked across the room to the windowseat, staring out at September yellows and greens.

"All right: I know you wouldn't marry anyone for the wrong reasons, not consciously."

"And unconsciously?" She did not look at me; she did not turn her head.

"Nor that either," I told her.

"You're lying."

"Who cares?" I asked, and waited.

"We went fishing together that July and August," she said. "I mean — real fishing, for money, not sports stuff. We set trawls. Sometimes we handlined, lived aboard, and it would be three four days before we would get back to the house and get cleaned and rested. I got so I liked it — even the stench of bait, the sleek load of fish, which meant cash. My hands grew scarred and toughened. I was proud of them. . . ." Her gaze drifted off.

"Yes?" I said.

"And then that fall, when the cold came, and the long nights, and the wind — blows, heavy blows — I began somehow staying ashore at the house. I recall no decision, no turning point. It just came about, seemed sensible for Hal — a warm house to return to."

"Sure. Why not?"

"But then — goddamn it, Charlie — from the day I began staying ashore, or almost that, Hal grew different. He—"

She stared past me at nothing.

"Well?" I asked.

"How can I say it without sounding like a disgusting intellectual snob?"

"Perhaps you can't."

"All right, then, but you know what he was like before, when I met him that summer at the Griffiths', and for some years before that, you tell me: his mind was alive every minute. We tore at ideas, probed at them, a bunch of us. You were there sometimes; you were in it."

"Yes, I remember," I said.

"Well, it stopped. Not instantly, of course, but quickly, very quickly, so much so that I was shocked. It was as if because, suddenly, I was a fisherman's wife keeping a fisherman's house for him that all the books he'd bought and read and shelved, all the discussions he'd gloried in, all the things he'd learned from everyone else (and he'd absorbed a lot) — as if all that didn't matter any more, didn't even exist."

"He was tired," I said, "damnably tired. Going on the water in cold, rough weather is exhausting work, and then the worry about money —"

"It hadn't tired him before, rough weather hadn't," she said. "Not the year before, nor the year before that, and you know it."

"Age," I murmured.

"Oh, don't give me that, Doctor. Not that fast."

"Was that all you married him for? Because of a vibrant curiosity about the world, about ideas?"

"Of course not, you idiot! Oh, Charlie, you are so thick sometimes! Or do you just put it on? But when a person changes, when something vital goes out of him —" She swung away from me and left the sentence unfinished.

"He was also worried about money," I said.

"Yes." There was a long pause. When she spoke again, her voice was little louder at first than a whisper. "I always thought, rightly or wrongly, I was no shirker. I work hard at whatever I do, no matter what it is. And I worked hard for him."

I nodded. "Hal knew it, too. He was impressed."

"How do you know?" She sounded belligerent.

"Because he told me. 'My God,' he said, 'work. You never saw anyone like her!' I wasn't surprised at his admiration. After all, Hal was mostly energy himself."

Silently Cathy stared through the window and across our tidal creek at the spruce woods.

I figured she could hear his voice.

"I didn't throw it around — the money, I mean." It was as if she were speaking to herself. Then she turned and looked squarely at me. "But I was never one to pinch either. Do you remember how bad the market was for lobsters, for fish, those first two years? I know, the prices were up a bit, but the expenses were up even more. For Hal it was another depression. I'd never known anything like it. There was struggle at the agency in Manhattan, but nothing like this."

I remembered all right. Always, when Hal had some money in hand, it went, but in those years there were too many places for it to go and not enough of it to go there. His coupé that had once looked luxurious and snobbish fell prey to decay and was replaced by a plodding, dented Dodge of uncertain stability. His shore clothes — his going-out-in-the-evening ones — became less startlingly flashy, as did Cathy's. And no matter how hard Cathy worked at the house, no matter how well she kept it, even improved it, that was no cash crop, and the sea was simply not providing enough.

The solution — which I observed but which neither of them really talked to me about — was for Cathy to return to New York for three months to work in the agency she'd left, an outfit that was delighted to get her back. After all, a copywriter who, they knew, was both imaginative and intelligent did not walk in the door every day or so.

The first time perhaps this move did not produce ostentatiously bad results. Hal was alone much, and lonely, of course, and though some of us tried to ease things for him, at least with our company, there were certain overtones, certain self-judgments we could not erase. I noticed then he sometimes accepted not just two highballs, but three, four even, before tackling the winding road back to his and Cathy's house.

He was delighted to have her come home, and she was delighted to be there. But then, a year and a half later, they — or was it she? — did a repeat. This time it was worse. Hal was no fun to be with any more simply because he drank too much, grew capriciously contrary and incoherent. And then, feeling my unspoken but I suppose obvious displeasure, he took up with Sam Schofield for his shore-time drunks, Sam — who had already been drunk half his life. And this time, Cathy's return could not mend everything at once, or rather could not mend everything. They were back together. Cathy, at least, I judged, was trying hard. Her married daughter and baby even came for a visit, which helped, because Hal liked them, but did not help enough. There were certain harshnesses, unpredictable spats, ones I witnessed, when Hal, for instance, struggling with the recalcitrant car engine, scarcely turning his head, would shout that he would go into town when he was God damn good and ready. And instead of sniping back, or just withdrawing in silence, Cathy would say: "Thank you for the courteous response."

And it was about then, shortly after that at least, that they launched the caretaking fiasco. I thought I saw Cathy's hand behind the blueprint, and I have discovered no reason to change my judgment. They had many friends, acquaintances, who owned the north shore estates. After all, these were the people through whom they had met, these owners of the gray and white and brownish mansions, with their attendant summer houses and stone piers that graced the sheltered shoreline between Rockhaven and the next island. Hence it was with little difficulty, when some worker dropped out, or some employee was unsatisfactory beyond tolerance, for Hal to acquire agreements for caretaking, first for one, then another, and yet another estate.

I never knew what went on exactly. I would see him sometimes driving out to one or another of the places, apparently with the greatest of regularity. But before a year was gone, I began to hear about considerable unhappiness on the part of the owners: closing incomplete with resulting damage from frost and leaks; inadequate repair work; and multiple billings, perhaps the result of careless bookkeeping. All of them found it an embarrassment, but finally, of course, someone spoke up, despite friendly relations, and then someone else, and so on, until caretaking, for Hal, as a business, was non-existent.

"In a way, that was the worst idea of all," Cathy said.

"What was?"

"Weren't you listening? I thought you, the kind physician, were going to help."

"I was," I said. "But my mind drifted."

"So, yours does that too, eh?"

"Never a doubt."

I was driving her to the graveyard because she had insisted on it, and we were following the twisting gravelly road past the old ice house, around the rim of the quarry, and across a perilously decrepit

Rockhaven bridge. "Moving to Connecticut [she said] was the worst."

"Worse than your going off by yourself to fill the coffers?"

"Much worse. Can't you see?"

"I'm not sure. Separation strikes me as the worst."

"But there was a separation there too. Think of it: you're a skilled lobsterfisherman, trawler too, who can respect his craftsmanship and therefore himself. And suddenly you're living in a Connecticut town, a commuter town, and not in the best section of it either. It's on salt water, of course, which is something, and you work at a boat shop, which is also something. But it turns out, as you must have known, that you're no boatbuilder, no carpenter really, and so you paint, and varnish, and clean up the shop, and tend the tool room, while your wife, going to the city on the 8:10 and returning on the 5:15 brings in four times the cash you do."

"I see — all too well, in fact." I brought the car to a stop at the right place. "Whose idea was that?"

"Whose do you think?"

"Don't torture yourself, Cathy. Don't."

"I wouldn't if I could help it."

We got out and stared at the grave. There were flowers still lying, in disorder now, from end to end of it, and about half-wilted. Rockhaven cemeteries, for some reason — probably because of the proximity of the quarries — have granite borders around every burial plot, so that they are starkly defined, lifted a little from the common clay of the rest of the earth. And there was a stone there, of course, at one side, for Margaret, none as yet for Hal, and no space for a third.

"I *would* be away — off in the West Indies — when he needed someone," Cathy said.

"Please. *Please!* Must you?"

"I told you — yes." She looked at the plot before us. "But I'll think of something."

"It's not immoral — to go to the West Indies."

"Not usually." She walked away a few steps and looked around her. Three gulls circled us momentarily, then swung away to the west. "Just coming to a cemetery doesn't amount to much, does it?"

"For some people."

"What, I wonder, did I expect? A catharsis of pity and fear? Or anyway pity?"

"Why not?"

"Because I'm not normal."

"Come off it, Cathy!"

"All right, then: I'm not like everyone else."

"Granted. So much the worse for them."

"You don't need to build me up."

"I'm not."

Swiftly a cloud blocked out the sun and threw us in shadow. "Take me away, please. I don't like it here," Cathy said. Back in the car, and until we were about halfway to the house, she was quiet. Then: "When did you find out, Charlie?"

"About what?"

"About the cancer."

"Too late," I said. Then, because I knew she would ask anyway, I went on: "That's one of the troubles with living on an island: one physician — suppose you've fought with him about a bill — and then fall and get a compound fracture of the leg."

"Hostile? Hal didn't fight with you about a bill."

"No. We didn't even fight. If only it *had* been a compound fracture, perhaps at least we would have met."

"Well then why?"

I drew a long breath, and for a second or two held it. "He was jealous." I looked at her.

She turned her head fully toward me. It was difficult to say whether she were looking at me or through me. "Jealous?"

"That's right, jealous. And over you."

"Oh, God Almighty!" She stared through the windshield. "But Charlie, for Christ's sake, why? Why? That was all over before he and I ever met."

I said nothing.

"After that, you never even touched me, to speak of."

"I know."

"Then why?"

"Like a virus, only more complicated, which makes it worse." I waited. "You were the one lived with him, married him," I said. "Did you never uncover ideas, suspicions?"

"Yes," she whispered. "Once in a while, yes."

"And unfounded —"

She nodded. "Always. Once he thought every fish and lobster buyer within forty miles was blacklisting him."

"So, you see?"

"Still it's hard to take."

"But why *you?*"

"Who knows? Because I was around, vocal — like you; because I was interested, not just in you, in everything, in everyone. I'm only guessing, of course."

"But he did come to you finally."

"No," I said, "he didn't. I drove past his place one day, slowly, the only way you can drive on that cowpath, and there he was trying to weed his garden. He was thin — startlingly thin, weak, bent over. And so I stopped to speak, in a way insisted he speak whether he hated me or not."

"And he spoke?"

"If you could call it that: a rasp, a painful, excoriated squeak."

She put her head in her hands. "Don't. Don't!"

"You asked," I told her.

She nodded.

"It was then I took him in hand, gently, whether he approved of it or not. And he didn't resist. Things had gone so far, he looked almost as if he were grateful, as if it were a relief to have me send him ashore to the hospital."

"Where he died."

"That's right," I said.

"While I was off to the West Indies."

"Stop indulging yourself."

"That's what you call it?"

"I do," I said.

"Very well, I'll stop. At least," she added, "I'll try to stop."

When we went into the house to have dinner with Mother, the sign was up by the telephone for me to talk with the operator, which I did. Mabel, who has grown quite efficient at judging cries for medical help, told me all three calls sounded of standard importance but that perhaps I could ethically allow myself a quick schlurp of soup at the table before I met the patients at the office. She would notify each of them. I wondered for a moment who was running the health care of Rockhaven Island, me or Mabel, but I figured this was a subject I might better not tackle on a day when I had troubles enough. So after a few minutes with Mother and Cathy, trying tactfully to jog Mother's memory just enough so that she might possibly recall who Cathy was, I went back to the car and drove the half-mile to my pseudo-clinic: one simple fracture of the wrist, the result of a fall on the cellar stairs; one laceration of the hand (three stitches) following a slip of his clam-opening knife, or so Mel Potter said; and prolonged wails and detailed complaints from Mrs. Tillmark who suffers from every known disease, plus a few I have never heard of.

When I got back, Cathy was alone in the livingroom, reading a paperbacked translation of *The Inferno*. She closed the book and returned it to the shelf, and for a while we talked of Mrs. Tillmark and of Mother's increasing senility. Then there was silence while Cathy really began to see the watercolors, and I stared at her, trying to fathom what was boiling beneath that brow. And when finally she looked at me again, recognized that after all I was in existence, I asked her to marry me.

"Try not to be frivolous, Charlie."

"I'm not."

She looked at me again, quite steadily. "By God, you're not, are you?"

I shook my head.

She stood up then and crossed the room, not fast — it was a kind of stately, obligato walk — and stopped beside my chair, stooped, knelt even, and put her hand gently to my face. "You're kind, Charlie. You're nice . . . nice . . . nice, and human, and affectionate."

"I also happen to love you."

"I know." She put her head down against my arm. "I know you do." Her voice became slightly muffled. "I won't even say I don't return that love."

I moved my arm and put it around her. "Well, then —"

Ever so slightly she shook her head where it rested against me.

"Why?" I asked.

She sat on her heels and grasped my hands. "Think of it, Charlie. Your mother's home, the one she's been running for some years now —"

"With a little help from employed neighbors."

"Yes, but hers all the same. And into that you bring Catherine, twice widowed, and it becomes *her* house. Or, if it doesn't . . ."

"My mother," I said, "whose life expectancy you and I can estimate in months."

"Don't be heartless."

"I'm not, really," I said quietly. "It's just true. You know that."

"All right, then: along comes one Catherine, middle-aged, twice widowed, and seizes her darling son."

"Happens all over the world, daily," I said.

"Not to people her age, and yours," Cathy said.

"A poor excuse."

"Anyway —" she swung around, almost quickly — "that's not the real obstacle."

"No?"

Cathy moved back to her chair and sat down. She stared across the room into nothing. "There is a loneliness — no, a loneness — for which no one has drawn a successful prescription."

"There are lots of things for which no one has drawn successful prescriptions, but we keep trying."

"Only you don't go in for witchcraft, for old wives' remedies."

"Maybe you think we don't. Anyway, once in a while one of them works."

"Or something works, by chance."

I was silent.

"Marrying you — old wives' remedy — that's not enough."

"Don't stretch an analogy too far," I said.

"It won't do, Charlie. It won't do," she told me. "I've done enough evil, failed enough on the island of Rockhaven."

For a long time — a few minutes even — we were both silent. There is a limit to how much one should probe at a wound. I stared intently at Cathy and she looked away. Finally she rose and said she was going to go to bed, and we said goodnight, our arms strangely and tenderly around each other.

In the morning I discovered she was not in the house, and explained to Mother that she had left me a note saying she wanted to take the six a.m. boat without disturbing us — as good a lie as any.

Not until noon did the misty precipitation of innuendo begin to reach me. I was in my office two or three hours. Then, at the drug store: "That Cathy Gustavsen — Hal's widow — I hear she was in town last night." I nodded, received a long, expressionless look. Then nothing.

At the post office: "That Gustavsen woman you met to the boat yesterday —"

"Yes?"

"You seen her last night?"

"Certainly. She stayed with us."

Laughter, and end of conversation.

On the strreet: "Hey, Doc! That woman of Hal's — what the hell you done to her anyway?"

"You tell me."

"Ha!"

Or: "You seen Neil Svenson this morning?"

"And why should I?"

Broad grin, half leer. "I guess you won't. He's probably wore out."

And then: "You don't never come down to Al Bunker's, do you, Doc?"

"Hell no!"

"Well maybe you oughta. Just once in a while maybe you oughta." Sly look.

Before long, I could put together some of the pieces. Besides I knew where to go to fill in the gaps, and (I think) how to sift out colorful lies from reports, though the reports, God knows, were colorful and painful enough.

Al Bunker's, a badly weathered, undistinguished shed about a hundred yards off Water Street, is Rockhaven's underground drinking resort, a kind of moral abscess on the butt of the community, a place for the most part ignored by the citizens of Christian Ridge, and frequented by a handful or more of the bored, the pitiful, the alienated — all desperately seeking some distraction from distraction, be it alcohol or sex or the roll of the dice.

It was there she went, suitcase in hand, apparently, near midnight, among men and a few women whom she knew, and who knew her, only rather distantly. They must have been astonished, I imagine, to see Cathy whom they had not seen in months, whom they had never seen at all at Al Bunker's. But a slug of whiskey, a second slug, and a third, and the astonishment surely vanished.

With whom she drank, and how long, and by whom she was pawed, and how frantically, I can imagine, though I prefer not to do so. The gossips agree, however, that Phil Stinson pulled Sam Schofield away from her and bounced him off the wall, and that sometime after one a.m., Neil Svenson — the weathered, broad-shouldered, dynamic epitome of high-line fisherman — flattened Phil and Sam both, and then scooped Cathy up like a bag of grain and carried her off in his car, presumably to some deserted road, or empty house, or wherever. I learned no more, then, except that, come daylight, Neil brought her, and her bag too, to the early boat and that both of them looked considerably scruffy.

Sombrely I went about the day's affairs: patients; ritual lunch and dinner with Mother, staying casual and pleasant, telling her nothing; in revulsion switching off the TV — an inadequate anodyne — and mixing myself extra highballs before, briefly, I could sleep. Then in the next day's mail came Cathy's note:

Charlie,

Contrary to the popular dictum, believe all you hear. You will not be deceived.

I was far on the lower path, the only one open to me, too far to move any way but onward.

Doubtless, even then, I blew it. Usually I do: the Catherine-pattern.

An attempt, absurd of course, to pay the bill, and I can't tell yet whether the check will bounce, has bounced.

Don't try to reach me, Charlie. The address, like the phone number, is going to go blank.

I write because I think you may understand, and I hope this note will help.

Cathy

I read it many times, folded it, unfolded it, read it again, sealed it away in my desk before I wore it out.

Do I understand? Often in the lonely suffocation of the night, I ask myself.

Perhaps.

And do I understand better, thanks to Cathy's note?

Perhaps, I have decided, but only perhaps.

THE VISITOR

Ralph Wheatley

In Oak Harbor we know better, we think, than to expect anyone to change his nature. If Herb Clintock suddenly stopped carrying off tools and gear that belonged to others, the neighbors would figure he was deteriorating and fast approaching death. If Crow Taylor cleaned up his boat and yard and quit poaching, we would know he was ailing. And if I stopped answering sick calls in a howling gale and an ice storm at two in the morning, Charlie Freemore, our first selectman, would without doubt telephone the Bangor State Hospital to reserve a cage for me.

So when I saw Raym Davis bringing in lumber and nails and paint, and then putting in good May weather building a porch — or railed sundeck I guess you would call it — just off his kitchen, I knew a kind of limited alteration was under way, and I don't mean just on the house either. It simply was not in character for him to do it, not his former character at any rate.

Some will say I am wrong, that a man never does change. And that is perhaps true, but a man may be like a diamond with many sides (if you can accept such an unlikely comparison), and all at once, thanks to some chance, some minor coincidence, a new side of him, once hidden, is turned to the sunlight.

Incredible? Well, consider Raym as a case history. I've known him since he was thirteen, as unruly and irresponsible as a good many like him. When he was sixteen, the high school, such as it was, and he gave up on each other, more or less by mutual agreement, and he started lobsterfishing on capital supplied by Abner Lawton, our local buyer. A year later or such a matter, he bought a second-hand mixture of metal and fabric that in loose terms might be called a car, and commenced a fairly routine sampling of the county's beer and bodies — meaning the live, human and female variety of the latter.

I was in no way surprised the next fall when I heard he had married Pete Greenan's girl, Alice; and in no way startled when within a month Alice came to me for prenatal care. She was attractive as young people are attractive, simply because they are young. But I could spot nothing particular that was going to outlast youth: no fire, humor, curiosity, excess energy — whatever those things are that endure better than good looks or being under twenty. I thought of Pete Greenan's half-finished house near the mouth of Minnow Creek, the one we all knew he would never touch another nail to, let alone a paint brush, where Alice had grown up with about six others — maybe half of them Pete's — in four rooms that leaked wind when it was fair, and wind and water both when it wasn't. And I could understand that she might not show any sign of sparkle or push. I wouldn't have either.

She had the baby — with considerable difficulty — in April; and Raym paid my bill, also with considerable difficulty, or so I judge, in the next ten months.

Eighteen months later she was back, carrying another one. This time the delivery was worse, but they were lucky I guess you call it — they both lived; and a few weeks after she came home again, I got Raym and her down to my office and I laid down the law: no more babies. Also the means of implementation — all in one easy lesson.

So they survived. I wouldn't say the kids thrived, but they grew, weathering the usual diseases. Raym seemed to work fairly hard, saved up his catches in the right seasons and was lucky in unloading them at a good price. The junk-heap, or maybe it was the third junk-heap, gave place to a car that was merely second hand, and Raym bought himself a used double-barrelled shotgun, and the car a chromium exhaust pipe.

It was Alice who was not better. There was no longer any youth, except in years, but that was not all of it. At times Raym talked to me about her: "Christ, Doc, she's crazier'n a hoot owl. I got to send her away."

I stared past him and out my office toward the spruce trees that line the deserted road to Fishhawk Point, and wondered how I could show him the way the sun runs through life, how before a man dreams it could even happen, his wife is dead and his children have rightly grown and left. But there is no way for a young fellow to believe that; he can't do it. Just as well, perhaps. Fishhawk Point, with its canted stones: I was still staring at its old deserted road. There are days I am almost ready to go down it solo and quit everything. Raym's wife wasn't as bad as all that. I looked at Raym's eyes, at the muscles of his face. "Who would bring up the kids?"

He looked down at the carpet between his boots and did a little half-silent cussing. "How they brung up now?" he said.

"They get loved and fed, don't they?" I asked. "They get their clothes changed and a washing now and then —"

"Now and then is right," he said.

"More than you can do when you're out hauling. You would have to have a housekeeper."

"Look, Doc: how would you like living with a woman trying to count to a billion? After you come home from work, after supper, middle of the night sometimes. I tell you she's crazier'n a coot."

"That's not crazy," I said. "Most of us have no idea of a billion. I take it she has, or is going to have."

"And then when she stops . . . She can't remember where she stops. 'Was it one million, two hundred and seventy-six thousand, four hundred and thirty-two? Or was it one million, two hundred and seventy-four thousand, one hundred and forty-seven? As if I gave a goddamn!"

I set out to tell him it might have made quite a difference if he had, but I have learned better than to rely on the direct attack. So I sat there, trying to think of what words to use. If I should say *neurosis*, or *disturbed* . . .? But I didn't. "We've never decided what *crazy* is anyway," I said. "Maybe there's something as strange, something I do or you do, as strange as counting to a billion."

He punched one fist into the palm of the other hand. "Goddamn it, Doc. Goddamn it!"

So finally he left. Trapped? Certainly he was trapped, and thinking over my patients and relatives, I have about concluded no one is worse off, except the condemned souls that aren't.

From all this perhaps you can judge that I was mildly interested this spring when I saw him building a deck and a rail where his kitchen stoop used to be. He painted it too, gray and green; then he drove a nail in the top of the rail where it made a corner, brought a kitchen chair out there for himself, and sat netting trap heads. I went past his place every day about that time because I was making regular house calls to ease Clara Greenough's pain — which was all anyone could do for her. Raym's house was at the top of a short, steep hill where the road curved just after it came to the summit, and since I had to slow down anyway, I naturally glanced over toward his place. It wasn't much of a house, but the location was good: it looked out over one or two other homes and yards, and then over the harbor and a number of the boat moorings.

The first time I saw him sitting there netting, I thought nothing much about it except that for reasons unknown he had gone to much trouble to build a place to do something he could just as well do in the kitchen, or in the workshop down at Abner Lawton's wharf, for that matter. Then, because I am an optimist anyway or I wouldn't even practice, I thought maybe he had built it to humor Alice; only Alice was never out there. Then I became aware that Raym almost always was, even when it was good hauling weather and he should have been out on the water. It seemed strange to me. It was true, of course, that Phipp Schuyler was building him a new boat down to his shop, one that wasn't launched yet, but after all, he still had his old boat.

And then by chance one day I mentioned the whole business to Phipp Schuyler, and he told me what it was all about; otherwise I would not have known, perhaps even until three or four hours later.

Phipp Schuyler

Well, in a way it is nothing to me what they do with their lives; whether they drown, shoot each other, swap wives, or go in for polygamy don't make no difference to me. And some weekends I don't know but it looks like they are setting out to do all four to once. All I do is build their boats for them, and just so long as one of them produces cash or some reasonable equivalent thereof, I don't have much to complain about.

You take Raym Davis, for instance: last fall he come to me, asked could I build him a thirty-four foot lobster boat. He knew damned well I could. It was just a question of how much boat he wanted, how much power in it, how much he was going to have to pay for it, and where was the money. We got through the first three parts of the question in good shape. He went back home and I figured that was the last of it. Then ten days later he was down to the shop again with a bank cashier's check for the first twenty-five percent. I kind of wondered about it, and yet I could see that perhaps he ain't too bad a risk. I suppose he owns his old boat, which should sell for something. And doubtless Abner Lawton, just to keep the lobsters coming, has co-signed his first note. The bank must have figured a chattel mortgage on the new boat would be good for the rest. Anyway, after I took on the job, he produced the other checks on schedule, all made out just like the first.

Thing is, I wondered if anyone up to the bank at the county seat knew about his Saturday nights. Not that they are necessarily a hindrance, though they might be. Nor are his blasts any worse than other people's — some of them, that is. The question is: are the other people borrowing thousands from a bank on slim collateral?

For a year or two now, soon as he got a little bit tired of being married, Raym begun to make a regular thing of turning up at Crow Taylor's Saturday nights. Crow and Belle — I guess she is Belle Taylor now whether she likes it or not — Crow and Belle run quite a lively outfit. They have the grocer deliver a case of beer there every morning, just like the milk. And sometimes it is not just beer they drink: I went there once one forenoon to get Crow to do some painting for me down to the shop, and before I even got in the door, Belle pushes a tumbler full of whiskey into my hand. The rooms was full of cigarette smoke, whiskey fumes, wine stench, stale beer odors, and indifferent git-tar music. All the worst people was present: Amy and Fitch Blake, Spider Philbrick, Herb Clintock, Nancy Teele, Phil Dexter, and such. They was anywhere from two to four to a room, draped over chairs, beds, floors, anywhere at all.

Well sir, for a long time that was where Raym Davis went straight as a die Saturday night and I don't know but between times. Doubtless still does, for which I can't altogether blame him: if I had to live with that thing he does seven days a week, I might do the same. But if the bankers don't mind his ungodly helling and sleeping around, then I don't. They are the ones likely to get stuck with the bad debts, not me.

Then last week he come down to the shop, after everyone but me had gone home, and spread out on the work bench the brass letters he had bought for the transom of his new boat. He put them in the order he wanted, and I stared hard at him quite a few seconds, scarcely blinking: "You out of your mind?"

"Not likely," he said.

But I wasn't too sure of it. "You don't have to put them on the boat."

"What?"

"Ain't no need to. Just leave them laying out here on the bench until the crew sees them tomorrow, and by suppertime — hell, maybe even before noon — it'll be all over the village."

Raym stared out the window at the gray water. "Whose boat is it?"

He can be some stubborn when he's a mind to.

"You might at least switch them around, like this," I said. And I put them in a different order: L I S E.

"Looks like some kind of bug," he told me. "Anyway, I already sent in the registration forms."

"Well, do it that way if you want," I said. "You're the one that's their neighbor, not me. You taking out any life insurance?"

But he wouldn't answer, just got up and walked out.

Ilse Fleming

It is a strange place, this, with its great rocks on the points of land, the drone of the surf roaring as if there were something wrong with my ears, the houses against the low hills at the sides of the harbor clustered, and last August when we first came, the haunting, rhythmic groan of the fog signals, different from, yet curiously like the warning signals at home. And there are the gulls slashing the cold air between us and the evergreens — pine, fir, hackmatack (strange name) — on the opposite shore.

No, Carl did not lie to me; it is a beautiful place. Nor did he deceive me about his work, nor the amount of money; he simply said there would be enough. He did not mention the stench of lobster bait that clings to clothing, but I suppose being used to it, he would not think of that. I made my own decision; I said I would — I, the silly girl who the moonlight nights loved because they were romantic, not caring about the British bombing runs, for at first of course I had never felt them — and finally every house on the block burned but ours and the fire chief's. His was next door to us.

Even in the cellar, where we lived for long months then, the radio sometimes worked, and early we knew the Americans were coming, from the rumors knew it too, from the conversations in the streets. And like nearly everyone we were before the last days out, because we were so ordered, building road blocks, carrying those stones — heavy, sharp stones — and clumsy, splintered, flesh-tearing timbers from the destroyed houses. Mother worked always fairly close beside me, but there was that old man, old enough to have fought them before in the earlier stupidness. I remember we were bending down, trying to place a rock — it was too heavy for me, too heavy for him too I guess — and he laughed. "Which way do you think the Americans will come?" he asked.

"On the road. After all, it is from the west," I said.

"No. They will cross the fields, naturally."

"Oh, it is not a thing I would know about. I did not think of that."

"Neither did the captain," he said, "or the senile major or colonel, or whoever is running this local foolishness. They will cross the fields."

And they did.

Like many others, my parents looked forward to the Americans' arrival, for it would mean the end of fighting, and to war. But for me the Americans were like the moonlight, romantic. What did I expect, I wonder: clean, untarnished young males in newly pressed uniforms, all rich?

There was a certain unpleasantness — hours, days and nights of it at first: the sounds of the heavy boots banging hastily along the pavements, the shots nights, daytimes too, singly and in great bursts — because of stupidity, even after the radio announced it was over, ordered it to be over, some sergeant, some corporal *Dummkopf* waiting at a street corner with the men under him, insisting upon killing and guaranteeing that others kill him and those with him. Suicides. Idiots.

Then when that was over, still the boots in the streets, the knocking and coarse shouts at the door: "Macht auf! Macht auf!"

"Die Mädchen! Wo sind die Mädchen?" And one who could not recall even what country he had reached: "J'voudrais des jeunes filles." Or others simply yelling in American, which I find in the books is not exactly English, and if one did not understand, or like Mother not to understand pretended, yelling louder and louder.

"No. No girls here. Only old women," she would tell them finally. And it was a good thing she had no attractive clothing, no hair-do, or make-up, or they would have been after her instead, for she was — is, I hope — a very charming woman, who can also, when necessary, be very very bitchy, which is where I get it, of course.

But once the occupation was complete, there was less unpleasantness. There were even good things: a little glass back in the
windows, the return of my father's piano from the country — a
kindly American captain saw to that — living upstairs once more,
rugs. And then because Father — or was it Mother? — had been
accepted so-to-speak by the Americans, there were guests, providen-
tial guests who learned soon enough to come bearing gifts, who
seemed to like to hear Chopin, who surely liked to hear Gershwin,
and among them was Carl, who came not to listen, but to look — at
Mother perhaps, but mostly at me.

I must not blame him. He was fair. He is not a bad man. No one
obliged me to accept him as a suitor, and if I am not wholly pleased
with the results, I have only myself to complain of. His uniform
helped, of course, and the commission. Then there were those
broad shoulders, the tremendous muscles — what girl was going to
object to them? And that quiet of his, that silence in front of any
group not his own fellow fishermen, and a sparseness of speech with
anyone, including me — a quiet that in a foreign land with rather
formal traditions, manners, impressed us as a species of charming
reticence. What I did not realize was that it was almost eternal, that it
was — what shall I say? — like the lid of a pressure cooker holding in
all kinds of things he could not say, partly because his world had
foolishly trained him to be ashamed to say them, partly because he
did not have the words. And it is true some words have not been
invented yet; still, there are ways . . .

The neighbors, I find, are often — but not always — like him.
Not Renée, of course, but she is not a native, and only by unfortu-
nate accident a neighbor. The others are not unkind, not thought-
less, but contained, constrained even. His relatives too, of course, his
brother, his sister-in-law —

We were together at Christmas, and thinking how terrible it was
going to be, and remembering home, I bought the wine, the straw-
berries — frozen, but no matter — and mixed a *Bowle* for them. I
laughed: they were so surprised that it tasted good.

Carl always gulps liquor — bang, right like that, as if it were the
manly way to drink, whereas with *Bowle,* of course, it would be the
way to over-drink. So I teased him, sitting in his lap, making him sip
from my glass only. I was wearing the green dress, earrings, my
Mexican beads — a combination he can never resist, although I am
not sure he knows that. And so things went well. Dinner was happy,
almost gay, and afterwards I sat on the floor with Carl's nieces and

nephews, joining them in banging drums, quacking toy ducks, driving wooden pegs with a little mallet.

But one cannot remake human character in a single Christmas.

When we first came, it was from New York state where he had been for months still in the Army, and I had learned somewhat in American to converse, partly from talking and listening, attending movies, partly in that strange manner from books — when we first came, the yard and the garden were ugly, an ugly chaos. In my short lifetime I had had enough of chaos, but it was late in the season to do much. I picked up the bits of iron, the scraps of wood, broken glass, metal cans. I pulled weeds. Then this spring when the ground began to warm, I asked Carl to produce some garden tools. "You get the implements; I do the work," I said.

"Vegetable garden?" Carl asked.

"No. The vegetables we will buy, please. Flowers only."

Many days I lived out there, trimming the edges of the turf, cutting graceful ovals, crescents, encouraging the iris to flourish, striving with wild roses to teach them where to extend their thorns and blossoms, installing pansies, and inserting gladioli. *Dem Glucklichen schlägt Keine Stunde.* For me, then, time did not exist. And yet out of this happiness, from this content, sprang much trouble.

Raym Davis

Without doubt Phipp Schuyler is one of the best boatbuilders within two, three hundred miles. I don't know but more than that. I am still not sorry I am having him build me a boat, but there are times, like this afternoon for instance, when he makes me mad enough to spit in his eye. Even then I don't. I just clam up and walk away.

It wasn't really that he said anything that wasn't the truth or that he shouldn't; it's the way the bastard says it, in his smart, kind of bitter voice. The worst of it was, after I got up to the house I knew he was right; anyway he wasn't wrong. It would be all over town in about twenty minutes, which there is no need of, not yet anyway. So early next morning I phoned him down to the shop and told him if he wanted he could scoop them letters up into a cardboard box and stow them out of sight under his desk, and he said, "Yeah, I've already done that." He might talk himself, but then again he might not, or at least not much.

It all started this spring when I was setting there at the kitchen window netting a trap head and looked down into Carl Fleming's yard. What I saw give me quite a jolt to start with, because although Carl Fleming is an all-right fellow, he is as ordinary a cuss as any of us, and his yard, any time I noticed it before this, was an easy going mess of all kinds of stuff, just like mine. But not any more. It is trimmed up like the deck of a yacht now. The first day I noticed, the flags was coming out, and she had got some of them blossoms on stems that is like the sheer of a good boat, and then pansies. She was kneeling down, bending over, her fingers in the black earth. Long sandy hair, lots of it, kind of stiff and curly. Wasn't nobody going to see that one in hair curlers ever, on the road or to home neither. No need of it. And when she straightened up, for a few seconds I could see her face. I held my breath. I don't know how long I set there, twine in one hand and needle in the other, not moving even. Every motion she made with her hands said life to the trimmed grass, the dandelions, the earthworms I guess, even the bugs. I see the shadow of a gull winging across the grass, and them flowers around her lean a little, suddenly, in a light breeze.

Had I been blind all winter? I wondered, because it was five six months Carl had been back from the service, and I must have looked at her, I suppose, going or coming between their houses and post office or store. Maybe I had not really seen her, not in jeans or rain clothes, or then again maybe Carl had kept her in the house, anyway in daylight, which might not have been too stupid at that. Then I remembered there was some kind of a touse not long ago between Carl's wife and Reenie Grant; Alice had gone on about it one evening, but I get so I don't know what Alice says anyway, and I figured well, that was what Carl got for finding himself an outlander and settling her in a house next door to another one.

Even after she got back in the house I still set there staring at the light. Then I come back to the kitchen I had never left: Charlene and Bobbie was letting the dead yells out of them, like they do about two-thirds of the time, fighting over a wooden cart, and Alice was swaying back and forth in the rocker counting out loud, somewhere in the last half of the second million. It had been going on all the time, without doubt, only I hadn't heard it.

That was when I says to myself: "If she keeps it as good as that, she must be out there a lot. By God I am going to have me a deck where I can net trap heads in peace." And that same afternoon I measured up the space I wanted outside the door and drove over to town to get me the cinder blocks and the plank.

Phipp Schuyler

Well, he set out to take my advice — Raym Davis, I mean. Called me up from the house not long after he talked to me and asked would I scoop up them brass letters of his and put them out of sight and keep them for him, which I did. But his relapse into good sense wasn't long-lasting, anyway not long enough, for soon as I and the crew got anywhere near finishing up on his new boat, he come down to the shop, lined them letters up on the transom and screwed them into place himself. I didn't even know he'd done it, and wouldn't have found out myself til Monday morning if I hadn't happened to go up to Albert Grant's to see was he in the mood to work for me two three days the next week.

Albert is no boatbuilder and not much of a carpenter neither (never will be), but there come times when I can use him for rough work down to the shop, and where he almost never gets up out of his chair next to the stove if he can think up a half-decent excuse not to, he is nearly always available.

He was available this time all right, but so was that wife of his, Reenie; that is, if you call screaming at the top of her lungs being available. She don't pronounce her name like that but I cannot twist my tongue around it the way she does, so to me she is just Reenie.

That bitch.

Anyhow, seems Albert had been down to my shop late to pick up an old rusted hammer of his (or more likely something unrusted of mine) he thought he needed, and seen them letters spelled out on the stern of the boat. He come back to his house all feathered out, of course, to report to his wife, and about the time I knocked at the door and come in, she had not had a chance to open the emergency valve yet, and mister man, I want you to know I really caught it. You would've thought I was the one broke nine out of ten of the Commandments in one weekend, to hear it.

"That beetch! That beetch!" she screamed. "She will be after Albert next. Not a home is safe. That beetch!"

"Stop giving your call letters, Reenie," I said, "and tell me what this is all about."

Reenie's hands and arms were breaking all speed limits, heading in every direction at once. "Zat Hun! Zat Boche!" she shouted, so excited now she could not say a civilized *t-h.* "She who told me to go back to that house in Bordeaux wiz ze red light over ze door! She — she — who spread legs to les - Allemagnes - les - Italiens - les - Russies les - Français - les - Anglais - et - sans - doute - touts - les - autres . . ." It

all run together like that finally and I couldn't catch none of it, until
at last I got her to simmer down enough so Albert could tell me about
finding Raym Davis's boat named for Carl Fleming's wife.

"You see! You see!" she screamed. "What she has done — it is
indecent."

"God, I knew about that three weeks ago," I said.

"You said no-*zing*? You said no-*zing*?"

"What the hell could I do?" I said. "There's no law against
naming your boat *Ilse*. Besides, what do I care? He could name it
Reenie and it wouldn't jar me a mite."

About that time I dodged a skillet and picked up one of the
chairs to shield me from other implements.

I knew, of course, why Reenie Grant was so burned up.
Everyone did. Oak Harbor's Franco-Prussian War, we called it.
Albert got out of the army a lot sooner than Carl, no doubt because
the army was happy to get shut of him. He had one of them government allotments, where some MP bounced him head-first off a stone
wall trying to sober him up and curb disorder, or whatever, so with a
little federal money, and a large mortgage, he bought that indifferent little house and lot where they live now. It was quite a shock to
Reenie to find they was going to live in a place like that and not be
rich. Over across there, I don't know just what Albert told her, but he
must have lied to her in good shape. And by the time she got here she
was pregnant and broke and wished she had never fell afoul of him,
but there was not much she could do about it. She had a right to be
ornery and disgusted — no doubt of it — but there is limits.

Wellsir, then Carl Fleming comes home with a fair satchel of
savings, at least half of which he puts in the bank, and that blond
goddess he'd married over in Nuremberg or some such, and buys his
house on the land that butts up against Albert's. They ain't very near
to one another, and a good thing they ain't, but the plots do butt.
Everything was all right — neutral, you might say — until that new
plumbing Carl had had installed even before they got there quit
working. Naturally the Flemings went ahead and made use of the
out-house out to the back of the lot. Only thing was, Albert and his
wife was using it too as their regular establishment, and claimed it
was on their lot. Carl pointed to the old rotted fence posts and said by
God it wasn't. Then Albert said them old fence posts didn't prove
nothing — which is quite right — and the way the deed was drawn
they was all in the wrong places, and Carl said he didn't believe a

word of it, but neither one of them dug out a deed to clench the matter. And if I know the way deeds was drawn around here for a hundred years or so, it wouldn't have helped much if they had.

Well, anyway, one thing led to another, and first thing we knew, Reenie flew aboard Carl's wife up to the post office at mail time, yelling, screaming, and calling her a Boche and a Jew-killer, a goddamned Nazi who did not even own her own shit-house. Five or six of us was around waiting for the window to open, and it was exciting all right (I got to give Reenie credit for livening things up), but it was embarrassing too, as you would know if you could see Carl's wife. She is quiet, and slim, and has — I don't know just what you call it — dignity, I guess. She is not a person you yell at, unless you are Reenie. You don't know why; you just don't. And so when Reenie stopped because she was out of breath, none of us spoke. There was something some of us wanted to say, I guess, but we didn't know quite what it was or just how to say it. And then Ilse — that is Carl Fleming's wife — she spoke.

It is hard to tell you about her voice. There's a German tinge to it, of course, but it's just a light touch. She don't sound at all like us, but then she don't sound like the summer people neither; she puts every sound, every word in place, like it was a beautiful rounded pebble she picked up on the beach and would let you look at it.

"No, I am no killer of Jews," she said slowly, looking straight at Reenie. "Why do you not go back to France and into that house you came out of, the one with the red light in the window?" Then she turned her back, went out the door, and walked down the road to her house.

Now for a few seconds that took the wind right out of Reenie's sails, but a few seconds later she was all set to throw anything she could reach — stones, sticks, turf, or turds; it wouldn't matter. She made a dive for the door, but Doc Wheatley was standing nearby. He grabbed her, and no matter what she howled, or screamed, or shouted, he wouldn't turn her loose, not until she had calmed down and shut up.

Then Sarah Morris, who is postmistress, opened the window, and when all the rest of us had our mail, Doc Wheatley explained to Sarah, and she let him have the Flemings', what there was of it, and he went down to Carl's house to deliver it and tell Carl's wife we were sorry. Doc could do that — he was in a position to do it — easier than the rest of us. Later, he told me about it.

"I thank you," she said gravely. That was the word Doc used:

gravely. "I do not know what people expect. I was a young girl. I knew about death from overhead. I knew about death, at last, in the streets. But about the camps I knew not. What could I have done? When Hitler came to power I was little. Of politics I was no part, nothing whatever. It is kind of you. My thanks."

So I was not surprised that Reenie was boiling about the name on Raym Davis's boat. The Flemings' plumbing had long since been put in shape, but after all, if some broad-shouldered young lobster-catcher was going to fasten his eyes and thoughts on his neighbor's wife, he should have took aim at Reenie Grant, shouldn't he?

And now that Reenie knew the name on that boat, everyone in Oak Harbor would know it quick. There was no question about that.

Ralph Wheatley

I can understand it, Raym Davis I mean, and his new railed stoop over-looking her garden, and the name on his new boat. I understand him too well almost. It has been easy since that awful morning at the post office which everyone thought was so hilarious, although perhaps they did not really think it was funny. They were embarrassed, dismayed, but could not find quickly, at once, the words or the gestures to meet this quarrel which was different from the usual neighborhood feud, different because of the accents, and because of the terms that called up names distant but real, real with imagined horror: *Dachau, Auschwitz.*

"Jew killer! she said. No, screamed, not said. She had the wrong target, or course, but she too, poor woman, has in her way been cheated and betrayed. A grim life — being mated to Albert Grant — and had she made an eyes-open choice, seeing the man deprived of uniform, in his own world, in his native group, we could say, "Well, she made her bed," and let it go at that. It is true of both of them, of course. They chose blindly, and I doubt they knew it. Still, she is better off, that Mrs. Fleming, much better.

There was no question about my going down to her house. No one else would do it; I could see that. She had walked away almost in measured steps, her back straight, her head up — not stiff, not outraged, but dignified — a cover for the wound of course, while I clutched the other one, Renée, by both arms, bending them back, hearing and marvelling at the fire-hose fury of her French abuse.

The neighbors are laughing about it still, naturally, but they know too, I think, it is only funny if you can keep a certain distance.

The Fleming woman stood in the shed door after I had knocked, accepting the mail, unsmiling. What was there to smile about? *"Bitte,"* I said, handing her the envelopes, and then apologizing for Renée, for all of us.

The blue eyes were very thoughtful, very direct, but she smiled at the *Bitte*. In a few words, unnecessarily, she defended herself, offered her thanks. We parted. I started to walk away, then stopped. She had withdrawn into the house. I stared at the garden: beach-rock borders, clam-shell walks, roses, violas, daffodils and iris passed, and other plants yet to bloom. It was not fussy, not overdone, not lush; it was order, direction, design.

Now that I have listened to her, now that I know more, the flavor, the tone of her thinking, of her answer to life, a feeling rather than thought, that garden becomes more vocal; in an odd sort of way it plays almost, like a Mozart quartet.

She rang the bell at my office one day a week or so later. The hours were already over, the last of my walking and riding patients with their fevers of the blood and soul, their lacerations and bruises of flesh and feelings, having already left. And I might have let the door go unanswered, or so I think. But I let her into the waiting room and was starting for the parlor to shut off the record player because I do not like to talk through it, when I noticed how she stood, utterly silent, motionless. So I froze too, and we stood there playing living-statues through the last two minutes of "The Appasionata." When it was over, no comment. She just turned her head to look at me, and I opened the door that led into the office.

The medical business was neither startling nor important, but in recounting her history, she necessarily talked of her parents, her home in Germany, the war. "It must never happen again ever, anywhere," she said.

I waited. "Not even just a few little ones? Just a few to pay toll to man's evil impulses?"

"No. No. Not any!" She paused, and then, after the quiet: "Human beings are so cruel, terribly cruel. My neighbors — my neighbors at home in Germany, when one of their fliers, British, dropped by parachute, they surrounded him in the street and —" She stopped, her eyes staring past me at something else. "I do not know how they could do it."

"He had bombed their homes, killed, maimed their children —"

"I know. I know. And ours had done the same to them," she said softly.

I wanted very much to change the subject. "You liked the music," I said.

"Oh yes. An old friend."

"Perhaps," I said, "if you would like to hear more —?"

"No. No-o-o, I must not linger."

"If you and your husband could come some time —"

"I am sorry," she said, shaking her head. She actually smiled this time. "He would not enjoy himself."

I nodded.

And then she went, this young woman, the subject of town gossip because a neighboring lobster catcher had given his boat the same name as hers.

The trouble was that that night, the next day, and the days after that, I found she had not left. Her voice remained, repeating her words, slowly, gently, calmly, each one separate: *Human beings are so cruel . . . No. No. I must not linger . . . I am sorry . . .* On it went, and she would sit in the empty chair, staring past me, beyond the wall of the office. *I do not know how they could do it.*

Ilse Fleming

I did not even know of it until after everyone else, or so I gather, for no one talked to me of it. Or perhaps that is not quite true: one tried, I guess, and then lost her courage. I do not know how she is called. I was at the nearby store to buy some small matter where precipitately she asked if I were going to the launching.

"Launching?" I said.

"That's right, down to Phipp Schuyler's shop. Sometimes there are free drinks."

"Thank you, but I prefer to drink in quiet, in my own house."

"Oh," she said, and glanced at the storekeeper.

I remember now, or think I remember, at least, an odd tone in her voice, what I should call the tone of a cat, and a slightly strange expression on the storekeeper's face. It is understandable, all that.

Then toward the end of the afternoon Carl came in from hauling traps, and even while he was still getting cleaned up he asked if I had seen the new boat.

"What new boat is that?"

"The Davis boat."

"No. Should I have seen it?"

"Maybe," he said, and put the towel — dirty now and all crumpled up — back on the rack. "It's moored right out there in the cove."

I glanced out the window. I often do: I like seeing the birds glide, the boats churn past, the shifting color of shadows across the water. "Well, it is a nice-looking boat, new-painted," I said, "But to me it looks like all the rest."

"Maybe you ought to look at it closer."

"No. It is not of much interest," I said.

Then he took the binoculars down from the shelf and put them in my hand. "Try these."

He had made me curious now, and I held the glasses up, focusing on the boat until it swung in the tidal current and I had read the name across the end. I lowered the instrument and stared beyond the harbor and beyond the land to a place where a small cloud was drifting near the horizon. "Oh." I felt the blood push to my face and my cheeks grow hot.

"You didn't know?"

Slowly I shook my head.

"Maybe I'll change the name of the *West Wind.* Call her the *Alice.*"

"That is a well-sounding name," I said. "You are welcome to it. Or you could try *Renée* if you prefer French."

Carl made a face and a vulgar sound.

I could not tell if he were angry. Sometimes he can be angry and quiet. "I do not really know the man," I said. "He lives up there?" I motioned with my head. "He and his wife and somewhat noisy children?"

Carl did not answer.

"I see them now and then at a distance, but not to talk."

"They tell me there was beer at the launching," Carl said. "Lots of it, whether Davis could afford it or not. And between you and me, he can't afford it. Someone wanted him to break a quart over the bow for a christening. He said, 'No, by-Jesus!' He could put beer to better use than that."

"He is quite right," I said. "If he'll bring me an empty bottle, I refill it for him, from Lethe."

"What's that?"

"A river in old books. Drink from it: you forget."

"Not a bad idea."

I returned the binoculars to their place on the shelf and went to the stove to turn over the chops. Carl was sitting in his chair, staring at the floor as if he had found a bug.

"What do you do now?" I asked. "Do you go knock him down as if you were two characters in a Western?"

Carl snorted. "What good would that do?"

"Precisely. But I thought perhaps it was the custom. Or do you then beat your wife?"

Carl did not answer. He knows better, I think, than to try that. I went ahead, setting the food on the table, regretting that I was not pregnant. He did not seem exactly bitter, or sad, or jealous — after all, it is a compliment, a compliment to him too in a sense — but neither was he exactly joking about it. We were eating our supper. "After all," he said, between bites, "I do not own the name."

"Nor do I," I told him. "Anyway, not the complete use of it."

And then I began thinking about the way he had said *own;* I did not like it. What do they mean exactly, these words of possession? *Mein, dein, sein* — English is only a German dialect, with some additions; I had caught on to that — but still, in one human being many things are uncertain. *Own? My?* It could enclose responsibility, giving, concern, or it could just be possession, the way one possesses an instrument, a set of tools, a truckload of wood.

"I think you better not work any more in the garden," he said.

"No? Why not?"

"That is what did it. He looks on you from his house. He even fixed up that porch."

"Oh. Like God?"

Carl snorted.

"So," I said. "In America the world is less free than I thought. It is verboten now to work among flowers, with green grass, in the earth.

"I didn't say that. I just said don't work in the garden where you'll stir him up. Wait until he's aboard his boat."

"Then my life is to be fitted to *his* movements, my garden neglected for *his* sake."

Carl put on his shoes and went out. Up to the store, down to the wharf — I know not. There is nothing unusual about that. But when he returned, he walked over to the radio and switched off the station to which I sometimes listen when he is out. Carl does not like the music; I try to remember that. Then he tuned in the station that plays what it calls "country music," an insult, I hope, to the rural districts; also a newscaster who sounds much like Herr Goebbels addressing thousands of small minds in the old Sportspalast, only his is an American version, slightly altered, for thousands of small minds in the United States. I say nothing. After all, it is Carl's radio too, Carl's home, also Carl's house. He has every right.

Raym Davis

I supposed of course that not long after I fastened them letters on the hull, she would hear about it, and certainly Carl would hear about it. Carl, I figured, might possibly come a-hell-a-hootin up to the house looking for blood, and if that's what he should want, I could oblige him with it. Or then again, he might do nothing, say nothing, like I'd never put that name on my boat in the first place, just ignore it, which would be more according to his nature, I think.

She might not come out in the yard any more at all. I knew that was possible, especially where Carl wouldn't wanter her to — unless he is blind and deaf both, which he ain't. But she might come anyway. She must be as naturally curious as anyone else. And then I figured she would look up to see was I watching, to see was I there even. And I would look back; she would have to look at me at least once, anyway for a minute.

But I was wrong. Things went on just like before. I could not be on hand part of every day, naturally, because of my gear and the new boat, and selling the old boat, and hauling; but I had learned the times of day to expect her to be out there, at least when the weather was fit, and I stole some time now and then — too often, without doubt — to be in the right place. Yet everything was the same as before: I'd watch her moving about the yard, or kneeling, her hands among the plants and down into the dirt, and it was like I was suspended up in the air somewhere, floating. I had thought perhaps she would glance at me, smile, or at least look out of the corner of her eye, but she never did, never saw me at all so far as I could make out.

Back there when the day come for the launching I got me four five cases of beer to take down to the shop. I stopped Alice from counting long enough to tell her where I was going and why, and said she could come along and bring the kids if she was so minded. She was kind of put out over my butting into the count — she always grabs for a pencil quick and writes down the number on the back of an envelope — so she said no, she wasn't going down to no god-damned shop. I told her what I had named the boat, but she acted like she had not especially listened. "Who's that," she says, "one of your Saturday night whores?"

I set out to clip her one on the jaw, not to knock her flat, you know — just enough to blast the living hell out of her. But then I thought better of it. After all, it is just ignorance, and not anything she can help.

Down to the shop, Phipp Schuyler wanted me to smash a pint over the bow. "Ain't you got no champagne?" he said.

"God *damn* the champagne!" I told him. "If I was a boat-builder I might be rotten-rich enough to buy some."

"You could try beer," he said.

"I ain't going to have no beer and broken glass messing up the prow of my boat, not after you've just finished it."

"Kind of goddamn fussy, ain't you?"

"Come on: have a beer. Then get out there and slide her down into the water," I said. And I commenced opening bottles and passing them out to all hands as long as they lasted.

Some of Schuyler's shop crew and the fellows that is always hanging around with nothing particular to do, especially if you hand out something free, tried to give me a hard time about what I had named her, but that didn't jar me any. "You don't like that name, put on a better one," I said.

After she was afloat and the crowd had thinned out, I had Phipp put her out on my mooring in the cove. He would have to bring her back to the float at his shop a number of times to finish up, but that didn't matter. "I want to keep an eye on her from my house," I told him.

"And that ain't all you want to keep an eye on neither, is it?" he said.

But I didn't answer.

And like I said, all I had done didn't seem to make no difference to her. In a strange sort of way it didn't make no difference to me neither. I felt as excited as ever, and one day after she had left the garden and gone back into the house, I went inside and played with Charlene and Bobbie. I would build up a fort with blocks and make them stay at the other end of the kitchen to roll a ball at it, taking turns. Most of the time they missed, but when the ball hit and all them blocks would go kersmash there would be some goddamn laughing and shrieking.

"For Godsakes, you out of your Christless mind?" Alice asked.

"Not quite. Let's build her up again," I said, and Charlene and Bobbie damned near drew blood trying to decide which one would help me rebuild the fort. "Come on now. Both of you help," I said, "you on one side and Charlene on the other."

It made the kitchen look like even more of a mess, but I didn't mind that. Come to think of it, I didn't mind anything. I didn't even mind Alice's counting them goddamned numbers — anyway not so much.

And then one day she looked at me and spoke. It took me a couple three hours to get to the point where I could believe it. I was coming down the road to the wharf, and she must have been on her way to the store or the post office, or such a matter, and first thing I knew she was walking toward me up the hill and no way to escape. Not that I really wanted to, you understand, but at the same time I found I was trembling and taut. "What in hell *are* you," I says to myself, "some goddamn kid?" But it didn't make a mite of difference. On she come, walking straight, not too fast, and not too slow, just like she was a tall person, which she ain't, and before I had time to think, we was only a few feet from each other and she was looking straight into my eyes. Her eyes are blue. Then, knowing I had to say something, I says, "Hi," which was not too bright.

And she said, "How do you do?" and then something foreign I could not of course make out, but it struck me there was just the least suspicion of a smile around her lips. Only how does anybody describe her voice, her way of saying a word, her way of speech? I have heard it, of course, more since, and I can hear her voice inside even yet, any time I want. But I can't tell you about it — something soft, slow, gentle, like the sun rising, deliberate, out of the sea when you are out on the water before daybreak.

We passed each other, and the next day I was still so high I took Charlene and Bobbie and Alice out in the boat and ashore on one of the islands for a picnic. The kids even went in the water, which liked to give Alice a regular chicken fit, but I told her to calm herself. "They ain't going to drown," I told her. "Not while I'm watching 'em, not in eighteen inches water and no surf."

All of which was all right, but I knew it couldn't just go on like that, not for me: I couldn't stand it. I even tried doing something else, see if it would bring me back to my regular marks. I got me a pint Saturday night, drunk half of it right off, and went up to Crow and Belle's to see what I could find that was of any interest.

Wellsir, Madge Carney was there, and Phyllis Tainor, and Doris Smith; and where Madge was the liveliest and the most interesting looking around the thighs and breasts, I poured her a few drinks, and in about forty minutes got her back into one of the bedchambers. Which wasn't difficult.

She tripped on the edge of the rug, or so it looked, and fell flat across the bed where she rolls over face up. "What you wearing all them clothes for?" she asks.

One thing was certain: she wasn't wearing hardly nothing under that dress, stockings perhaps. Anyway, I outfitted myself to match as you might call it, and climbed up onto her. But it was a dull business, nothing like it had been once.

"Damn, damn, God damn," I thought, walking out to my car and wondering where I could go or what I could do next. The liquor didn't seem to have touched me. Christ, I couldn't even get drunk.

So I set in the car when I got back to the house and thought it out. I would have to go down into that garden and speak to her; I would have to explain it, tell her. And I would do it when the time was right, and I would not even look to see if Carl was out on the water or right there near the house. I was sure of that. I could not go up like a sneak. It had to be just the opposite. She was worth more, so much more than anything some snivelling little fool might do like that.

Ilse Fleming

He did not really surprise me that morning when he appeared in the garden. I think I had known he was going to come there: there was the name on the boat, of course, but I think it was less that than the way he had looked the day I met and spoke to him on the way to the post office. Yes, I knew he would come. And now, as I bent over, already on my knees, using a trowel in the black earth, I saw from the corner of my eye his trousered legs. I assumed it was he, at least; Carl would have spoken before this. So I did not hurry. I finished digging in the earth in that spot, put down the trowel, took off my gloves, brushed the hair back from my face, and looked up. Deliberately, I did not smile. There was nothing casual about it. I stood up, staring him in the face. "So —" I said.

There was a moment before he spoke. Then: "I had to come. It was too far away, there." He motioned up the hill to his house.

"So," I said.

"You don't mind?"

"When I do, I ask you to leave, and you leave — quick." He did not reply to that. "I must thank you for my name on your boat. It is a great compliment."

"I meant it like that."

"Others have been less pleasant."

He nodded.

I smiled then, for although sure of himself, certain of what he was doing, he seemed tense. But the smile frightened him; he took a deep breath. "And so we shall now stand here and stare at one another?" I asked.

"I could stay right here a long time," he said.

"You must stop that staring at me. You make me nervous. I am only a human being, an animal, you know?"

He shook his head.

"You don't think so?"

"No."

"What makes you so sure?"

He did not answer, but the answer was there in his eyes, his shoulders, in the way he held his head; and I felt a little ashamed of myself for having played up to it, created it, for having brought it on, which I guess is what I did. But I excused myself a little, telling myself to remember what my youth, my adolescence in first a bombed and then a conquered city had been like. If there had been more acceptable, presentable young men, perhaps . . . If I had had some one, or even two, in those years stare at me with bull-calf eyes of worship, but there had been not any, and the result — an empty place within, hunger. So I invited him into the kitchen for a cup of coffee.

And if now he, this one, had once tried to touch me, if he had put a hand on my shoulder there in the garden, or had grasped my arms in the house, I would have made him wish he had stayed on that new little porch up the hill. I would have sent him back, banished him — finis. But he seemed more somehow like a little boy, utterly, thoroughly male yet uncertain, consumed by awe, eaten by wonder. And my righteous self, the one that is supposed to say: "You have learned what the rules are. You know. Now follow them" — that too was silent.

I tried to get him to talk, but it was not easy for either of us. His answers were quiet but short, so that I would ask the questions — another, and another, and another. "Have you been a long time a fisherman?" "Where did you live as a child?" "Milk? Sugar?" "What is it about a boat? Why are they so important to you, to all of you?"

At first he knew not what to say to that, and there was a silence. Then: "They are like women."

I laughed. "You could be a little more specific perhaps?" But it was the wrong word. "How are they like women? What is like a woman about them?"

"Some of them are beautiful."

"Is that so?"

"But only a few."

"Of course."

"Like you," he said.

We were talking about boats, remember?"

"I know. They are all different."

"And all alike?" I asked.

"Yes, they're that too. But they're all themselves. There are little differences — the way they answer the wheel, round up to a trap buoy, rise to a wave, respond to speed, roll, pitch — things like that."

I was not sure what he was speaking of, described, but that, I judged, was because of my own ignorance. "I believe you. I do not know," I said. "I have never been in one."

"Never been on the water?"

"Not in one of these craft, these lobster boats," I said. The truth was I had asked to, wanted to, but Carl had not permitted it; he had an idea a woman aboard a boat was bad luck. It is just possible he was right.

"You will go out with me," he said.

"Now that would be very interesting for everybody in Oak Harbor."

"To hell with Oak Harbor!"

I stared at his eyes: he meant every word of it. And I do not pretend I was unimpressed. It was not just his physique. He was tall, broad-shouldered, muscular, but Carl too was all that. No, it was a slight, ever-so-slight intonation in that voice, a certain wonderment in the eyes, as if, suddenly — I hesitate to say it — he had found God. And do not mistake me: I am not confusing myself with Jehovah, nor even with Aphrodite. I simply happened to be the focus, the light at the right time and place. But it is quite a wonderful thing, being by chance that lightning on the road to Damascus, even if just an erotic one. I looked at him kindly. "You will do something for me?"

"Anything," he said.

"I want you to go now."

"But I'll come back. I'll come back when I want."

"No. Carl might be here."

"I don't care if he is. I didn't care if he was today. I don't care —"

"But I do," I said.

He looked downcast, and I felt sorry at dismissing him like that. I thought for a moment of stepping close, of awarding a kiss — but no, there were plenty, I was sure, who had done that, had done much more. And just what do you do as the attendant, the transient bearer of the holy light? Burn forever it cannot. Yet neither should one smother it, dash it out. It should glow, soar, subside in its own time, and then, like the bird from ashes, somewhere, some time, spring to birth. I lifted my hand and gently, softly, brushed the hair back from his forehead. "Thank you for making me feel like a woman again."

I pushed open the door, and he went out.

For a time I drifted around the house, not touching the floor quite, and then subsided, facing the large window, and the harbor, and that new powerboat with its name announcing something to the world.

Ralph Wheatley

They never quite stop surprising me — the neighbors, I mean. I don't count the reports of things far away, good or bad, because they are never quite real to me, nor to anyone else who is at a distance either, if they would admit it. I mean things right here in Oak Harbor, on my doorstep. Just about the time I am convinced the human race is not only rotten but headed the wrong way and beyond hope, and I should have studied veterinary surgery in the first place — just about then one of them will turn to and commit something acceptable, if not downright good, and once more I have to suspend judgment and start the examination over.

I told Father Blaine one day, when he asked, that on Mondays, Wednesdays, and Fridays I was a transcendentalist and knew God was in Man and Nature both, but on Tuesdays, Thursdays, and Saturdays total depravity got the upper hand and I was a Calvinist. "And what about Sundays?" he asked. "Sundays I hold with original sin and an all-merciful Father," I said because I knew it would please him and let him laugh — both at once. But it left me back where I started.

All of which I bring up because of *l'affaire de tortue* that hit Oak Harbor, or anyway hit me and a couple more with some force. Ordinarily the men here don't run across sea turtles or any other *Chelonidae* that I ever heard of. This one must have been sick before Herb Clintock and Joe Teele ever hooked onto it. Drifted a thousand miles east in the Gulf Stream, I suppose, and then got afoul of one of Herb's and Joe's trawls. It seemed to strike them halfway between disgust and amazement. Anyway, they hauled the creature aboard and dumped it over on deck on its back to guarantee it would be harmless, though I doubt it had so much as one meagre snap left in its beak even then. And when they got back in port and had sold the fish at Abner Lawton's, they nosed their craft up onto the cove beach near the wharf and dumped their creature overside into shoal water. In theory, then, he could have got away, but I guess there wasn't enough kick left in him by that time to hobble along the bottom, let alone swim a stroke.

Herb and Joe put their boat out on the mooring, and by the time they had rowed back, four or five fellows from the Fishermen's Lunch were down there, not to mention some from the fish factory. It was that crowd standing around something that drew my attention and brought me down there. The tide had ebbed, leaving the creature on wet sand, and Aaron Dexter had picked up a rusted old flounder spear somewhere. It had only one prong left to it, but he was using that to poke under the creature's shell behind its front leg. "Come on, move, God damn you. Let's see you waddle. Move!" There were four or five bits of gore on the beach and more aft on the pebbly rocks the turtle had moved from. It kept its head pulled in as long as he was jabbing and tearing at that open wound, gouging the flesh, but when he let up for a while, it poked its head out in a sick way and swayed it drunkenly from side to side to take in the universe. Some of the men laughed.

"Jesus Christ! If I didn't look no better'n that, I'd drowned myself!"

Somebody shied a beach rock. Then somebody else tried another one; it struck the turtle on the side of the head and bounced *plop*, as if it had bounced off an inflated tire. The head withdrew.

"Two-bits you can't do it again, Joe."

"Not without being right on top of him he can't."

"Try the other side, for godsakes."

That was the way they talked, and I spoke up then, saying something they didn't like, and instead of making things any better, it made them worse. One or two looked at me like I was from another planet and said as much, which is all right with me: I don't care what they think of me, good or evil. But then Carl Fleming did the thing he did, and I did what I had to do. It wasn't very pretty and it wasn't dignified, and I know the town will never forget it, me standing there shouting and screaming, and no one doing what I said, until finally Raym Davis stepped up beside me and said, "Doc, I don't blame you a damn bit. These mindless bastards are lower than a bunch of cannibals."

I stared at him a few seconds to see if he meant it.

"What can I do to help, Doc?" he said.

So I told him, and he did. Then, later, on the next tide, he brought his boat in, hooked onto the carcass and towed it off into deep water.

Phipp Schuyler

I don't suppose none of them would have done it to a man, at least not in the regular course of events, and although I can understand the Doc's point, same time I can see how the men feel too — Carl and Joe and Herb and all them fellows. There they are out there hauling in fish and lobsters damn near every day of their lives, and killing the fish, or anyway letting them die, and saving the lobsters to be boiled alive. How's that for humanity — boiled live lobster? Don't bear thinking about, does it? Well, they don't think about it, nor about the fish neither — cold-blooded creatures all of them, and killed for food too, which can't be sinful. So what the hell difference a turtle make?

I wasn't with them, really, but I see this small crowd from up to the shop, and I stepped down onto the wharf to catch what was going on. Al Grant and Spider Philbrick and Fitch Blake and all that bunch was there and I don't know who else. They'd been at it some time, I guess, tormenting that miserable creature, and when I got there, somebody let fly a rock and hit the thing in the side of the head. It was about then I heard the Doc saying, "Now that makes you feel pretty good, don't it?"

"I notice you didn't hit it," Aaron says.

"That's right," Doc tells him. "I grew up a number of years back."

"Come on, Doc. Don't be like that," somebody said.

"Dry up, Doc."

That was the way it went, and then right while they was talking, Carl Fleming grabs an old flounder spear out of Aaron's hands and makes a stab at the critter's head just coming out from under its shell, spears it right in the eye. The head pulls back under, spear point and all, and there is Carl, trying to yank it back out when Doc Wheatley steps up quick to him and knocks him flat: one blow to the jaw, and no notice.

Now, mister, I want you to know that was a bit of a shock to the rest of us. We are not used to seeing it, not every day of the week. Carl picked himself up saying nothing, and the others backed off a ways, silent, staring at Doc Wheatley like he was a freak of some sort.

Doc stood there beside that critter, his face red now, yelling, "Kill it, one of you, will you? You've had your sport; now kill it. God damn your Christless souls, kill it!"

"Who says to, Doc?" somebody asks kind of quiet.

"The Town Health Officer, that's who," Doc said. And since that's him, there wasn't much of any answer to that. So nobody moved, and nobody spoke, and things was beginning to feel damned taut and unpleasant, when the Doc sees Raym Davis, who was standing off to one side almost under the wharf, and the Doc looks at him, and Raym moves over for a short conversation which I couldn't hear, and then Doc says, "Raym, go up to the house for your rifle and come finish this miserable beast."

"All right."

"And do it fast," Doc said.

Raym didn't run, but getting back there with the rifle didn't take long neither, and he put one shot through what he hoped was the head, and three or four into the body.

"Thanks," Doc said.

Raym nodded his head.

"And when the tide comes, will you tow that thing off the beach and get rid of it?"

And the Doc walked up to his car without once looking at any of the rest, though they stared at him; and Raym carried his rifle home to clean it, in silence; and finally the others drifted off in ones or twos, and if there was any talk I couldn't hear it. I went back to the shop, hacking and spitting now and then, trying to get an ugly taste out of my mouth, but it didn't work.

Ilse Fleming

Carl never told me about it — the business at the shore with the sea beast and him and the doctor. But then, in a way, that is hardly strange. There must be much that he never talks about, for he talks little. Still, in a small place almost everything goes from tongue to ear sooner or later, and so I learned. It was puzzling at first, a neighbor asking me when we met on the road how Carl was.

"He is his usual self," I said. "Why do you ask?"

"Oh, nothing," she told me, but there was a shadow flickered across her face. And it was the same with many others for a time, except for Mrs. Morris at the post office. She too hesitated to speak until the day I said, "Oh, then, never mind. I do not wish to bother you. I can always ask the doctor himself if I must." I had heard some comment that included the doctor.

She seemed upset. "Please, please do not do that."

"No?"

"He is troubled enough."

"About what?"

She looked thoughtful, looked away from me and at the wall of the clean but dull room which the mail window and the mailboxes face. "It is time for me to close up now. Why do you not come back to the kitchen and I tell you what they say?"

So over a cup of tea I became a receiver of gossip, some of it doubtless here and there with fragments of truth sprinkled. I told myself it was all a thing of no great importance, that there was no reason truly for Carl to tell me of it, especially where there was perhaps a certain embarrassment, and then suddenly I realized Mrs. Morris was saying, "And Carl, your husband, said nothing of this?"

I looked at her eyes: "No, nothing," I said, knowing now that that word would also go all over the village. But I did not really care that it did. What I did care about, I suppose, was seeing Carl and me suddenly in the eyes of this neighbor who was, though perhaps not friendly, certainly not malicious. And clearly, to her, it was significant that Carl had not told me, so that for a moment I looked at my life in a different way and saw that precisely because certain events were embarrassing, or shameful, or even just upsetting — for that very reason, he should have talked with me if he could. And presumably he could not. Suddenly I knew a great emptiness, an aloneness, and was sick for Nuremberg.

"What is the matter?" she asked.

I was silent.

"Are you faint? Can I get you something?"

"No. no. Thank you," I said. "It was just that, for a minute, I went away from us here, from you and me."

She looked perplexed.

"I mean in my mind, in my imagination," I said, and lifted one hand vaguely to my temple.

"Oh. Oh, yes." She looked relieved. "I understand. Will you have some more tea?"

"That would be very nice," I said, and let her guide our talk into other matters, none of them of any importance.

But after I went home that day, and the next, and the next, that moment of emptiness, that moment of deep concern kept recurring, and thinking of this, responding to it, I arranged in the days that followed to give Carl many opportunities to talk. I could not probe; I felt it would be of no use to him for me to do that. The word had to come from his side of the gap. I had not thought it was a gap. I had not thought about it at all. But now I found not only was it a gap, it was becoming a chasm. Sadly I received his silence, and felt — what should I call it? — shunted, relegated, deserted almost. There was great pain in the experience, and when I was alone, I bent, weakly no doubt, to flowers, flowers springing from the crumbling, blackened earth.

Raym Davis

I am not myself, not what I ever was before. I know that, though it is hard for me to say it even just to me. I wonder sometimes, what is it I am afraid of? Not Carl Fleming, I am sure of that. Not of her, certainly, but maybe afraid of hurting her, for I feel like she would hurt easily, bruise, and that feeling keeps me from moving almost, from doing anything.

But when she went into the garden again, I moved quickly enough until I stood beside her and she looked up, smiling. "You do not waste any time."

"No." I said, "not when it is you."

"Please."

"Please what?"

"I feel so public out here in the light and air."

"Why do you care?"

"Come."

And inside the house she turned to look at me and did nothing, nothing at all. "You do not want coffee?"

I didn't know what to say, so I guessed: "No."

"It is just something one does, of no importance."

She moved close to me then, and I held my breath while her arms went around me and up over my shoulders. That hair was under my chin. I could feel her breasts pressed against me, and when I folded my arms around her she made herself small, huddled against me, like a bird sheltering itself from a gale. We stood that way a long time, almost quiet. Then I moved my hands, and could feel her shaking her head.

"Not yet. No. Wrong time. Wrong place. Just hold me, please close and tight."

"When?" I asked.

"Take me out in the boat some time."

"When?"

"I'll tell you when. When it's the right day. Oh, hold me close now. That's all. I am lonesome."

"I'll do anything you ask." I bent my head to reach her lips, and tasted the tears.

Carl Fleming

Slowly, very slowly, I see much now that I did not see before. She is alone, very much alone, lonely in a way that even I am in no position to help — though I am the one that courted her on a foreign continent, in a strange city, where I was the foreigner — the alone one, you might say, yet not so alone as she is now, for I had friends, my outfit with me; for her there is no outfit.

I know, I think, more than she herself, more than anyone here perhaps understands about her. Think what it was for her back there in the Third Reich, in a country clearly losing a war, in a city bombed, burned, mostly wrecked, where only her father's house and the fire chief's next door — at least in her district — were upright and no more than scorched. And there I came, seeing her casually at first, accidentally almost, and loving her instantly, moved by that hair, that gentle, dignified voice struggling with school-learned English (but much better than my gutter German), that slender, graceful figure that summed up in a strange way, new — entirely new — to me, all the dreams. the visions of the past fifteen years at least, all the majesty of sea and mountains I had waked to look at daily as long as I could remember, all the glory of sun and wind, the moonlight and storm — all the things, the nourishing, necessary things I had been starved for in the military life here suddenly signified, embodied in one youthful female.

No, it is no wonder I came back, staring at her, unable even then at first to speak — it has always been my trouble; oh, if I could only

speak! — but at least I could smile, could finally touch her hand, her
shoulder. . . .

But what has her life been here since we married, since our
return across the Atlantic? Think back. The months — years it was,
finally, two years — in upstate New York, during which she was
learning to speak — no, more than that: learning to think — in
English words, English sentences, and for the rest, for a time anyway, she and I, isolated among army men and army wives. Why? Was
it something about her, or about me, or about both? I never was
much for talk, never. Silent, or almost silent, I.

And Ilse? What did she have? What dignity, what quiet, unas-
suming majesty that yet made all feel she was a visitor, a visitor
somehow noble, from another planet, not insultingly superior, not
self-serving, but simply, quietly aloof in a gentle, yet kindly and even
human way. I do not know, yet there was the result: we were set
apart.

And then we came here; I brought her, as I had told her I
would. There was no deceit: I had described to her, as best I could,
Oak Harbor, the way of the lobster catcher, the way of life among
neighbors, except that I could not really explain it, could not paint a
picture of a place, a year, ten years, a life on the Maine coast, not to
someone from an inland European city. Where would you begin?
What would you say first? What would you tell, describe, in what
order? I never found out; I am not an artist.

So here, now, a year — no, a year and a half — later, our
neighbor, our fellow lobsterfisherman and competitor, falls in love
with her, or with, rather, that unnamed cloud that floats with her,
around her, or rather floats around the imagined image that she
brings out in men like Raym and me, once one of us has been
touched. So I know what it was like for him, too, because I have been
there. It is no new territory.

I am not even sure she is mine. Oh, yes, she is my wife, I her
husband, according to certain recorded papers; but somewhere,
somewhere between the vision, the dream and what is real, I think, I
believe — no, I know — we have lost one another. And so, no wonder
she is alone, lonely. No wonder, perhaps, that she does not actually
definitely reject his call: her youth, her young-time of flirting was cut
short by war. No wonder, too . . . Yet what does a fellow do? I cannot
go back now, cannot re-do, cannot catch up.

Only this I know: if he makes one more, one-half a move, to take
her, to shift her even farther from me — or, for that matter, me from

her — than each of us is already, if he does that, anything like that. or rather, anything deeper, closer, more intimate, more final than that — so help me, Christ, I will murder the son-of-a-bitch.

Ilse Fleming

Very well. So I have done wrong things, many wrong things. I do not deny it. I wish only to explain, to myself at least, I suppose, so I will know where I stand. For much of the fault, the responsibility — not all, but much — is my own. I have, therefore, no one to blame but myself — which is all right for me, for whatever I suffer, but for him? Even for them?

And since Carl would not speak, would not answer a question, would not give the opportunity when he could avoid it — since he closed me off, shut me out of his world, I went out to the garden again to weed, to cultivate, to bring color and life in some small proportion at least to the bit of life-giving earth around our house. And within minutes, that other was standing behind me, as I knew well he would, of course. I stood, and looking him in the eye, said: "Now I will go off with you in that boat, the one you named for me."

"Now? This morning?" He looked happy, but surprised none the less.

"Why not?"

"While everyone watches?"

"I care not. Let them watch. Let my neighbor Renée watch and be jealous. I must go to the house first: I have a lunch for us already prepared."

He rowed me out to his boat in the cove, the two of us in a short, squat, flat-bottomed craft that I felt any moment might turn over or sink. But it did not. And the larger vessel, which did not even tilt with our weight on one side of it, gave me a sense of firmness, almost as if I were back on the land.

What noise from that engine! What deafening racket! Yet also what speed, what throwing of white spray to the four winds as if nothing would ever matter. We bounced, I felt, from wavetop to wavetop, and finally I moved close to him, grasped his arm. He put that arm around me, held me, and asked: "Frightened?"

"No. No, I love it!"

"Steer, then," he said, and let me stand, grasping the wheel, feeling the exciting pressure from the rudder. He was behind me, his hands firmly on my hips, and suddenly I shuddered, shuddered pleasantly, luxuriously, from a sense of control, or power. He kissed my neck, and I laughed. He slid his arms around me, his hands clasped at my waist, and whispered into my ear which way to turn the boat, until, suddenly it seemed to me we were in the calm waters of an island cove, and he slowed the engine, then shut it off entirely. Such heavenly silence! And we glided, glided across smooth, rippleless water. It was as if I felt it, as if we were gliding across a luxurious, exciting epidermis, and little ripples of joy suddenly ran the length of my spine, both ways at once. I leaned back my head against a strong, muscular shoulder and closed my eyes. His arms tightened deliciously, his hands over my breasts. Then I twisted, insisted, turned about to face him, threw both arms around his head and pressed his lips against mine, pressed my body against his as if it were for forever. I moaned, running my hands over his back. "Schatz! Geliebter!"

"Wait," he said. "I must drop the anchor, or we are ruined."

I laughed and released him. "We are ruined anyway," I said. And while he was forward, doing what he must do to secure a vessel, I shed my clothes, carelessly, rapturously. Returning, he held me softly but firmly in his arms, then led me to the cabin below, where there was a single berth, where he too presently became naked, and where I welcomed him, in quiet joy, between my outspread legs, as if all the world, the cosmos, were suddenly one, as if he and I scarcely existed as people and were only the universe.

Then we lay, quietly, his weight upon me, heavy, but in its way delightful, and he whispered softly words that would only seem silly were I to repeat them, but that to my ears were holy and joyous.

I remembered, later, that doing this was, to my mind, supposed to cure him of his love-ailment. Afterwards he was supposed not to care, but to realize that taking me, or having some other female, came to very much the same thing; he was supposed to grasp the thought that all cats are alike in the dark. Yet things did not go quite such a way, and I cannot pretend that immediately I was sorry they did not, for he knelt beside me, touched my flesh with his lips, as if he, or both of us together, were at some kind of a shrine, a shrine holy not with a past, but with a future. And all the way home while, under his direction I steered the craft named for me, his arm was firmly around me, his lips near my hair, and his voice gently, quietly directing me when, and where, to turn, and just how much. And when, almost silently, at the shore, we parted, we stared for a few seconds deep into each other's eyes, or perhaps more than that.

Carl Fleming

The minute I got up to the house and went through the door, the second I looked at her and looked at her eyes in the afternoon light, and she at mine, I knew what had happened. Don't ask me how; I just knew it. "So," I said, "you made a gift of yourself, did you, to our friend up above." I jerked my head in his direction. "You lay down and made him welcome, eh?"

"Yes," she said quietly. "And one of our neighbors, who saw us go, or saw us return in his boat — one of them reported to you, no doubt."

"Not by a damned sight," I said. "You told me yourself."

"Ah." she hesitated. "I suppose so. What is it? The way I am standing? The way I hold my head?"

"I don't know, but it is something. It speaks clear."

"Then you knew, knew it was about time. You are not surprised even."

"Shut your goddamned mouth," I said. I crossed the room toward her until I stood quite close. The sunlight was suddenly hazy, the way it gets sometimes toward the end of a soft, quiet day, and I knew then this was a weatherbreeder, that the gale was on its way, within hours. Funny I would think of a thing like that at a time like that. She had closed her eyes and was waiting, like I was about to strike. And just because she did that, I guess, I could not do it. But she waited quietly, waited even for that, as if it was a way of paying a price. "Oh, you bitch! You goddamned bitch!"

"Yes?" she said. And waited. Then she stared at me. "Is it worse than what one might do to a turtle?"

I swung around, almost blind for a moment, smashing over one of the kitchen chairs, and left it there flat on the floor, broken or not, and the hell with it. "I'll show you! I'll show you, goddamn it!" And I took my carbine down from the top pegs on the rack, and reaching into the wall cabinet for shells, loaded it. I looked back.

She had closed her eyes again. Her face was white. She was waiting. And part of me could not help admiring her — what I had begun doing some years ago, admiring her for this, and that, and the other, and then, without limit, loving — and now? But I could not hate. I could not even strike her, let alone move the muzzle, and I stamped out with the loaded carbine and quickly walked up the hill to the Davis house.

Raym Davis

As luck would have it, I was looking out the kitchen window at the
sun dropping into some of the steamy, fog-like clouds, and thinking
bad day tomorrow, though God knows I didn't care, where I had just
had the best day I could ever remember. I had come home in a good
humor, and no wonder. I'd looked at the figure on the calendar and
told Alice, who asked from the other room, how many thousand she
had counted since yesterday, and I had played a kind of roll-on-the-
carpet, knock-em down ball game with the kids. And now through
the window I see Carl Fleming heading toward the house — stride,
stride, stride — with that carbine of his under his arm.

I remember saying to myself, "My God, he's ready to shoot," but
I never thought about, I never even started to reach for my rifle up
there on the wall not eight feet away from me. Instead, without
saying one word to Alice or the kids, or even thinking about it, I
stepped out the kitchen door onto that porch I'd built, then down
onto the grass, and walked toward him just as fast as he was coming.
When we was about twelve, fourteen feet apart, he stopped, and I
stopped.

Don't ask me why I did what I did, because I don't understand it
myself. I couldn't hate him; I couldn't even blame him. Neither
could I go out there to meet him with fire arms. It was like if I did I
would be cheapening something, putting a smear right across what I
never wanted to spoil. And so I stood there and he stood there. And
after a while I said, "Well, what about it?"

Then he began mumbling, "You bastard. You goddamned
son-of-a-bitch," until I said:

"What are you aiming to do about it?"

He paused then, staring at me like his eyes could drill right
through me.

"Are you going to shoot or ain't you?" I said. "Because if you
are, do it. And if you ain't, unload that carbine and take it home
empty before somebody gets hurt."

He just stayed still for many seconds, which felt like a lot more,
looking at me with bitter, gloomy eyes that didn't even seem to blink.
His hands opened and closed, one at a time, easing and tensing their
hold on his rifle. But he never quite put his finger in on the trigger.
Then about the time I begun to wonder was we going to stand right
there solid through to Sunday (because I didn't dare move now; I
didn't dare step forward nor turn away so much as an inch neither)

— about then he spat at me, growled some cusswords (not anger so
much as disgust), closed the safety catch on that carbine and walked
home fast.

I went right on standing there for a time, waiting for the
trembling to stop, but instead it got worse, and at last I went back to
the house, snapped the cap off a bottle of Black Label, and set there
at the table, sipping, to see if that would some way calm down the
shivers, which at last it did.

Ilse Fleming

All the time he was gone, I tried hard to pretend that nothing
mattered. I did up the dishes from yesterday, and dusted a little but
not too thoroughly. Once or twice I admitted I was waiting in fear, in
horror of hearing a shot. I could not have stopped him; I was sure of
that. I could not even, apparently, draw him to aim upon me instead
of upon someone else. I put his supper in the oven to keep it warm,
as if he had just gone to the store for something forgotten, or to the
post office.

Yet there was no shot, not that I heard at least, and when he
entered the house, I stiffened (not that I wanted to but I could not
avoid it) and waited. He looked not just grim, but despondent, and
instantly I moved toward him. He pushed me aside —

"Out of my way, whore!"

— and put the hateful weapon (hateful to me at least, as all
weapons are hateful) back in its customary place.

I took his supper out of the oven (none for myself; I did not
want it, not yet) and set it on the table. He was standing at one of the
windows, staring out at the harbor, at perhaps the darkening, ever-
cloudier sky, and the growing ripples on the water.

"Carl," I said gently, "your supper."

He swung around fast. "God *damn* the supper! What in Christ's
world would I want with that?" He strode to the table (*strode* I think is
the accurate word for the way he did it), scooped up the plate, glass,
food, drink, and flung all into the sink.

Ah-h-h, I said to myself, *and why not?*

Then he went down the short hall to our bedroom, entered, and
with a loud noise slammed shut the door behind him. I knew there
was no lock, but the lock was there all the same, in effect. So I cleaned
up the mess in the sink, took a blanket from the hall closet, and lay on
the couch we have in the kitchen as if I were about to sleep. Only of

course for a long time there was no sleep, and I lay there reviewing the days past, the good, and the evil, and the indifferent, listening to rain now and to the wind gradually rising as the world darkened, and at last the dour roar of surf too beyond the shelter of the harbor. At daylight it became worse, roaring and blasting.

Carl was awake and up by then, but would not speak, would not let me lift a hand for his breakfast. He pushed me back, brusquely, out of the way so that I fell across the end of the couch. I sat there, hearing both wind and surf, and watching, while he made coffee, fried eggs, cooked bacon, warmed up baked beans. There was no use to talk — I could see that — and so I was silent, until, having eaten, he put on his boots and foul-weather equipment. I stood up and moved toward him.

"Carl, where are you going?"

No answer.

"What are you going to do?"

"No business of yours."

"Carl, you're not going aboard? Not going on the water?"

"Shut your goddamned mouth."

He went out, slamming the kitchen door behind him, and a moment later the shed door behind that.

Abner Lawton

I was down there to the wharf that morning the same as I am down there damned near every morning. It grows monotonous, of course, but it is the only successful way to run a lobster-buying business, at least in a harbor like this one. If I think even one or two of my fishermen are going out in a strong westerly (as they can all right if they've a mind to take the punishment) I know I got to be there when they come in, to buy their catch, and fill bait buckets for the next day, gas tanks, or whatever. On a day like the one I'm speaking of, I take it for granted no one will cast off his mooring and go outside, of course, but even so I feel I ought to be down there. The fishermen that take their job seriously will be at work in the big shed at the shore end of the wharf, and they may want to charge up ganging, or laths, or trap nails, or machine oil, or I-don't-know-what. Anyway, it's best to tend the stove myself before some of them dim-wits throw every-thing I own in there just to take the dampness off the place.

So as I say, I was down there that morning the same as ever, listening to the mostly aimless talk of Don Morris, Joe Teele, Bill

Ames, and Aaron Dexter, and putting in my own two-bits' worth from time to time so's not to be overlooked *al*together, when in comes Raym Davis, and when one of us says "Hi," or "Morning" to him, he don't do much more than grunt, and instead of going to work on his gear, or holding up one of the studs while he talks, or anything like that, he stalks over to the window and stares out at the rain the goddamned easterly is blasting against the panes, and says, "Didn't none of you fellows see Carl going out aboard of his boat?"

"No. Did he?" I said.

"What if he did?" Bill Ames asked.

"Probably wants to see will his engine still start under that leaky cabin," Joe Teele said.

"It started," Raym told them.

Something about his voice made me look out the window, and then I see what he meant. Carl's punt was there on the mooring, but no boat. "Well Jesus Christ," I said, "where's he gone to?"

"Outside," Raym said.

"You see him go?" one of the fellows asked.

"Sure did," said Raym. "But what of it? His punt's there on the mooring; he ain't hauled out; there ain't no place but outside *for* him to go, is there?"

"Not unless he sunk here in the harbor," Bill Ames said.

And then all of us was quiet, while I looked from one to another and then another, and they looked at me, all except Raym himself who was still staring out that window, saying nothing. And I knew what they was thinking and they knew what I was thinking — about Raym's naming his boat *Ilse*, which couldn't mean but one thing. And now, for one reason or another which we didn't know about but thought perhaps we could guess, we couldn't see but what Carl was the last man whose safety Raym should be worried about. For there wasn't one of us but had heard about that German wife of Carl's — the one with the sandy hair and the silky voice — going aboard Raym's boat the day before and disappearing with him for two three hours at one of the islands, or had actually seen them going out of the harbor or coming back into it.

So it was almost embarrassing, us standing there with nothing to say really, just waiting. Still, there was a small, quiet part of my mind that said, *Yes, it could be like this. It could be that a man headed due west for the dish of gold, and damnation to boot, at the end of the rainbow, all to once hears something or sees something in a way he never heard or seen it before, and before he even knows it, his compass swings around 180 degrees and he heads east.* But there wasn't no way for me to say that or explain it to anyone (Hell, I couldn't even explain it to myself.), so I kept my mouth shut.

Then after three or four minutes which felt like hours, Raym turned away from the window, crossed the workshop and went out the door onto the wharf. I followed him out. He was turning toward the water when I stopped him: "Raym."

"What?" he asks.

"Where you going?"

"Out aboard."

"What for?"

"What's it to *you?*" he asked.

"You ain't going to cast off, are you, Raym?"

He looked me right in the eye, steady. "No, I ain't. Anyways not yet."

"Don't you do it," I told him.

He grunted and walked off toward the float, launched his punt and went out aboard of his boat, where he run the engine awhile, pumped out, and apparently done some other housekeeping chores below decks. I didn't pay much attention to him after that. He knew as well as the rest of us that Carl might have wanted to save a short string of shoal-water traps before this storm pushed them up on a lee shore, and it could easily take him an hour or two to do it.

About eleven-thirty Aaron and Don went home to eat, and Joe Teele and Bill Ames and I opened our dinner buckets and set around in the building, talking about nothing much between bites of our sandwiches, and listening to the gale tear at the shingles over our heads. Then Raym comes back in and sets with us a while, doing nothing.

"You fasting or something?" I asked him.

"No. I didn't bring no dinner," he said.

"Going to starve, ain't you?" Bill said.

"Have some of mine."

"Thanks, no. I'll go up to the house soon, see if Alice got something for me to eat."

"She better have," Joe told him.

"You're right about that," Raym said.

But he never made it, because before he even got up to go, the door to the building swung open in a kind of gingerly way and in come that Ilse woman like something you think about in a picture, her hair windblown; her blouse, skirt, and footgear wet from the rain; and her kind of breathless, standing there uncertain, I guess, and scared, I am sure.

We was all taken aback. No question about it. For usually no woman comes into the building down there on the wharf. They go past it, yes, on their way to go aboard a boat or to come ashore from one, but they don't come into the work room. There is no rule about it; it is just custom. So we looked up, and there was a moment when none of us spoke.

"Please. Please," she said. "I know it is strange, but he has been gone now a long — too long a time. I do not know — where he went. Perhaps you can tell. Perhaps you, some of you —" She waited.

"Can go look for him," Raym said.

She stared back at him for a moment, her eyes wide, like she was frightened, then nodded her head.

"I'll do that," he told her.

She took a deep breath, closed her eyes for a moment.

"You ain't going alone," Bill said.

"No. I'll go with you." Joe reached for his foul-weather gear. "We both will."

"Have you called the Coast Guard?" I asked.

"No. Is that what one does?" She looked bewildered. "I do not know what is customary in such circumstances. I —"

"I'll call them," I said.

"Thank you. Then, in that case, is it necessary that these others —" She gestured toward the three of them.

"Best to do both," I told her. "No one can look everywhere to once. And these fellows, they know where Carl's traps are, where they're likely to find him."

"I am most grateful —" But suddenly she stopped, for the men were going out, and Raym had hesitated there just for a moment, his eyes searching hers and seeing, I would judge, only fear and distress.

Then they were gone, and she looked at me sadly.

"You'd best go back to the house, get yourself dry and warm," I said.

And she stood there for a moment, dazed, before she left.

Ralph Wheatley

It was the kind of event to beget stories, and those in turn to beget more stories. There was too much there just in possibilities for anyone to expect our gossips, or those who weren't gossips perhaps but just plain human, not to wonder about. And once they began to wonder, some of them began to embellish, and then there was one more story, and one more, and one more, until finally a man was hardly prepared to believe anything. It was no wonder, of course, if they imagined wheels within wheels: every one of them knew Raym Davis had named his boat for his neighbor's wife, knew too the wife was that strange, foreign, dignified person with the precise manner of speech, and nearly all of them quickly heard about Raym's taking her off in the boat somewhere for three or four hours before her husband come in from hauling the day before that easterly struck us. Also there was talk about Carl and Raym squaring off with a thirty-o-six in the hands of one of them, though nobody seemed to know which, or why nothing came of it. And then for Raym Davis to be the one to go to the rescue outside in a howling gale — that was more than the town was prepared to digest readily.

I couldn't myself, which was why I detained Joe Teele past the end of my office hours the next day, after I made sure the contusions and lacerations he'd suffered bouncing around out there in Raym's boat didn't mean fractures underneath. I told him he was apparently still in one piece, and then asked exactly what in hell went on out there yesterday anyway.

He sat in his chair and stared at the floor for a minute, then said: "You mean you want to know everything, every little thing that might mean something or not?"

"That's right. Take your time," I said.

He took it. He stared at a space right beyond me, right through the office wall, and out there to sea for all I knew, and it did not seem to make him any more comfortable. Finally he said, "Well, we both of us said we'd go —"

"Both?"

"Bill Ames and I. And Raym never offered to stop us, nor her neither. In fact, she thanked us —"

"Of course."

"Yes, of course. Why not? But we could have done better, you know? We could have taken two boats — mine was hauled out — but we could have gone in Bill's, and Raym in his."

"Would it have made any difference?"

Joe waited, then shook his head. "Don't know. I suppose he would've set foot aboard any boat but Raym's; that is, if he could've made it, which ain't likely. Then again, Bill's boat ain't so rugged as

Raym's; the whole thing could've been much worse." There was a long silence. Then finally he got started, his voice going quiet, soft, not quite whispering, as if he were afraid the world would hear what he might say and for some reason ought not to hear it, telling how they had rowed out to Raym's boat, fighting the wind and the rain in a couple of punts, how they had warmed up the engine, cast off, and headed out of the harbor, the bow of the *Ilse* even there slicing the seas almost up to the guardrail.

And when they got outside of course the seas were much heavier, the boat pushing her nose right down into them, then rising high above before the following plunge, the spray each time pounding the deckhouse windows until they feared any minute the glass might crack. Yet they kept going, working slowly — God, nobody knows how slowly — from point to point, and at last out to the southward, offshore, where they knew well Carl had gear. Once they sighted the Coast Guard boat — in the intense rain they could not see far, nor much — which was moving toward another section off shore, as quite properly it should. They cruised out there in the seas — almost every one of them breaking just as if it were over a ledge — an hour, and then another hour, until at last they gave up, I guess you call it, and took a course for what they hoped would be Oak Harbor Head. And they had not come back more than fifteen minutes' worth, when they came up on Carl Fleming's craft, apparently broken down and rolling and pitching to beat Jesus, or so he said.

Joe stopped then, as if he were seeing things.

"Well?" I said.

"You know what it was like?" he asked. "Or can you see what it must've been like, trying to talk from one boat to another, with the seas what they were, the pitching and rolling not just of one craft but of two?"

"I'm trying." I told him.

"And then, with all that," he said, "Raym wanted Carl to jump, to save himself and let his boat go to the devil. Raym, of all people —"

I nodded.

He told how they had shouted back and forth, shrieking against the wind, the seas, the rain, three in one boat and one in the other, trying, no matter how sensibly nor how foolishly, to get one man to save himself, or at least try to save himself, the two craft the while careening, bouncing, and in real danger of collision; and how Carl had cursed Raym and said he'd be goddamned if he'd ever set foot aboard a craft with a whore's name like that, until finally Bill had screamed, asking if they threw a line would he take hold of it for a tow. They couldn't make out his answer, but they threw the line anyway, and Carl caught it and inched forward precariously, with pained slowness, to the bow of his boat, and made it fast. Then, once again he was aft and at the wheel, and they commenced towing.

But the line would not do the job. They must have payed out a hundred fathoms of it (he said), and still when the towing vessel was riding the front of a sea and the towed one sliding down the back of one, the strain was too great and she parted. So then they doubled back, picked up the broken towline (the while Carl Fleming's craft was lying side-to-it, rolling like a hunk of driftwood), put a good double-hitch in the line and made fast an anchor to it amidships. This time she held. Yet holding, Joe told me, wasn't enough.

He shuffled his feet and looked away toward the baseboard of the room. Then: "It wasn't no fault of Raym's — what we done out there, I mean." He spoke quietly, as if he were looking inside himself as he said it. "Nor Bill's nor mine, nor even Carl's, I guess, though there wasn't no sense going out on a day like that. Poor judgment. But —"

"Well?" I said.

And he told, speaking slowly, quietly, about their headway being so slow, so minute that half the time they felt they weren't moving at all. An hour passed, and the rain slacked off and the wind picked up, roaring, until some of the seas were breaking for nearly a quarter-of-a-mile at a stretch. And it was then he began to sense the terror. "I wasn't sick," he said. "I mean, I wasn't seasick. It was worse than that. It was like my whole insides turned over all in a jumble, and I looked aft and there we see Carl, and Carl's boat — I couldn't believe it — I didn't want to believe it, and yet I see it. I watched one of them seas — a goddamned monster I tell you — curl its tongue and pounce down onto that craft of Carl's like it was just a chip of wood. It filled the whole cargo space in one plunge, must have pushed right down into the cabin, because she sank right off, like a rock. And next thing we knowed, our towline was hanging down almost plumb, then dragging, starting to haul our stern under, and Bill grabbed Raym's hatchet and slashed us loose, because if we hadn't we'd have been filled and swamped the same as Carl was."

Joe put his head down almost on his knees. "It ain't right what they're saying," he told me. "It ain't right. We doubled back, risked our goddamned lives to do it, too, but there wasn't no sign of nothing

to speak of, just some bits of gear afloat, a bait barrel, a glove, his gaff
— stuff like that. I know the stories going around, about Carl's
woman and Raym, and I don't dispute it; it's possible. But Raym
done all he could, goddamn it. He done all the right things, as well as
a man could know how to do them. Sometimes, on the water, there
ain't no right thing. They ever think of that?" He drifted off into
silence.

"Thanks, Joe," I said. "I'm sorry. I shouldn't have put you
through it."

"That's all right, Doc. I guess I'll live for a while yet," he said,
and he got up out of his chair and put on his cap.

Raym Davis

The first of it I just set there in Abner Lawton's building on one of
them crates he has instead of chairs, sort of waiting for myself to dry
off and for my muscles to unbend, trying to forget what I had seen.
But it didn't work: the pictures of an hour, an hour-and-a-half ago
was still in my mind. Bill Ames and Joe Teele was there in the
building too, resting the same as I was, except they talked; they could
tell about it to Abner Lawton who was standing near the door, all of
us knowing that one or another of us, or doubtless all three, was
going to have to tell it over and over, perhaps as much as twenty
times, in the next day or two — that is, unless the town had changed
its nature altogether.

But I couldn't talk. I couldn't even sort out my feelings right. I
could see that craft of Carl's, and that son-of-a-bitching sea open its
jaws and clamp down on his boat like it was nothing, and a few
moments later it was going to do the same to us, except Bill grabbed
the hatchet and cut us loose so the stern could rise just in time to save
us. Even then, though, we shipped an almighty amount of water.
And I thought *My God My God we made it,* but I couldn't even think
that without all of a sudden feeling worse, worse and worse about
what happened to him, not us, *him* of all the goddamned people! It
was like I was carrying a weight heavier than any I'd ever felt, right
here in my chest.

So I heard them, but I didn't listen. I just heard the sounds and
set there staring at Abner Lawton's boots until I found Abner was
almost shouting at me: "Raym! Raym!"

I looked up. "What?" I said.

"I been talking to you and you don't even hear me."

"No, probably not," I told him.

"Who is going to tell her?"

"Tell who?"

"That woman of Carl's."

"Oh, yeah," I said.

"You don't want someone should just come in off the road with gossip."

I shook my head.

"Raym, Bill will go if you want him to. He was with you. He says he'll do it."

I was only about half thinking about what I said even then, but I looked over at Bill, who nodded at me. "That's so," he said.

"No. I got to be the one to do it," I told them. I could see that all right.

"Then you better get at it," Abner said, "because you know what this town is like."

"Yeah, I know." And I got up and went out the door and started up the rise, slowly, toward Carl's place.

I stood there at the kitchen door for a few seconds before I knocked. Then when the door opened it wasn't her; it was Adele Morris, who must've got her daughter to take hold up to the post office while she was gone. For once I felt glad to see Adele. She looked me in the face and knew already, I guess, but she said, "Well?"

I shook my head.

Adele took a deep breath. "I was afraid — Come in," she said.

Ilse was in the kitchen, quiet, calm, sitting beside the table, her hands in her lap. I tried to look at her, but it was too much, and I had to look away, out the window, where all I see even there in the harbor was the jeezily seas, whipped by the wind, and tossing everything that was at a mooring. They tried to get me to set down, but I said no, no, I guessed I would rather stand up. Then I told her, right off: Carl was lost. The boat was lost too. There was nothing left.

Silence. I thought it would kill me.

I glanced up and she was staring at me. It was worse than if she had begun to bawl, really. "Look," I said, "we tried. Bill Ames and Joe Teele and — we tried. The Coast Guard was out there too, but we was the ones found him. We towed —" And I tried telling them about the line snapping, and how we picked it up, and how finally that goddamned bastardly sea — so big I couldn't believe when I looked at it — and then circling back, which almost finished us, and nothing, nothing — "You ask Bill Ames or Joe Teele," I said. "They was there. They will tell you the same thing —"

"Raym! Raym!" she said. "Nobody doubts you. I believe you. We both believe you."

Only how could she know that?

"It is difficult for me to realize," she went on. "So suddenly, to take on so much —" She fell silent, and looked at the table, where there wasn't nothing to look at.

Then they tried again, both Adele and her, to get me to set down, to have a cup of coffee, but I told them no, it was not the right time for that, and I had to get up to the house. "You understand," I said, "how we — Jim and Joe and me, how we feel —" I couldn't go on, but she said:

"I know, Raym, I know." It was like a whisper.

I stood there for two three seconds, but there wasn't really nothing more I could say, so I just turned around and went out.

Ilse Fleming

Strange land. Instead of becoming more familiar, more natural, as one would expect, it grows, for me anyway, stranger daily. So this is how death comes here, at least at times. I was accustomed to it — hated it but was accustomed to it — from fire, from piercing, shattering metal in the night. Yet for all the horror, there at home it was something real. There was that to put the hand to, to see, to touch. But here, this way — simply disappearance. I have been deserted, and struggle to convince myself the desertion is genuine.

The aloneness, though, is real enough. Even the efforts of neighbors to lessen it does not change that. And those neighbors, once so distant, so formal, so cold almost, now attempt kindness. I do not scorn this; they mean it. They are truly sorry, imagining themselves, as some of them could be, somewhat in my place. Mrs. Morris, she of the post office, first of course, for she had been thoughtful, helpful, ahead of all the rest, and she had stayed with me, knowing, almost, the result before the event. She is here often, trying to get me to eat. And a Josie Ames and Doris Teele, wives of those men who were there, were involved in what is to me the disappearance. That woman also, the one who questioned me in the presence of the storekeeper, is no longer cat-like; her feline affinity has evaporated, or so I hope. And one Mr. Schuyler who, I am told, built the boat, *that* boat, has asked me to call on him for any heavy lifting, or skilled, mechanical repair work, which was generous, though there is a look in his eyes which is not generous, which is, if I read it aright, the glance of the hunter, the hunter of a kind, with no kindness. Even Renée, Renée of gross insults from the gutter grown, has brought me politely a covered dish, food — no less. Many have done this, the Ames and Teele women, and how many more I know not. They bring it here to me, who, much of the time, is almost unable to eat. Yet the gesture is understandable; it speaks well, beyond words, for it is not just sympathy, not just kindness, but unity, oneness: food, life-giving, life itself, and the return of life, even when it, the food, encompasses death. Sometimes I am not sure I make sense. Yet here I am, now, flooded with food, and no appetite for it!

Then there is the physician, who understands much, but not enough, and — again in kindness — tries to tell me what decisions to make. He also introduced me to a lawyer at the county seat (took me there in his car in fact), a lawyer who explained to me the property rights of widows in relation to those of other kinship, and the odd complexities that reign when there is simply a disappearance, no proof of death. I admit the importance of property rights, but they seem, somehow, for me, much of the time beside the point.

And then there is one Raym Davis, who brought the report on a dismal day of sadness and never came back. I could imagine various reasons, from noble to decadent. But which reason was it, or reasons, that held sway and led him often to pass this house en route to the shore, and to *that* boat, without so much as turning his head? Of this I thought frequently and much, among other sadness, so after I had made certain decisions and packed most personal belongings, I watched for him one morning, went to the door, opened it as he passed thirty meters away, and waved, and by that gesture obliged him to look. "Hello!"

"Hi."

"Come here. I want to talk with you a minute."

He came up to the door then. "Come inside."

"With the whole town watching?"

"It did not bother you that it did, once."

He followed me then into the kitchen where I turned to face him. "You have neglected me."

"I did not know — I was not sure — There are so many things —" He could not finish.

"You mean you thought in my sorrow and grief, in my guilt perhaps, I would throw you out."

"Maybe. Not quite like that, but —"

"But close to it?"

"Something like that," he said.

"And you felt that way perhaps because of your own guilt, guilt not over the woman, but over the death."

He squeezed his eyes shut. I had made him wince. I stepped close to him and put my arms softly around his neck. "What more could you have done?"

"I don't know. I think about it. I wonder. If only I —"

"Then stop. Please stop. Forgive yourself."

There was silence, and I pressed my body against his so he would feel my breasts. "I am going home, Raym," I said, "going back."

"Back?"

"Back where I came from."

His arms closed tightly around me. "I wish you wouldn't."

"Wouldn't what?"

"Go home."

"So what would you have me do? What would you have me do that is bearable, and possible, and would work?"

For a few seconds it was as if I could sense his thinking over the three — bearable, possible, workable? I could feel him shaking his head. He did not know any more than I did. And we stood there, clinging to each other, in silence, as if Oak Harbor, and sin, and death did not exist, until at last I pushed myself gently away from him, my hands still on his arms, and said, "Before I go, I am going to give, and take from you, a gift."

He stood there, silent, questioning me with his face.

I took his hand. "Come with me, Raym. Come into the bedroom with me," I said, leading him. And he did not resist.

Ralph Wheatley

The moment I saw the letter —*Luftpost,* and the German stamp — I knew of course who had written, and immediately, even before I had opened the envelope, began seeing, hearing again those conferences I had had with Frau Fleming after her husband's death. She came to me seeking advice. She had talked by telephone with Carl's relatives who live east, sixty or seventy miles along the coast. There were questions — detestable questions she said — about property rights, about what went to a wife; even about whether, or rather when, one who drowned, disappeared at sea, leaving no trace, was legally drowned. And so — miserable, harsh, crass as it seemed — would I give her the name of a lawyer, one I had known, one I could trust?

I not only could, I did. And the next day, since I had to be at the hospital anyway, drove her to his office at the county seat for a conference. She was, understandably, very quiet at first. I had expressed my sympathy to her, sympathy in the face of traumatic loss, and she had thanked me, but one can not, should not at least, keep on with that subject, for if one does, it becomes at last a revolting self-indulgence. Then eventually, on our return journey, after she had talked with legal counsel, she announced she was going back to Europe.

"Go back?"

"Yes, why not?" she asked.

"To whom?"

"Oh, to my parents. They will be glad." She was staring ahead through the windshield, but not, I think, at anything within sight. "They did not want me to marry a foreigner, to come away to a strange land in the first place."

"It is not necessary. You do not have to do that," I said.

"No? You think not?"

"That's right. I think not."

"One must live," she said. "Have a means to live."

"There is work."

"What, for instance?"

Because I did not know where to begin, I was silent.

"It is different if you were born, grew up here," she said. "You pack cans in the fish factory; you clerk in the store; you —"

"Not only that," I told her. "There are other things, skills one can acquire, typing, bookkeeping."

"You do not understand," she said. "I speak well perhaps, a talent I worked hard to polish, but my education, such as it was, was warped by the Nazis, then crushed by the bombing British."

"You could learn."

"Now, after all this? Remember, I am living among neighbors who do not forget. They are kind now, for a while now, but they do not forget."

"You think scandal is permanent? You think they never tire of talking about it? Do you think there is one of them who is not touched somewhere, some time, by the harsh tongue of gossip?

They live through it — live it down, if you wish."

"I suppose so," she said. "But it is their territory. Do not forget: I am foreign-born. Do you not, honestly, think now I have made trouble enough?"

"There is Renée. She too is a foreigner.

"Yes, and you would all be no worse off if she left."

"There is something in that," I said. "But with you it is different."

For once, she laughed. "So I would like to hope. But after all, I have none to blame but myself. Others' troubles, mine, are my own doing."

"Yours alone?"

"Almost, yes."

"You take on too much."

She shook her head.

"If only you could cry! Do you ever weep?"

"Often, yes. In the loneness of night," she said. "What did you expect?"

We held another conversation later, because I made the occasion for it, but it was not very different except that I offered to lend her — give her, even — money on which to live while she acquired a skill, an occupation. "The community needs you. The evergreens, the rocks, the gulls, the waves across the water — they are enhanced by your presence."

"Do not be ridiculous, Doctor, please," she said.

"They are enhanced for me."

"Very well. I thank you. Still, you must not say it. There is one thing you can do, though."

"Yes?"

"Day after tomorrow, you can drive me to the airport and say goodbye."

"If I must."

She smiled. "Thank you," she said.

And now, with the letter in my hand, the letter thanking me for my help and saying that in a little while she thought she would get used to being in Germany again, I played those conversations back through my memory. Then I got in the car and drove to the shore looking for Raym, whom I found just this side of Abner Lawton's wharf on his way, I suppose, to his house. I stopped, opened the door, and asked him to get in.

"Now what, Doc?" she asked. "It ain't one of my kids, is it?"

"No, not yet."

"Hunh?"

"I just thought you would want to read this." And I handed him the letter. "Especially the last sentence," I said.

He took the paper and studied it, reading slowly, and when he got to the end he read it twice, and twice more. I grinned to myself, for the final sentence went like this:

> When you see Raym Davis, you may tell him his daugh-
> ter, or son perhaps, will grow up a European, but that I
> will try now and then to expose her to American speech.

He looked up from the letter, neither glad nor sad, but perhaps in wonder. Then he turned the paper over to stare at the front. "No address," he said.

"That's right."

"Do you have the envelope?"

"No," I lied. "I threw it into the stove before I thought."

He stared at me for a moment.

"You can keep the letter if you want," I said.

"Thanks, Doc." And he folded it, stuffed it into his pocket, got out, and walked off up the rise of ground, past the closed Fleming place, and on toward his own house.

A MEMORY FOR MOTHER'S DAY

Again, and again, and again I dated Fay Pierce, or called on her at her house. Box score: no runs, no hits, no errors. Or perhaps there were some errors at that, mine or somebody's.

I was a friend of her brother's, her mother's, her father's, before she and I ever met. Mr. Pierce was a rising corporation executive who had been transferred to the New York Office from his native South. I came to know his son, Phil, at the suburban day school we both attended, and after he had taken me to his house once or twice, I kept going back.

I had grown up in an atmosphere of lingering New England puritanism, and the easy-going tone of the Pierce household, the way Phil addressed his parents as Joan and Billy, the way each of them gently ragged the others delighted me. "Now you come right in here and sit down, Ted. I want you to tell me what excuse you've got for staying away as long as this."

Her gentle drawl helped her, no doubt, to be charming, friendly and sociable, attainments for which, however, she really needed no help. She was a tall, large woman, who seemed genuinely interested in people, especially the person with whom she talked, but her interests ranged beyond that. Chaucer, washable wallpaper, the theatre, raising goats, heresies in politics, economics, or religion (but not race; we steered clear of race) — talk with her about anything

157

and you came out with the pleasant feeling that you were an intelligent conversationalist. Not a few women have that talent, but most practice it through adroit listening; Mrs. Pierce did it and still talked. It was difficult to visit the Pierce home and not presently find yourself facing Mrs. Pierce and involuntarily directing to her more than to anyone else nearly every remark. Nor were the visits with her ever brief.

This state of affairs never seemed to irk Phil and Mr. Pierce, or if it did they never showed it. I am sure they were often uninterested in the subject, but if people around them were sociable and happy, that seemed to be enough.

Nine-tenths of the time Phil was outstandingly frivolous, and his mother frequently needled him for it. "When in heaven's name, Phil, are you going to stop being an idiot?"

"Well, I don't know, Joan, considering the parents I've got."

"I hope someday something will come along and make a man out of you."

"Be right nice if she is a brunette," Phil said.

"You are the biggest fool in the county, Philip. I would like to stir up you and Ted and divide the mixture. It would make a man out of you and a human being out of Ted."

I was not prepared in the least for Fay's return home from finishing school. Mrs. Pierce had talked about Phil, about Mr. Pierce, whom she spoke of as Billy, about the South, about poetry, novels, painting, music, but never about Fay. I cannot recall that I even knew of her existence until I found her there suddenly, a part of the family. It was an extremely pleasant shock. She had her mother's courtesy and mother's accent, without adding any cuteness to it. She had dignity and at the same time managed to be vivacious, and if she had not beauty, she offered a close approximation, so close that it was hard for me not to keep re-appraising her figure, her eyes, her hair.

When I went to the Pierces' after that, I was looking for Fay, but no one would recognize the fact, unless, of course, any of them did recognize it but chose not to admit it. I was too reserved, too cautious to make my purpose explicit. Sometimes they assumed I was in search of Phil, without ever quite saying as much. More often I was cordially welcomed as a visitor to all of them. Then no matter how much Fay claimed the attention of my eyes, it was Mrs. Pierce who claimed my ears and my intellect. It was she with whom I laughed, she with whom I argued, she inevitably to whom I listened. I do not mean to say that Fay, or Phil, of Mr. Pierce were stonily silent (the idea is beyond belief), but they were clearly the straight men in the act.

If I invited Fay to a dance, or for an afternoon on the river, she accepted with courteous delight. Nearly always, she remained gay and charming, and nearly always I felt that I knew her not one degree better than I had before. No doors opened. No straits of the personality, no bays, no broad oceans were to be explored, neither hers nor mine. In the conceit of youth and masculinity, I approached the conclusion that there was nothing there to explore and ignored the probability that she was shutting me out.

I called one night when she was home alone. Never had I passed a more boring evening with a beautiful woman. She persuaded me to compose her note of acceptance to a bid from the Junior League

Another evening a young woman of independent if not nonconformist temperament, but of unassailable social standing in the town, called at the Pierce's with not one escort, but two. Both boys were in the uniform of private military schools, and although none of the three said as much, it was clear that their intention had been to get Fay to go out. My presence apparently served to block the deal, and after a decent interval they said their goodbyes and left. The door had little more than closed before Fay jettisoned both charm and dignity.

"Who does she think she is expecting me to go out blind on a few minutes' notice?

"Fay," Mrs. Pierce said, "it was most thoughtful of her."

"She's got no more taste than a tabby cat."

"Please, Fay. That's enough."

"You'd never catch me running around with those babies in monkey suits!"

"Try to be generous, daughter."

"That's easy enough for you," Fay said.

By the time I left for college I had resigned myself without pain to being a friend of the family and no more. That my position was fixed became, I believe, notably clear during a vacation when I was at the Pierces' for lunch with Mr. Pierce, mother, and daughter. À propos of very little, it seemed to me, Mrs. Pierce suddenly, in charming and semi-humorous tones, said: "I declare, I don't know what we're going to do for a husband for you, Fay. If you don't find one soon, girl, I'm going to hang out a sign."

Perhaps it was the best way. I don't know. I do remember that I felt painfully embarrassed, not for myself (I was supposed to be only Mrs. Pierce's appreciative audience) but for Fay. I looked down at my plate, or out the window, and I heard Fay laugh. Almost immediately Mrs. Pierce turned the conversation to something else.

After lunch Mr. Pierce prepared to leave on a business trip, and some dispute, some minor quarrel arose between him and his wife. I was not shocked by it; I was merely uncomfortable, and cannot remember what it was about. It continued through the moment of departure. Mrs. Pierce would not kiss him goodbye nor permit herself to be kissed. She would not descend to a farewell of any sort. She was disciplining her husband. Finally, almost good-naturedly, he picked up his suitcases and went out.

Fay was sitting on the couch across the room from both of us. She lifted her feet from the floor, put her arms about her knees, and with the expression of a teasing twelve-year-old in a mean moment, intoned singsong: "Ha-ha! I hope - he - never - comes - back - again! I hope - you - never - see - him - again!"

Her mother's face turned white. She rose, walked quickly to the door and out to the front porch, but she was late; already her husband was driving away from the house. Fay rocked back and forth on the couch, laughing.

I was unable to forget her laugh, and after that visit I never really wanted to go back.

TWENTY-FIVE OUT OF TWENTY-FIVE

I was about fourteen when I stared for a second or two down the aimed and loaded double barrels of Frank Blaisdall's shotgun. Terrified, I dodged back into the concrete shelter where I belonged, turned the arm of the trap to the northeast, and waited for Charles to pull the lever, release the spring, and launch clay pigeon number twenty-one on a graceful flight over the meadow — all of which presently Charles did. Then came the familiar report of Mr. Blaisdall's twelve-gauge, and the pigeon, almost precisely at the top of its trajectory, was shattered.

Mr. Blaisdall, unlike his rare guests, nearly always hit, and I used to wonder, since he knew he could smash twenty-five out of twenty-five scaling black saucers, why he bothered to drive fifteen miles out into the country to do it. No sport in that.

Later I did not ask why he and Charles had taken such a long time preparing to fly that twenty-first pigeon, and Mr. Blaisdall said nothing about my foolishly sticking my head up into the line of fire. I was thankful for that. He and I endured a neutral and rather formal relationship. I liked earning some money at easy work. I liked sitting up front in the limousine with Charles in uniform while he drove Mr. Blaisdall to the trapshooting. I liked handling the clay pigeons, the smell of burned powder, and the thunder of the shotgun blasts. But I did not like Mr. Blaisdall; in fact, in a muted manner, I saw him as the Enemy.

161

His name had been often on my parents' lips after he had bought the large and spacious lawn of Mrs. Johnson's adjacent to ours and, to make way for his house, had promptly sent workmen to cut down the majestic linden tree that graced its center. That gigantic linden, whose lower limbs bent gently to the earth on all sides, had provided for the really important people in the neighborhood a greenish cave where Indians, thieves, or at times Robin Hood's men gathered to plan their exploits. The very atmosphere of the place, with its thorough seclusion from Mrs. Johnson, gardeners, mothers, and police — some of whom from there we could momentarily spy upon in safety — inspired and excited us, providing much of that sense of adventure that seemed essential for living. And then this old Frank Blaisdall came along and ruthlessly destroyed it.

Nor did he stop with the removal of only one tree. He seemed to have a yen for cutting them down, or for hiring others to cut them down, whether the trees were direct obstacles to the building of his own house or not; and the day his workmen aimed their axes at the base of a mature and, in its season, inspiring dogwood tree near our boundary, my parents, who had had enough, or rather, more than enough of neighborhood destruction, went forth precipitously to protest: *Woodsman, spare that tree!/Touch not a single bough.*

That was not precisely what they said, but it was clearly what they meant, and the workers, suffering mild shock as witnesses to these apparently respectable neighbors overtly butting in on somebody else's business, waited while their foreman telephoned Mr. Blaisdall, who must have said, "Let the tree stand," for that was what they did.

The Blaisdall house, an expensive, run-of-the-mill, not even eclectic this-or-that of the mid-nineteen twenties, was slow to materialize. I remember printing with my finger on the snowy surface of a pile of lumber stacked near the foundation: "Damn Frank Blaisdall." That I really put the *n* on *Damn* I am uncertain, but surely it was present in intent. Later, other boys and I played dramatic and semi-violent games in the half-built skeleton of his house — if he *would* cut down our linden tree, we had to get *some* fun out of it — and leaning against the side of the workmen's tool shed, experimented smoking pine needles wrapped in toilet tissue. After we had (a) set fire to the shed, and (b) had conscientiously put the fire out, Frank Blaisdall, or perhaps his contractor, felt enough was enough, and put a watchman on the night shift.

Even without our intervention, however, the Blaisdall place seemed never to be finished. What had once been the Johnson barn became a garage equipped with a furnace, and the loft was made into an apartment where Charles could live. Mrs. Johnson's former vegetable garden was landscaped to a pleasing smoothness, then plowed up again, harrowed, rolled, and re-made into a miniature nine-hole putting green. Three times at least I saw Frank Blaisdall skillfully tap his way around that starched and ironed course.

Then there was the matter of the fence: between our barn and a deserted chicken coop, and past the Blaisdall garage (across Blaisdall land) ran one of the informal thoroughfares for neighborhood youth. But our rapid comings and goings displeased Mr. Blaisdall, or his wife, or daughter Jean, or Charles, or the cook (or perhaps all five at once), so Mr. Blaisdall called in a carpenter to construct a sturdy fence, a move that would have been his undoubted right, had not the fence been thirty inches over on my father's property.

My father, not wishing to descend to confrontation, nor yet to be done out of several square feet of earth, wrote Mr. Blaisdall at his office, indicating the carpenter's mistake, and asking, not that the fence be moved, but only that its owner write, stating that it did not mark a boundary. A satisfactory letter came back, or one that would have been satisfactory had Frank Blaisdall rather than his secretary signed it. The letter was returned with a specific request. The second reply was signed by Frank Blaisdall, Jr., a partner in his father's real estate business. Only on a third attempt was the site of the boundary unequivocally established, as was also the measure of my father's trust.

Through all this, however, I still rode out occasionally with Charles and his employer to the trapshooting, where Mr. Blaisdall continued to smash twenty-five out of twenty-five flying saucers. En route now he somtimes talked, from the back seat of course, to Charles and me, who made polite and casual responses. Mostly his talk was reminiscences of his Rhode Island-farm boyhood, of his duck shooting, his pigeon shooting, his crow shooting. At least I knew then where he had gained that marksmanship, though I did not think much, one way or the other, about it.

Inevitably a certain amount of gossip quietly, almost casually stated, crossed the dinner table at our house. Mr. Blaisdall, who clearly had plenty of money, and had made it known in an oblique way that he would be pleased to become a director of the local bank, was never given the chance; Mr. Blaisdall, who had hinted wherever he tactfully could that he would like to join the Ridgemont Country Club, had been kept out of it. And did these bits of information explain, perhaps, why Mr. Blaisdall had established a new bank to compete with the old one? why he had organized and largely financed a new and quite attractive country club? Mr. Blaisdall was doing business with the community, acquiring wealth from the community no doubt, but was he part of it?

Overtly my parents never quite asked nor answered such questions, though the questions hung over us. For them (my parents) it was important, it was convenient, it was only acceptable to maintain at least amicable relations with near neighbors; hence my mother now and then dropped in for an afternoon visit at the Blaisdall residence. On the occasion of my first return home from college, she asked me to go with her, ostensibly to be nice to my one-time trapshooting acquaintance, but probably more to show off her son-the-college-student.

Mr. and Mrs. Blaisdall were on their sun porch, a place indistinguishable from a second living room, where for a short time we sat and talked. Mrs. Blaisdall asked me about my college interests, which turned out to be literary. What writers, particularly, did I like?

I am not sure now what I answered: O'Neill? Shaw? Conrad perhaps? But I am in no doubt what Mr. Blaisdall said in a rather crackling, deliberate voice:

"The best reading there is is in *Boy's Life.* I've subscribed to it for years. I always read it. The very best. . ."

And sure enough, there on the table in a neat row lay several copies of *Boy's Life.*

"I subscribed for a long time," I said, "and enjoyed it very much."

"You should again. Don't stop. The very best. . ."

It was the conversation that, momentarily, stopped.

Then Mrs. Blaisdall regretted her daughter was not present to see us: "Jeanne went back to Paris just last week—"

Before she ever went to Paris, her name had been Jean, I noted in silence.

"She loves Paris. So Frank and I are alone again. But we don't mind that, do we, Frank? We have been alone much in our life together." She smiled a little, and reached out to touch his hand on the arm of his chair near her. Not only was the gesture tender — it was an appeal.

Mr. Blaisdall did not move his hand. His gray, solid expression did not change, nor did he shift his head. He was simply silent, and my mother desperately said something to change the subject.

I never saw them again, I think, and I do not recall my parents' report — if any — about their departure. After October 1929, and especially after the bank holiday in 1933, I saw when I came home many changes. The Blaisdall real estate firm had disappeared, and the new bank — like many others the government closed in 1933 — was not permitted to reopen. For years its windows remained vacant. The new country club changed hands twice — each time for back taxes. And the Blaisdall residence, as well manicured as ever, but without its putting green, was a funeral home — an aseptic kind of monument.

For years I was intensely busy whittling out a life, and gave almost no thought to Frank Blaisdall. Then recently, perhaps because I am approaching the age he bore when foolishly I stared into the loaded barrels of his shotgun, I have recalled these bits and pieces, and think I know why so often he coralled two servants and drove out into the country where — with shotgun stock firm at the shoulder, the barrel grasped, and finger poised near the triggers — he would shatter twenty-five out of twenty-five clay pigeons as they sailed gracefully above the gently rolling New Jersey landscape.

STORM WARNINGS:
a Tale of the 'Thirties

I

Arch Lockey says I am crazier than a Quoddy cockroach. "A young fellow your age," he says, "and you ain't been to the movies since you come here. You ain't been to a dance, or the pool room, or the Green Front — No girls, neither!"

"It wouldn't do no good if I went to the Green Front," I said. "I ain't twenty-one."

"Them fellows to the state store don't know twenty-one from twelve," Arch said.

"Anyway, I don't drink."

"Well, that may be, but when I was your age — say, you know, sometimes I think you're sick."

"Don't count on it," I said.

You would not think a man like Arch, with all the acres he has in potatoes every year, with the potato houses he has, the trucks, the tractors, and the big house with the hardwood floors, bathrooms, oil heat, glass wool insulation, and a two-car garage — you would not think even just kidding he would talk that way, probably about his daughter, to the hired help, but Arch does it.

His daughter is not much older than I am. She is tall, and almost blond, and her face is freckled in a nice way. You can tell right off there is fun in her, as well as good sense (she is a lot like Arch). You see her in one of them bright-colored dresses or a green skirt and a white blouse, and begin to think what she would look like without it, and the thoughts are pleasant.

Many fellows stop to the house evenings to take her out, most of them boys from her school, although a few are older. Sometimes they drive up in expensive cars too, but Helen has never said nothing or done nothing to make anyone think that made a difference.

She has been decent to me ever since I come here. Once in a while she will ask me to do her a favor, like going somewhere in the car to pick her up, and then she jokes and laughs quite a lot on the way home. I know she will go to the show, or a dance, or basketball game with me whenever I ask her, providing she has not already said she would go with somebody else, and Arch will let me have the Buick to take her in, but so far I haven't done nothing about it, and it's hard for me to believe I ever will.

That is what gets Arch started, I guess. "The trouble with you down-easters," he says, "is that you live in them ocean fogs half the time."

"Only in summer," I told him.

"Well, that's too often," he said, "and winters you're raked by the damned northwesters six days a week."

"It don't never blow northwest here, I suppose," I said. "And forty below into the bargain?"

"If you don't like this county, just hop aboard the Bangor & Aroostook any time you want to get back to the seacoast."

I grinned. "I never said I didn't like it."

"It raises the best damned potatoes," Arch said, "of any state in the Union."

"How long's Aroostook County been a state?"

"Well maybe it ought to be, at that," says Arch.

"There's some of you act like it was already."

"At least we don't have the salt caked onto us so we have to scrape it off with a knife come spring."

"Is that so?" I said.

"Since the day you got here, you ain't raised one bit of hell," says Arch. "It don't seem natural."

"I thought you was hiring me to help with the work."

"What work was that?" Arch kept right on looking at the stick he was whittling.

I swore a little, and laughed.

Arch and his wife treat me the same as I was one of the family. He pays me, well — not much — but enough, and has me live right there to the house. I am lucky to be with him and I know it. I've got Helen to thank for that, too.

The night I landed up in this country it was darker than the lower cellars of hell, and I don't know how many degrees below zero. Half the thermometers in the state had hit bottom, shrivelled up and died, or so they tell me. A gale right off the north pole was sweeping everything and piling the last two days' snow into man-high drifts.

I had newspapers stuffed into my boots and under my belt. My collar was up, my earflaps down, and still the drifting snow was going down my neck and stinging my flesh like so many hornets, and my fingers was numb inside the mittens.

The drivers had been good to me, but then one of them had had to drop me off somewhere out in the middle of nowhere, and I was standing in the lee of a snowbank the plow and wind had built up well above my head, shivering and shaking and wondering if maybe I'd better begin to pray when the widespread lights of a sedan bore down on me like they was coming in for the kill.. When the door swung open, I didn't hesitate. "Thank you, sir."

She laughed.

I'd already seen, of course, the mistake I'd made. I slid into the front seat and closed the door behind me. "Sorry," I said, "in the dark, I —"

She laughed, but not at me exactly. I could see she was young and that probably a lot of men turned on the street to look at her, but that did not make me feel no better. In a way it kind of shut me up.

It was warm in the car though, and clean, and I liked that. She had the radio on, and getting in there from out in the night was like stepping from a bumboat aboard of a yacht, only more so. First I stretched out my feet and then kind of leaned over toward the heater and put out my hands.

"You must be froze," she said.

"Pretty near to it."

"Your folks up this way?"

"I have no folks." In a way it was a lie, but I meant it.

"Oh." She let the radio music fill up a long gap and we rode together through the night, shut off from the world, cozy and warm, the dashboard light throwing a slightly greenish glow in the car, and out front the headlamps stabbing at the tall drifts, and the wind and snow beating against the windows.

"You going into town?"

"I guess so." My voice must have told her something, because she said, "One town as good an another?"

"All alike," I told her.

We swung a left- and a right-hand turn and up what I could see was a main street. There was several stores, a couple, three barber-shops, a movie theater, a pool parlor, and two lunch rooms. The schools looked bigger than the town and twice as wealthy. I guess I was staring around quite hard.

"Any special place you want to be dropped?"

"Anywhere," I said.

"Do you happen to want a job, or don't you hold with working?" she said.

"I like the eating that goes with it. It gets to be a habit."

She stopped the car in the middle of the road outside a pool parlor. I saw she was smiling; it was a friendly smile, as if she wanted to help. I looked the other way.

"Go in there and ask for Arch Lockey," she said. "Once in a while he hires someone."

"Thanks."

"Thank him, if you get it," she said.

"And thanks for the lift."

"Goodnight."

"Goodnight."

And then I was alone in the middle of the main street, all the gear I had in a canvas bag under my left arm, and the wind-driven snow swirling up around me as her car pulled away quickly and went out of sight. I looked about at the snow-shrouded and almost deserted town. Well, there was the pool parlor. It was nearest. I might as well try that as anything.

I walked toward it, and between the road and what I supposed must be a sidewalk, climbed a snowbank not much larger than a small mountain. I slid down the other side. The poolroom windows were frosted over solid, and the light shone dully out onto the snow. Inside there was a thick fog of blue smoke. From the looks, all the loafers and half the solid citizens of the town was in there, warming the chairs or nursing billiard cues. A few was playing checkers or sixty-three. Twenty or thirty eyes looked me over as I closed the door behind me, and I stared around the room slowly until I come to the tobacco counter and see the proprietor leaning over the back of the glass case. We stared at each other a split second and he nodded his head just enough so I could know he'd done it.

"Hello." I took a step or two toward the counter. I knew he wouldn't ask me what I wanted to buy, because half the men that come into a place like this haven't got no intention of buying anything anyway. "I'm looking for a fellow named Arch Lockey."

He jerked his head toward the chairs to one side. I turned. There was eight or ten of them in chairs leaning against the wall, and for a moment I hesitated.

"The big one," the fellow behind the counter says.

Well, there was only one of them, and he was looking right at me, his broad shoulders and big arms straining the seams of a lumberjack shirt. I walked toward him. "Arch Lockey?"

"That's right."

"I come to see if you needed any hired help?"

"Who told you about me?"

"Girl give me a ride in a Buick sedan."

A couple of men nearby chuckled, but not Arch. He would have had more expression if he'd been talking to a stray dog.

"What color sedan? Green?"

"It was pretty dark," I said.

All the time, Arch was watching me, watching my eyes, and now and then glancing at my boots, the canvas bag, my mittens and jacket. "Where you from?"

I told him the name of my town.

"That's on the coast."

I nodded.

"What you doing up here?"

I didn't know how to answer him. I didn't know how to begin, or to finish, or nothing. So I just looked at him. There was a long wait.

"Well," he says, "maybe it *is* none of my business. You look cold and hungry; we better go home."

I followed him out to his pick-up truck and he drove out of town across the tracks, past the last of the sheds and buildings, and about four miles between the potato fields hidden under snow. Every second or two the wind reached out of the night and grabbed at the pick-up; I could feel it slow down, and in spite of the heater warming the small cab, I shivered.

I was surprised at his house being so big and well-built. I suppose I'd looked for an old farmhouse. But it wasn't until I got inside and see Helen that I realized the sedan parked in the yard was the same one I had come into town in.

Arch, who had asked my name, introduced me to his wife and daughter. Helen just looked at me, her eyes laughing. She said nothing about having given me the ride or having told me to see Arch for a job, and neither did Arch. Mrs. Lockey seemed to take it for granted I was to stay right there. She made me feel at home, and after supper showed me where my room was. The three of them was going out somewhere, and I turned in and slept like I was dead.

Next morning we had a breakfast large enough to keep a medium-sized whale going a week. Helen wasn't up yet. Arch sat around puffing on a cigar, talking with his wife, and stroking the long-haired cat that had jumped up in his lap. Now and then he looked at me and said he didn't believe the young fellow was getting enough to eat. When his wife paid no attention to that, he said, "It's too bad the food's no better here; you'll just have to put up with it."

She slapped him the next time she walked by, but nothing seemed to have jarred her any.

After a long time, I said, "What about that work?"

"Work?" says Arch. "Oh, yes. Well, I suppose we ought to have a look at it maybe." And he took me out and showed me his potato houses and more potatoes than I supposed ever existed.

A week or two later Arch decided the market was as high as it was going to go, and before long I was muckling onto hundred-pound bags of Green Mountains in my sleep. But once his crew, of which I was a damned small part, had loaded the cars he had ordered out on the siding, there was even more time for Arch and me to set around and talk.

I never get put out none over what Arch Lockey says to me, and he knows it. If I watch him real close while he is insulting me, I can see a kind of sparkle deep back there in his eyes somewhere. I know now it is there, without looking, because I can hear it in his voice. It makes me feel good inside, like the sun coming on, suddenly, in March. That look, and the keen, dry cutting edge of what he says burst in me like a bomb going off in the night air above the fair grounds, making my spine tingle, making me grin broad but silent. And I say, "You son of a bitch!" And Arch laughs.

Arch used to tell me he would be Goddamned if he see why I come to Aroostook County. "For a time I figured you had a girl in trouble down there," he said.

"Is that so?"

He was staring at me and I stared right back.

"But now I don't think so."

"No?"

"You ain't like that. You give none of the signals."

"Hm-m."

"You will tell someday," Arch said, "only you will not tell me."
I kind of grinned.

"When you tell, it will be to a woman."

"How do you know so Christless much?"

"It's a gift."

"I guess it must be," I said.

Without knowing he does it, Arch goes a long way to make up
for Elwood. But there are other things that Arch don't know. He's
got no idea, of course, that every time I see his wife around the
kitchen, she reminds me of Corinne. And if I tried to explain what
that does — well, I won't.

And Arch can't know that sometimes when I lie in bed in the
silence and darkness in my small room under the steep roof — that
sometimes I smell the bait and hear the clank of the hoist lifting
herring out of one of the smacks, that I hear the gulls screaming, and
the powerboats warming up before daylight. Or I listen to the
generator hum all night long down to the canning factory, and
underneath, the waves slapping at the barnacled spilings, at the old
mussel shells and clam shells and junk.

Sometimes it is the blasts from a tanker's whistle as she feels her
way past old Grayback in a fogbank. Or I hear the rumble of the
Icecap's diesel, just the *Icecap*.

And then I get thinking about the house, and about the night
she argued with Elwood to let me join the *Icecap* on one of her trips to
the eastward. When I get to that point, I always know there will be no
sleep the rest of the night. I lie there staring at the black roof, or the
windowpanes covered with ice, but what I see every time is the *Icecap*
swaying gently at the factory wharf in the winter darkness, now and
then straining a little on her spring lines, and rising and falling an
inch or two maybe with the surge reaching in from outside the
harbor.

II

Jagged chunks of ice that night drifted past her at the end of the fish
factory wharf in the coal-black water, and a crust of old snow lay over
the roofs and fields. It snapped and crackled under my boots as I
walked down the frost-rutted road in the winter darkness, passing
the post office and two three shapeless factory rents where everyone
was to bed. No lights showed except the ones that glared out from
the boiler-room windows onto the trampled snow and ice of the

wharf, the white all grimy and sooty now where Eggshell Adams had wheeled soft coal in to the fires from the outdoor bunkers. But the coal dust made things look warm and friendly as well as grimy, and I was glad to set down my clam hoe and hods, and open the big doors under the sign that said "No Admittance." Inside, the tall, hot boilers stood like the funnels of some ocean liner, reaching thirty feet up to the dim, blackened roof. The bare, hanging light bulbs almost blinded me the first of it, but then I saw Eggshell, slumped in an old green chair with woven lobster warp for the seat and back.

He looked up over the edge of his comic book, and every joint in the chair squeaked. "Hello, Tommy. What the hell you doing down here the middle of the night?"

"Just walking."

"You ain't going to find Nancy down here nowhere."

Eggshell was wearing a part of one of his wife's stockings pursed up into a knot to cover his bald head. I looked away at the fire doors where the coal blaze blinked at me through the bolt holes.

"Let me stay overnight, will you, Eggshell?"

"What they do? Kick you out up to the house?"

"No," I said. "Can I stay?"

"Why not? It won't cost the company nothing."

"Not a cent," I said. "The Old Man don't want me to sail aboard the *Icecap*. I figure if I'm down here early enough, he can't stop me."

"Be aboard himself, won't he?" Eggshell said.

"You get me up early, I'll be ahead of him."

"How early?"

"Soon as Tarbox shows up."

"I thought you was in school," he said.

"Well, I ain't now." I just stood there waiting for him to put up an argument.

He spit some tobacco juice at a bug on the wall and looked like he was thinking it over. "I guess it don't make very damned much difference. How do you know Tarbox ain't aboard already?"

"No lights in the ports."

"Asleep."

"Look, what difference it make to you if I bed down with the roaches?"

"Not a damned bit. Just thought you'd rather be in a bunk."

"Well, I wouldn't. At least you've got a good can up above."

"That's for the women."

"No women in the factory nights."

Eggshell picked up his comic book. "Not yet."

I put my hands on the iron rungs of the ladder which was built into the wall between the boilers, and started to climb. The coal dust come off black and gritty against my palms, and with every step the air grew hotter. Above the boilers was an iron catwalk, and at the end of it a door four feet high led to a hallway and lockers and washrooms connected with the rest of the building. I went in there and stripped off my coat and jacket and a couple of shirts. I switched on two bulbs, filled the basin with clear hot water, helped myself to soap, and washed my hands and face.

Then I rolled my coat for a pillow, shut off the lights, and lay down on the floor. I don't claim it was soft, but the roaches stayed away, and it was warm without being hot. A lot better than the boiler room itself.

I had not wanted to go aboard the *Icecap* because even if Tarbox was there in the cabin, I was sure Jappie and Wid would be there too. Not that Jappie and Wid were not all right, but they could never keep their mouths shut, and if I was to talk Tarbox into letting me go with him, I wanted to do it alone. I didn't want anyone else to know if I failed.

What I couldn't understand that night was why the Old Man didn't want me to sail with the *Icecap* at all, and why Ma (Corinne, that is) took up for me. Almost always it had been the other way around. When I wanted to quit school early this winter, Corinne fought it like a horse mackerel.

"What's the good of it?" I asked her. "What am I learning there that'll ever help me along shore or on the water?"

"I don't know," she says, "but you'll find it's something."

"If I can't see what it is now, I doubt like hell if I ever will."

"Oh, stop talking foolish," Corinne says. "If you quit, you'll regret it."

"God *damn* the school," I said.

"I can't see it makes much difference," Elwood told her. "He can clam on the flats here this winter, and next spring I'll take him with me lobsterfishing."

"There ain't money enough in neither one to go around," Corinne said, but she had lost and she knew it. The Old Man's word settled things that time, and Corinne was so mad with him she hardly spoke for a week.

But they was just the other way around about the *Icecap*. The *Icecap* is a smack which belongs to the company that owns the

canning factory, and all spring, summer, and fall they use her to
bring in herring from the weirs here, there, and every place. But in
winter they shift over the factory machinery and put up clams.
Diggers bring in clams from all parts of the coast in two counties.
Sometimes, to get more of them, the factory managers let Tarbox,
who is captain of the smack, take a crew of five or six to some islands
farther east. They get a good chance there to dig and load their
clams aboard the smack. The men split up the cost of food, and
Tarbox takes a percentage from each one for transportation. I
began to figure there was a place for me next trip. Then Elwood put
his foot down. "No sir," he says, "you ain't going. Not by a goddamned site."

"Why not?"

"Because I say not."

Corinne had been doing the supper dishes or such a matter, and
when she says quietly, "That ain't much of a reason, is it?" I was so
surprised that I was silent.

"Reason enough," the Old Man tells her.

"When he quit school you said he could go clamming with you
winters."

"He ought to be home once in a while," Elwood said. "Hardly
ever is."

Corinne snorted.

"Besides, this is different. The *Icecap*'s no fit place for a boy —"

"You mean because Jappie and Wid, or that bunch might be
aboard?"

"Maybe."

"He's around with them down to the shore anyway," Corinne
said. "I guess it ain't going to hurt him."

"God damn it," the Old Man said, stamping both feet and
getting up, "will you leave my business to me?"

"I will when it's all your business," Corinne says.

He went out swearing and slammed the door. I kept staring at
Corinne. I was still surprised, and suddenly I remembered how I
used to run to Corinne and throw my arms around her when I was a
kid. It was a long time since I'd done that, and I wanted to do it again,
because for this once she had been on my side and I hadn't looked
for it. But I did nothing of the kind. I just sat there, staring, and
thinking how she knew all right, all about me and Nancy and everything, how she had said she'd like a permanent herself, and how
when I gave her the money she had said, "Thanks, Tommy," in a

way that told me how bad she felt. I wanted to say something about it. I asked myself, "Can I say it? Can I say it now? What will I say, anyway?"

And then, instead, she said, "You do what you want, Tommy. It's a rule. Do it your way, not all the time maybe, but some of the time."

I guess I mumbled something.

"Why don't you go to bed now?" she said. "Get up about midnight and go down to the wharf. Hang around there until Tarbox turns up and get him to say you can make the trip. Elwood won't make such a fuss if he finds you've already shipped."

"Yeah, all right," I said.

"And Tommy —"

I stopped and waited.

"Make Tarbox think you expect him to take you. Don't ask no favors. You're a good digger."

"Sure. Goodnight, Ma."

"Goodnight, Tommy."

So there I was, at half after midnight, down to the factory wharf with my gear, my clam hoe, and a hod, and trying to catch a sleep up above the boiler room. I guess I caught it all right. The next thing, Eggshell was rolling me over with his feet, shouting, "Get up, you goddamned article. It's four o'clock."

I was pretty groggy at first, but I never missed a rung coming down the ladder. Then I was standing in the room next to the boilers, where the generator is, blinking my eyes in the bright light from a naked bulb and trying to shake the fuzz out of my brain.

Eggshell poured me a cup of coffee out of his thermos, and that helped. I went to the door and stuck my head out into the night. There was five or six million stars within reach and it was crisp and calm. The breath rose out of my mouth and into the night like a little ghost. "This is a corker," I told Eggshell. "It'll be flatter'n a flounder outside. The *Icecap*'ll slide over this like eels through a lead pipe."

Eggshell looked like he had swallowed a sour pickle, and shook his head. "Weather breeder."

"Can't we have no good days without there being weather breeders?"

"Not in February," Eggshell said.

"You are some damned gloomy, ain't you?"

"It was too good yesterday; it ain't going to stay."

I was getting my clam hoe, hod, and sacks together near the

door when Tarbox come in. He was a tall, dark-haired, easy-spoken fellow, who walked and moved like he was double-jointed all over.

"Hi, Eggshell. Hello, Tommy. Up before breakfast, ain't you?"

"Looks like it," I told him.

"You and the crew going east today?" Eggshell asked.

"Good chance, I call it."

"Maybe," Eggshell said. "Glass is falling."

I went before Tarbox. I wanted to catch him outside. I tried to think what I would say to him and how I would begin saying it, but I couldn't get an idea to stay in my mind two seconds. I crunched around in the snow, scuffing it under my boots, taking in the night and the *Icecap* in her berth at the side of the wharf, and then suddenly Tarbox was coming out the door and standing there quietly like he was waiting for me to speak. He snapped his cigarette to the edge of the wharf, swerving it across the sky and out to the edge of the wharf like a shooting star.

"What you going to do now, Tommy?"

"Going clamming."

"Where to?"

"Down to East Cove, if I don't go with you in the *Icecap*."

Tarbox kind of grunted. "You quit school?"

"Sure." For a minute I thought he was going to lecture me like all the rest, but he stuffed his hands in his pockets and thought it over.

"You'll get clams to East Cove. Why go with us?"

"I'll get more if I go with you."

"I don't know about bunks."

"You got a pipe berth in the fore peak."

"Full of junk, and darker'n the devil's hip pocket."

"Don't care if it is."

Tarbox chewed on that for a minute. Then he started across the wharf. "Come on. Let's get aboard," he said.

I picked up my gear and followed Tarbox out onto the wharf. The *Icecap* hung off from the wharf a few feet, and Tarbox had the bow line in both hands, leaning back on it to haul her in close enough so we could jump aboard. I give him a hand, and a minute later we had her where we could reach out, grab a stay, and swing down onto the deck.

I'd thought at first that the pipe berth was going to be cold, because I knew it would be farthest from the galley stove, but it wasn't. It was forward all right, as far forward as anybody could put it, but it was slung quite close to the deckbeams and was warmer than the rest of the bunks which was built lower down.

There was five main bunks in the cabin, and when Tarbox switched on the light, I could see, and hear, that Wid was asleep in one and Jappie in another. Tarbox kept that place cleaner than an old maid's parlor. He had linoleum over the floorboards, and kept it scrubbed, and the paint most places was free of marks and splotches. Jappie and Wid were a messy and dirty pair, but they knew enough to have things clean when they shipped with Tarbox. There wasn't even no dust or ashes around the stove.

Tarbox tended the fire right off, shaking the grates and refuelling. I went forward, unlashed my berth, and stowed the gear which was in it in the lockers Tarbox pointed out for me. Then I asked was there anything he wanted me to do, and when he said no, I turned in. I wondered when the Old Man would show up and what he was going to say when he found me aboard. It couldn't have bothered me much, though, because soon I slept, and when I come to, it was to hear the Old Man and Tarbox going right to it.

"Look, Elwood: what have you got against it? You let the boy quit school, didn't you?"

"What if I did?"

"He's got to make a living somehow."

"He don't have to make it here."

"What you trying to do: keep him a kid all his life?"

"What is it to you what I'm trying to do?"

"Nothing. The boy asks to go with us and I figure he's a good clammer and say he can go. I call it between him and me."

Elwood must have been looking at the other bunks. "Wid and Jappie?" he asked.

"Uh-huh."

"Who else?"

"Lysol — if he ever gets here."

I looked up over the edge of my berth just then and see the Old Man look at Tarbox so ugly you'd think he was about to hit him. But when he spoke it was quiet: "I'll get my gear."

"I'm sorry about the boy," Tarbox said.

"He can go if he wants. I'll just get my gear."

"Sure?" Tarbox asked.

"What do you think?" Elwood said.

"Sorry," Tarbox said. "I wasn't going to bring Lysol, and then Wid and Jappie got after him and talked him into it before I knew what was going on. He didn't sound like he was fierce to come neither. But he's been a lot of times and I couldn't say no to him."

"You could have told me," Elwood said.

"Hell, he ain't aboard yet. Take it easy; he may never come."

"I'll wait — on deck," the Old Man said.

"Try the engine room," Tarbox suggested. "And start warming her up. I told Lysol five o'clock; if he ain't aboard by the time I've had coffee, he can jump off the wharf for all I care."

His name was not Lysol really; it was Lyle, only nobody called him that. I did not know what it was the Old Man had against him. I wondered, but there was nothing to go on. Myself, I hated the sight of him.

The Old Man darkened the hatchway for a second and then was gone on deck. The engine room was aft, and there was a separate hatch for that. Because the *Icecap*'s cargo hold was amidships, there was no through passage below decks.

III

A few minutes after we heard the diesel and felt that steady vibration through the vessel's timbers, Tarbox set down to the hinged table to swallow a cup of coffee and smoke a cigarette, and Jappie woke up and sat on the edge of his berth, growling and yawning. He reached across the cabin with one foot and pushed Wid in the face.

Wid grunted.

Jappie pushed him again. This time Wid come up howling: "You one-lunged, louse-ridden, bald-headed seabird! Keep your stinking feet out of my face."

"Ah-h, go back to the reservation where you belong." Wid jumped his berth and pinned Jappie against the blankets."You gandy-gutted blue heron, I'll twist your Christless neck for you."

Tarbox looked up from his coffee. "About time you no-goods roused out. You lay in them bunks much longer, you'll rot."

"Coffee," Jappie said.

"Christ, we got to have coffee," Wid said.

"Who's stopping you?" Tarbox asked.

Both men went up on deck for a few minutes and then come down and commenced to eat. I crawled out of my corner, and Tarbox says, "Hi, Tommy. What'll you have?"

"What have you got?"

"Well, will you look what we've shipped, for godsakes!" says Wid.

"This trip is ruined," Jappie said.

There was baked beans, cake, coffee, bread, jam, cereal, tea and doughnuts. They was all store-bought, but I ate plenty anyway.

Tarbox had sent Wid and Jappie on deck to cast off the lines, and was on his way up to the wheelhouse, when there came a hail from someone up topsides, and I heard a couple of booted feet hit the deck. Whoever it was went down, too, because I could hear that. Wid was shouting and cussing up there, and I jumped to the hatchway ladder to have a look.

Lysol, as big and rugged as ever, was sprawled out on the cargo hatch like a starfish. He had a pint on each hip and an opened fifth in his hand. He got up, laughed, swore, and began telling Jappie to keep his mouth shut. Didn't I hate the sight of him! He was too big and too broad, and too much man altogether.

While he was standing there, Tarbox reached over and snatched the two pints out of his pockets. Lysol swung around like he'd been shot. "Hey!"

"Don't worry," Tarbox said. "You can have them later."

Lysol calmed down, and Tarbox handed the pints to me. "Take them below, Tommy, and put them out of sight."

I stuffed them into the top of my trousers where my belt would keep a good grip and went down the ladder. Lysol stared at me making off with his liquor. A kind of funny look come over his face, and then he laughed. While I was hiding the pints under my blankets in the fore peak, I heard Tarbox calling to Wid and Jappie to cast off the bow and stern lines. Then the wheelhouse door slammed, and a moment later I could feel and hear the *Icecap*'s propeller churning in reverse. We was backing away from the wharf and out into the harbour.

I went up on deck. Wid and Jappie were coiling the bow and stern lines, and Lysol squatted on the edge of the hatch-cover, watching them. Tarbox pushed down the window in the weatherhouse and motioned for me to come over.

"You'd better go below, Tommy, and tell Elwood."

"Tell him what?"

Tarbox looked me straight in the eye. "You know what."

"Yeah."

I went aft and climbed through the hatch to the engine room. The Old Man was down on his prayer-handles, a wad of cotton waste in one hand, cleaning up around the generator. I squatted on a tool box and watched him. He didn't say anything. The engine made so much noise that nobody would want to talk over it unless he had to. Finally I got the Old man looking at me, and I said, "Lysol's aboard."

"What?"

"I said Lysol is aboard."

Elwood stopped working and his lips moved without making a sound, or so I thought. Then he shouted, "When did he come?"

"Just as we cast off."

"Why in hell didn't you tell me?"

"I was below decks," I said. "Before I'd had time to think, we was under way."

The Old Man heaved the cotton waste into a corner like he was throwing a rock at a rat. Then he mounted the ladder. I followed him on deck, but he went into the wheelhouse and slammed the door in my face. I couldn't tell whether he meant to or whether he didn't know I was behind him, but I stayed out anyway.

Then I could hear him beginning to jaw at Tarbox, and Tarbox answering back. I stepped away a little. I could not hear what they was saying and I didn't want to. It was enough for me to hear the sound of their voices. I hated to have them fight. There was Lysol setting on the hatch cover, and he was the cause of the whole mess. I walked aft so I wouldn't have to look at him.

Everywhere the water was calm and gray, and the sky almost the same as the water, overcast and solid. We was sliding along past a headland that forms one side of the harbor, and when the Coast Guard station come in sight, I see that a red triangle above a red square, with a black square centered on the red one, was flying from their staff. I looked for a ripple on the water, and except for our wake I couldn't see one. I could feel no wind neither. The air was sharp and below freezing, and inside the wheelhouse the Old Man and Tarbox was arguing.

I was sorry I'd come. "Maybe the Old Man will make him go back and set us ashore," I thought, wondering what was wrong with me that I had fought so hard to go and now here I was wishing I was home again.

When Elwood left the wheelhouse, he looked as disgusted as ever. He walked past me like he never seen me at all, and went down the engine-room hatch. I stood out there in the middle of winter not knowing which way to turn; I didn't want to go forward where Lysol was, nor below with the Old Man, and I felt I wasn't supposed to enter the wheelhouse without Tarbox asking me.

I saw red spar buoy number two slide past our port quarter and noticed the *Icecap* had swung somewhat to the east. We was clear of the headland, and there was a ripple on the water now. A light, sharp breeze cut across my face, and the heat from the *Icecap*'s exhaust pipe, which ran up above the top of the wheelhouse, felt good behind me. Hot and steady, the exhaust banged away over my head, and through the soles of my boots I could feel the deck vibrate.

I was commencing to shiver, and I was beginning to hunch my shoulders like a chicken caught outside the shed in a blizzard when Tarbox glanced aft for some reason or other and see me. Perhaps he was looking to check up on his compass against the land, or maybe he was looking to see if he'd clipped a lobsterfisherman's buoy, or such a matter. Whatever it was, he opened the door a second later and hollered to me, "Get in here, you damned idiot!"

He didn't have to speak twice. The lower part of the exhaust pipe, as well as a coil from the galley stove, heated the *Icecap*'s wheelhouse. There wasn't a lot of room in there, but there were a couple of high stools, a place to spread out a chart, a place for the radio, and of course a binnacle and compass. The wheel itself took up a lot of space. Tarbox had out a chart showing our part of the coast, and his dividers and parallel rules was laying across it.

"Have a seat, Tommy."

"Thanks." I twisted my feet under the rungs of the stool and looked around at the headlands, the islands, and the lead-gray ocean we was sliding along the edge of. I forgot about wishing I was home again. It felt good to set there like you was God-Jehovah surveying everything and not have even so much as your nose out in the cold.

Tarbox was silent for a while, and I watched a couple three gulls circle us and then take up astern in the hope we would throw bait or orts overside. A little smoke swirled out of the galley stovepipe, and now and then Wid or Lysol opened the hatch cover and stuck his head out for a second or two, but no more. Tarbox jumped a cigarette out of the pack he had pulled from his pocket and hung it from one side of his mouth. "Tommy."

"Yeah."

"Elwood says he won't bunk forward with the rest of us."

"That so?"

"I don't see nothing I can do about it."

"Not without you take him home."

"I ain't going to do that."

"No."

"You don't mind?"

"I guess it makes no difference to me," I said. "Where'll he sleep?"

"There's a bench down there in the engine room."

"That thing?"

"M-m-m," Tarbox said.

"That's harder'n South Bunker Ledge."

"At least that."

"But if he says he'll sleep on it, he'll sleep on it."

"I know," Tarbox said. "You want to take his berth up forward, go ahead."

"I guess I'll stay where I am," I said.

Tarbox kept one hand on the wheel and began twisting the dial on the radio. Pretty soon we got a Boston station coming in clear: "Now a word from our sponsor, The Boston Five Cent Savings Bank, with —" I just shut my ears to all that stuff, and the forecasts for the city and suburbs. But then he says: "Eastport to Block Island: east to northeast winds increasing to thirty-five and forty miles an hour, with higher gusts. Snow late today. Visibility poor. Northeast storm warnings are displayed. Block Island to Cape Hatteras —"

That was all that mattered. I watched Tarbox and could not make out if he was listening to the forecast or if he wasn't. He kept his gaze on the compass, on the horizon, and on the bow of the *Icecap* as it moved slowly one way, then the other. When the Old Man come on deck and entered the wheelhouse, Tarbox snapped off the radio. The fellow had been talking about one of them government agencies that help the farmers.

"That's right," Elwood says, "give everything to the farmers and goddamn the fishermen."

"Ever know it to fail?" Tarbox asked.

"Not yet."

"Well then, go farming."

"To hell with the farming," Elwood said.

I moved off the stool I was setting on to give the Old Man a chance, and he says, "That's all right, Tommy. Keep it." He acted a lot calmer, and like he was over being mad almost. I had thought it might be crowded in the wheelhouse with the three of us, and I had thought of getting out, but after that, I didn't.

"Looks like dirty weather," the Old Man said.

"I guess so," Tarbox said.

"What's the radio call it?"

"East northeast winds. Small-craft warnings."

"They are crazier'n hell. If it don't snow, I'll eat the weather report."

Tarbox grunted.

"Look at that overcast."

"I know," Tarbox said.

The Old Man dug out his pipe. "Hell, this is no day to go down east, clamming."

"Oh, I don't know," Tarbox said.

"It's going to blow a harmonious, living tornado. And snow — a regular white whore's bastard."

"That's nice to know," Tarbox said.

"You wait. I ain't fooled on weather. 'Small-craft warnings.' Holy Jesus!"

"M-m-m . . ."

"I don't think but damned little of going out on the flats in this."

Tarbox looked down at the compass card and shifted his feet. "Maybe you don't need clam money as bad as I do."

"I do, and you know I do," the Old Man said. "I owe everybody I look at, just the same as the rest, but I figure I'd rather owe them than not be here to look at 'em."

"If it comes on bad," Tarbox said, "we can still slide in behind Grayback or Conway Island."

"About as much shelter to them as a barbed wire fence."

"Oh, I don't know," Tarbox said evenly.

"No, I guess you don't."

"We might get all the way to Trafton Island before it's too tough."

"You are optimistic as Jesus Christ."

Tarbox said nothing. We both knew he was going to do exactly as he had in mind to, so there was no use arguing.

After staring at the water a while, the Old Man went back to his engine room. Tarbox showed me where there was a bunch of cotton rags and had me go over the brass on the binnacle and the controls. Then he made me rub down the brightwork in there. The way he acted, anyone would have thought the *Icecap* was a yacht.

"Tommy."

"Yeah."

"Take the wheel for a while."

"Sure." The wheel was extra shiny where man after man had hung onto it for years, and the wooden handles had been warmed under Tarbox's grip.

"Keep her on east by north," Tarbox said.

"You steer right and we'll make the bell at the east end of Crown Ledge, split it right in two."

"Good enough."

Tarbox went out on deck, and aft. I watched the compass card and the little black triangle, east by north. Whenever the tip of the triangle slid past the black line on the white wall of the compass, I would nudge the wheel in the same direction. Then I would watch the *Icecap*'s bow, and as soon as it began to move across the horizon, I would inch the wheel back the other way to balance the swing. Of course, the compass card moved very little at all; it was just the boat and the compass wall which moved, but that was the way it looked to the man steering. Between times I would glance at the water to make sure I was not running something or somebody down, and after a while I had the triangle pretty near balanced on the black line, clinging right to it like it was glued there. A person can do that steering while it is calm, and so far it was calm enough, although there was more air moving and more wavelets across the water than there had been. Steering is a sleepy job when it is like that, and before long I was fighting to keep my eyes open. I reached over and slid one of the windows down to let the cold air in.

Tarbox came forward and went down the hatchway where the rest of the crew was. A few minutes later he came out carrying blankets for the Old Man. He stopped on deck to speak to Jappie who stuck his head up through the hatchway after him. Then Tarbox went aft. Jappie looked around at the weather, spit over the rail, and ducked back into the cabin.

It felt to me like an hour passed before Lysol climbed on deck and come into the wheelhouse. It had breezed up by that time. The wind was cutting across the *Icecap*'s deck and I had all but closed the wheelhouse window. A light chop was slapping against our port bow, and once in a while a gust would knock the top off one of the waves and roll it, churning down into the narrow trough. Lysol turned up the collar to his white and black jacket as he crossed the cargo hatch. Inside, he said, "Hi."

I made some kind of sound and figured he could take it any way he wanted.

"Tarbox said for me to relieve you some time or other," he told me. "Might as well do it now."

"Yeah."

"Had a long trick?"

"Not too long."

"I was afraid you'd get thinking about some girl or other and hit a rock."

Lysol had punched right to the nerve that time, but I would be damned if I was going to show it. I ground my teeth for a second and then said, "That so?"

"M-m-m."

I stepped back and Lysol took the wheel. "East by north."

"I know," he said.

I put my hand on the knob of the door.

"Don't hurry," Lysol said.

I knew I shouldn't. I knew I should stay right there and chew the fat with him if for no other reason, to show he had not hurt me, but I did not have the stuff to do it. It got close in there with Lysol, and he was not dirty neither. But I'd as soon have been shipmates with a whole boatload of horse dressing.

"I'm going to turn in for a spell," I told him.

The wind hit me the moment I stepped on deck. Every second, it seemed to me, it was blowing harder. Whitecaps were beginning to dot the water everywhere. I turned my head aside a little on my way to the forward hatch, and once I was sure I saw a snowflake whisk through the air before me.

Below decks, Wid and Jappie had the checkerboard out between them and was hopping each other.

"Hello, Tommy."

"Hello."

"Play you some checkers in a minute," Wid said. "Jappie is wearing out."

"Wearing out hell! I could play the two of you to once."

"Tommy can play the winner."

"Not me," I said.

"Going to have a mug-up?" Jappie asked.

"No. I'll sleep."

"What, again? That's all you done since you got here."

"Yeah."

"Sleep? What's that?" Wid asked.

I went forward of them and their bunks and turned in. I pulled a light blanket over me (it was warm in the forecastle) and swung my face to the planking. Wid and Jappie went on playing checkers and growling at each other; the *Icecap* pitched and creaked gently, and I began daydreaming myself to sleep, the way I had a lot of times in the last month.

IV

It was always the same dream, and by the time I was aboard the *Icecap* it didn't hurt so much as it had once. I don't know why I did it, thought stuff over, that is. Maybe I just wanted to torture myself, or maybe I was drifting back to a time when I was happy and then more than happy, and everything in the world had been in its right place. I couldn't help it, anyway. Only you can't stop where a dream is happy; you have to finish it, and next thing you know you are up to the present again.

I always began back at one night Muriel (that's my sister) and I was fooling in the kitchen. I never hit Muriel until she began to bite, but I would twist her arm some. I had done it that evening, and she commenced getting back at me by plaguing me about going out on the flats clamming with Elwood and Phil and Mac. I hadn't been at the work long, and she teased me about my thinking I was a grown man.

"Why, you're so tired when you come in," she says, "you can't lift a teacup off'n the table."

"Is that right?"

"You make out you're as good as the men, but I guess you'd better not brag on yourself too much."

"You're so cocky about it, go out and dig a few clams of your own," I said. "You was teasing the Old Man to give you money to get a permanent."

Muriel was drying dishes while she talked, but when I said that, I see her stop. She looked right past me and into the automotive parts calendar.. "Well," she says, "why not?"

"What now?" the Old Man said.

"We could do it, Nancy and I could. I don't see nothing to stop us."

"I guess you'll see something if I've a mind to stop you," the Old Man said. "I don't want you bumming rides to Marshfield every day in the week."

"Please?" Muriel said.

"What do you want one of them damned permanents for?"

"Elwood, don't be foolish," Corinne said.

"I ain't," the Old Man said. "Or that is, I didn't think I was."

"I'd like to get one myself," says Ma, "but I ain't going to spend the money."

"Please," Muriel said.

The Old Man grunted.

"You can't hold the girls down forever, you know," Corinne said.

"I ain't aiming to hold down but one. What Nancy does is Mac's business."

"You might as well let them earn the money to spend on themselves," Corinne says.

The Old Man didn't answer at all, and Muriel grinned because she was sure she was going to get her way, and after supper she goes over to Mac's to tell Nancy.

Well, the next day the tide was so we could begin digging around nine o'clock, and Mac and Phil and the Old Man and I set out the same as usual, only Mac's punt is gone. There was the girls in it a third of the way to the clam flats on Barnacle Island already. I looked to hear some swearing from Mac, but he just laughed. Nancy is his daughter and I guess he thought she was just about the center of all there was anyway.

"Looks like I got to walk," says Mac. "The kids got my punt."

Phil took Mac with him, and the Old Man and I went in his punt the same as always. There was a breeze that day, but it was not cold. Phil and the Old Man made better headway than the girls, and after a while we was up abreast of them. They shouted to us, laughing, and I told them they'd have to rouse out earlier'n that to keep up with us.

"What do you mean, *us?*" Muriel says. She was setting on the stern thwart and Nancy was rowing as hard as she knew how to try to keep up with us. Their hair was streaming out in the wind, and Nancy would shake her head to keep it out of her face, but she didn't stop rowing.

I see Mac look over to the Old Man from the other punt, and wink, and the old Man kind of grinned, though to tell you the truth, I didn't see what they was proud about. I thought it was kind of a mess, having the girls go clamming with us.

They didn't dig right on top of us, anyway, which was something. I guess they was afraid I would tease them, and maybe the others would. They went off on the flats a short ways where we couldn't tell when they stuck the hoes in if they was turning over any clams or not.

We kept on digging until the flood tide drove us, and by that time I was some glad to quit. We put the filled burlap sacks into the punts, and the girls loaded the hods they had filled into Mac's punt, and we all rowed back to Oak Harbor to steam out the meats and clip the necks from the clams and have them all ready to go to the factory. You get more for them if you steam them out. This time the Old Man and Mac and Phil got thirteen or fourteen dollars apiece; I got ten; and Muriel and Nancy got about three.

It looked like the girls would have to clam some more and wait another week to go to Marshfield and get their permanents. But that night I see the Old Man slip Muriel a few of them lettuce leaves when he thought no one was looking, and Mac must have done the same for Nancy, because the next day the two of them sets off for Marshfield. They caught a ride on the mail, and Lysol, who had driven to Marshfield for some Old Mr. Boston, brought them back.

Muriel's hair looked like all wire springs to me, and I told her so. She didn't think but a little bit of what I said, neither, and flew aboard of me some wild, fists flying and fingernails and all. For a second she had me backed into a corner, until I could grab her wrists. I twisted one of them til she was all turned around and down on her knees begging me to quit.

But about that time Ma made me stop. "And no more plaguing Muriel about her hair," Corinne says. "Of course it looks funny before it's been combed out."

Saturday it snowed again, and the Old Man couldn't do no work. He set in the kitchen and knitted trap heads, and before long Corinne begun telling him she wanted to go to the dance that night. The Old Man, he cussed and growled about it, but I see he was going to go all right.

I took a bath that afternoon, once I finally got the washbasin away from Muriel and refilled the hot water tank in the stove. I dug a clean shirt out of the drawer and rubbed some polish over my shoes, and dressed, and called myself ready to go to the dance. I had spent most of my clam money, but I figured I had enough left to stay with the rest of the crowd that night.

Before time for Al Ames to get around with the truck that everyone rode to the dance in, Nancy come over to our house so as to be there and go with us. I was listening to the radio when she come in, and I looked up and thought, "Godfry Mighty, who's that?" And then I see it was Nancy. I had never seen her looking that way in my life and I could hardly believe it was her now.

"Hi," she says, and Ma and the Old Man both says, "Hello.'

I didn't say nothing.

"Take off your coat," Corinne says. "Al probably won't be here for half an hour."

"Where's Muriel?" Nancy asks. She was laying her coat over the back of a chair.

"In her room," Corinne tells her.

The Old Man was taking a good look at Nancy. "I should think you'd be cold," he says. "Hell, you ain't wearing enough to flag a wheelbarrow."

"Elwood!" Ma says.

I could have slapped the Old Man, but Nancy just laughs and swung around on her toes kind of, and went into Muriel's room. I looked after her and just set there staring. She was not the girl that had been going to school with me at all, or that had gone clamming with us neither. Her hair was different, naturally, and it looked beautiful, not like Muriel's, though I got to admit Muriel's looked a lot better that night. There was something about the way Nancy was wearing her new dress, all black and red, and the way she moved and laughed, and her legs that looked sleek, and the red polish on her fingernails . . .

It seemed like an hour to me before Nancy come back into the kitchen. When she did, Muriel come with her, and I kept reading the comics on the last page of the paper, or that is, I pretended to, so that no one would know I was looking at her any more than usual.

When Al Ames got to our house everybody was ready and waiting. He took Corinne and the Old Man in the cab, and the rest of us climbed in back. We each give Al a quarter when we got in to pay for the trip. Muriel was first. She went to the forward end of the truck body and we followed her, walking on the blankets Al had spread over the hay on the floor of the truck. It was dark inside and we couldn't see nothing, but we could tell by the voices who was aboard. Muriel planks herself down next to someone and Nancy sits next to Muriel.

"Come on, Tommy," she says, "just about room for you in the corner."

I suppose Nancy spoke the same way she always had, but it didn't sound like it to me, and it made me tingle, kind of. Maybe I had ridden next to Nancy in cars twenty times before, but this was different. I slipped into the corner and hardly dared move for fear I'd touch her, and all the time I was afraid I never would. She and Muriel kept on talking and laughing about one thing and another, and I couldn't say a word. Al stopped a couple three times to take on more kids, and the truck got crowded. Our legs was all crisscrossed, and Nancy had to move over against me when the others pushed.

"You got room enough, Tommy?"

"Sure," I said, but I didn't have much room, and I was pretty excited because I didn't. Nancy felt warm pressed against my side, and I begun wishing Al would miss the road or something and drive about forty miles extra.

There would have been more room if I had put my arm around her. I made up my mind the next time the truck took a sharp curve, I would do it. I waited and waited, and when Al finally lurched around a bend I would draw in my breath and not move a bit.

Maybe she wouldn't like my doing it. Maybe she would say something out loud and everyone would laugh. Or maybe she would set there not moving or saying anything, but just stiff and straight so I would know she hated it.

And then Al drove the truck over a bump where the snow had piled up and hadn't ever been plowed. Half of them in the back screamed. We was jounced so hard we went right clear of the blankets, and Nancy grabs my hand. I moved her fingers around so they was clasped between mine, and they stayed that way. I couldn't talk. There didn't seem to be nothing I could put into words. I wished I could see Nancy, but I was terribly glad she couldn't look at me. When the truck stopped to the dance, she give my hand a squeeze, and says, "Thank you, Tommy."

I guess I must have stammered.

"What?"

"Just, just nothing," I told her. And she laughed, but it was a nice laugh all right.

The first of it, that night, I didn't go nowhere near her, but I watched the whole time, even when they turned the lights down and almost out for some of them waltzes. I was sure Nancy was the prettiest girl there, so I was not surprised, in a way, when Clayton Graves, and Lysol, and a couple three other men danced with her. Girls always dance with girls to our dances until they are old enough for the men to dance with them. And this was the first time I remembered seeing Nancy dance with anyone except other girls. But then, I had not been to dances for some time and I mightn't have known.

My chance come when Dale Carter, who plays the fiddle in the orchestra, gets up and shouts for everyone to choose partners for a contra. I can dance a contra, the Lady of the Lake, or Soldier's Joy, and I like them. We call them the old timer's dances, but I don't know why, because we are still dancing them, and have never stopped, although we don't dance them quite so well maybe. Nancy and I was up near the head of the line, and when he had what he called plenty of couples on the floor, Dale yells, "First and every other couple cross over." Which they did. Then the orchestra started playing and we were off.

They played "The Devil's Dream," and "Oh, Them Golden Slippers," and "Redwing," and kept right on playing. I thought there was nothing on earth like it, and dancing with Nancy I was sure there wasn't. I swung her until the room was whirling. We went down the lines and crossed over and started up the other way. I swung the others too, of course, but they was nothing like Nancy. She would laugh while she was dancing, looking right in my eyes. The music and dancing give me that high, funny feeling inside, so I was ready to dance right through to daylight, and with her there in front of me, and my partner and all, I was more excited than ever.

Suddenly Dale yells, "Swing your partners," which meant the contra would be over in a few seconds. I twirled Nancy like she and I was the blades to a windmill. We kept going faster and faster, and then I see her feet was swinging right clear of the floor. She was leaning back on my arm and the only thing was going to keep her from falling, if anything was, was me.

I put my other arm around her and tried to stop swinging. I was quite dizzy and it was hard for me to stand, but I managed to do it, and hold Nancy up besides. Only for a second or two I didn't let go. I kept both arms around her. She was gasping for breath and laughing, and she leaned against me and says, "Oh, Tommy, I thought I was going to go down flat. Honest." But she didn't try to push away right off, not until the music stopped and maybe a little more. It was only about the time it would take you to count to seven, and in a room full of people at that.

We danced another contra together later that evening, and I was feeling so good I didn't even care when Lysol took the last waltz with her. I was a little worried when I see him helping her on with her coat and kind of going out the door with her. I supposed at first he would give her a ride home in his car. Anyone really couldn't tell whether he was taking her home or not, where he and Nancy was in quite a crowd going out the door. We was no sooner outside than I heard somebody saying, "Lysol, you got time?" meaning did he have time to take a swallow of rum.

"Ever see the time when I didn't?" he says, and slipped out around the dance hall with some other fellows.

Nancy didn't act like he was leaving her, neither. She just walked along to the truck with some other girls, and by the time they got there I was alongside. Nancy didn't say nothing and neither did I. Everyone was climbing into the truck, taking pretty much the same places they'd had before. In the darkness there was a lot of talking and laughing and some singing. I set down before Nancy did, and when she sat next to me I had my arm around her. She moved a little closer and leaned her head back. I could feel her hair against my face and neck. "Tommy, did you have a good time?"

"I sure did. Did you?"

I could feel her nod her head. "The best time I ever had to a dance."

I knew that without her telling me. And I may have been kind of crazy, but I was smart enough to know it wasn't account of me neither. I'd seen what kind of rush she'd had during the dance, and I was sure it hadn't often been like that before, if ever. A funny thing, too — I was proud of her.

We did not say much the rest of the way home, and I didn't mind that. Everyone else was shouting and singing away. Al seemed to be taking the curves on two wheels and generally through snow-drifts, and when he stopped to let someone out, he done it so sudden it felt like the whole load of passengers was on top of Nancy and me. But that was nothing. After what seemed like about two minutes to me, Al stopped near Nancy's house.

"Shortest twenty miles I ever rode," I said.

"I got to get out, Tommy."

"I'll come with you."

She didn't say I shouldn't, so I followed her. Muriel never see who I was until I was halfway out of the truck. She sets up a holler then but there was so many others shouting that I pretended I didn't hear her, and the next minute Al had driven off down the road and left Nancy and me standing together in the snow.

We stood there and watched the truck driving away even after it had stopped to my house to let out Corinne and Elwood and Muriel. The tail light swayed back and forth, and the sound of the exhaust and of the kids inside singing got fainter and fainter until it sounded real far away and soft through the stillness. Then it was gone altogether. "Ain't it quiet," I said.

"I got to go in, Tommy."

"I know."

We walked up to Nancy's house, only Nancy would not walk in the path; she walked where the snow was unbroken, making it fly up ahead of her a little, and we could hear it crunch crunch under our feet the way it will in cold weather. When we got to the door she turned around for a minute and we stood there. The only sound there was in the whole world was Mac's cow getting up or laying down or something out in the barn.

"I wish it wasn't over," Nancy said.

"There'll be another dance next week."

"Not just the dance."

I thought about that for a few seconds. She wasn't looking at me; she was kind of looking past me at the snow and the night.

"Nancy, tomorrow night?" I said.

She nodded. "After supper. Don't come in, Tommy. Just wait."

She was standing on the doorstep. To look at her face at all I had to look up at her, and I was perfectly ready to do that. I wanted to thank her for talking to me and standing there in the snow with me and saying, "Not just the dance." But I didn't.

"Goodnight, Nancy," I said.

"Goodnight." She turned away then, and went into the house.

I walked down to our place like I weighed a couple of pounds less than nothing, kicking snow in front of me and listening to the quiet and seeing the shadow of the spruce woods and the houses under the starlight, different from the way I'd ever looked at them before. I hadn't never thought they could be especially beautiful until then.

Corinne had left a light on for me downstairs but everyone was to bed. The chamber up over the kitchen was mine, and I undressed there and crawled under the bedclothes. I pulled the pillow sideways and put my arm around it and did a lot of thinking. Or maybe you call it dreaming, though I was not asleep. There are things about a pillow: it don't laugh at you, or say what you don't want to hear, or talk about you to other people, or anything like that. So you are not afraid of it, and I was still afraid of Nancy a little then. But pretty soon I was asleep.

V

For a while I used to think about the days that followed that dance, and even about the hours. I would remember what Nancy and I did together step by step, and what she said and I said, and in a way it was

the same as thinking, suddenly, in January, about the taste of straw-
berries.

The first day I forgot there was such a thing as clamming, and
the Old Man went off without me, of course. I felt a little foolish
about that, but I really didn't care then. I lugged water for Corinne
and split firewood. I lay around the house with a comic in front of my
face and thought about Nancy and wondered if it wouldn't never get
dark, even in December.

Muriel set out to plague me a couple three times about jumping
out of the truck to Nancy's the night before, but when I didn't get
angry about it or even try to grab her by the wrist, she quit. And
Corinne and Elwood never said nothing.

Along the middle of the afternoon, Ma sent me up to Mac's to
get an extra quart of milk, and I didn't growl none about doing that.
Sophie, Nancy's mother, was getting the milk ready for me in their
kitchen and talking steady belt the same as always, when Nancy come
in from the other part of the house. We both says, "Hi," or "Hello,"
or something just like the world was the same place it had been
twenty-four hours before, but at first I didn't dare to look at her, not
really look at her.

Then finally I did, and she was looking at me, right in the eyes. I
see suddenly what her eyes was like then, the same as if I was staring
into forty fathoms. I thought sure Sophie must hear me draw my
breath or notice me start, but she never. Too busy talking. Corinne
says that spiel ain't come to a full stop within the memory of man,
and that if Nancy and Mac don't say much it's account of neither one
ever got a chance to practice.

That night when I got my things on and started to go out,
Muriel had already left to go coasting. I was worried she might stop
in for Nancy, which she always used to, but I found she hadn't. I
waited twenty or thirty feet from the door to Nancy's house. There
was a tree or two there and some bushes, so that anyone wouldn't see
me unless they was really trying to.

I waited what felt like half the night before I so much as caught a
glimpse of Nancy through the kitchen windows. She had her jacket
on then, though, and a few minutes later she came out.

I held my breath. She stopped on the top step right where I had
said goodnight to her before, and she looked one way and then the
other, not like she was really expecting anybody, but more like she
was trying to decide which way to walk. I moved then so that the
branches shook a little and her eyes were on me in a second. I come

out and across the path to meet her, and she come down off the
stoop, and there we was standing face to face again in the snow and
the night.

"Hello," we said. I mean we both said it, and you would think it
could not mean anything, wouldn't you? But it meant a lot to me just
to hear her voice and know who was speaking for me to listen. I took
her hand and she answered me with her fingers. She looked off to
one side.

"The kids are all coasting over there, ain't they?"

I nodded. We could hear them shouting and laughing. It was
queer to think how a couple of nights before I'd have been fierce to
be with them.

"Let's go this way," she said.

It was a path that led up to the main road the same as the other,
but went through the trees and over the ledges. It was icy in places
and we would slip and slide, dodging the branches, and Nancy
laughed. When the path widened out and come to the road, she and
I each put an arm around the other. Now and then a car would meet
us, but we would just step off the road to give them room and pay no
attention.

"You only danced with me twice," Nancy said. It was like she
had been thinking back and just then noticed it.

"They don't play but a few of them contras."

"You could dance the others."

"No, I couldn't."

"Tommy, you could learn."

"I should doubt it," I said.

"You will learn, won't you?"

I laughed.

"Tommy . . ." She stopped and we both turned so we faced each
other.

"All right, I'll learn," I said. Something about the way she was
looking when I spoke made me do it. If I had thought about it for a
second I would have hesitated and thought a lot more, and never
moved. The way it was, I didn't think. She put her arms out and held
me off, but not very hard. "Nancy," I said. I didn't have to try then.
She melted right up against me. It wasn't til several minutes later we
went on with our walk, and from then on it was interrupted quite
often. I don't know yet where it was we went, down East Point Road,
I guess, but I know I never seen the snow so fluffy and light on the
spruce boughs, like it was then, nor the snow in the open places so

exciting, nor any winter night, ever, that was tender and gentle and soft.

It was late when I left her to the house. There was no kids coasting over on the highway, and almost everywhere the lights was out. I held Nancy off at arm's length a minute just so I could look at her.

"Tommy, what's got into you?" she said.

"I feel new," I told her.

She smiled. "Did you feel new last night?"

"I felt new last night too."

"Did any of them ever tell you you were a sweet boy, Tommy?"

"It doesn't matter," I said happily.

"Did they?" she asked.

"Maybe Corinne, once."

"Oh, Tommy!"

I had never known saying something could be like that. Even after she had gone in the house and I was walking home it was not so bad because it was interesting looking at the points of land, the bay, the fences, and trees that I had never seen before in life, and the minute I hit the bed that night I was asleep.

I went clamming the day after that, and the next and the next. Not that I felt especially clammy, you understand, but I wanted money. I looked through the catalogues til I found a suit I liked, and I got that marked, and the price, and then some shirts and shoes and socks. I had to work that week because the next week I would be back in school and would not have the same chance. Then nights of course I went to see Nancy.

There is no need to tell you about every night because if you know, you know, and if you don't, you don't, and that's that, except maybe the night of the snowstorm. It was not a heavy snow, and perhaps there was nothing very special about it, except us. I waited for Nancy the same as always, and when she came out she had the hood of her jacket back on her shoulders, and her hair blew in the wind. Her skirt blew too, pulling tight against her legs and streaming to leeward, and the light snowflakes flew past her. She ran to meet me and took my hand and we started up the path quick.

As soon as we was out of sight of the house, she stopped and put her arms around me and kissed me like she had never done before. It is not too easy to explain. It was harder, yes, only that wasn't all. She was fiercer. *Good God, is this Nancy?* I thought, and for just a split second I got the idea there was something wild about her, like an animal, and I was frightened. I would be frightened again now, and so would anyone who has brains enough to hold a hat on.

We let go of each other soon, and Nancy didn't say nothing. We just went up the path to the road. The tree branches swayed over us in the wind and the light snow blew in our faces. It did not feel cold out, just frisky. Nancy would run ahead of me sometimes and I chased her. Then she would dodge off the path and I'd reach out and try to catch her. It made her laugh and the laughter in the spruce woods was like music.

Finally we left the highway and went up a side road that goes to Ned Anderson's place, and when we come near his barn, Nancy creeps into my arms like she was hiding from something. I felt her hands slide under my jacket. Her fingers clutched the flesh near my shoulders, and she stood close to me and kind of buried her face in my neck.

"Tommy . . . Tommy . . ." Her voice sounded very far away and sad somehow. We went into the barn then, and I helped her climb up on top of the hay. There was a hollow place there, and it felt warm and springy and like she and I were alone on earth.

I thought I had never known before how much I loved her or how much I could love anybody. I hadn't known. I had never been one for going to church much, or praying, but there in the barn I see all of a sudden how I was supposed to feel in church. I felt like I was almost nothing, like I wasn't important at all, but Nancy was the whole world and the stars too even, and everything there is.

I bowed my head, kissing her, and it seemed right, taking off our clothes (most of them anyway) and coming together like other animals do. It was the way I wanted things. I cannot explain it right and no doubt never will. Only maybe you know . . .

We lay there for a long time, whispering and laughing, and I took her home, if anything, earlier than usual that night just to be safe.

There were other nights, of course. Though after school started again I did not go to see her so often. She thought that way it was better, and to tell you the truth, I did. I was clamming so hard after school, and sometimes, when the tides was that way, before school in the morning, that I was about dead by night.

But I had to keep up the work. I did not have enough for the clothes yet, and I wanted to get some lobster gear besides and put down traps in the spring and summer. And except for Nancy I would never have bothered. She and I had a good time at the next couple dances, though they was not really like the first one. I danced with her a lot more, and I did not mind when Lysol or the others danced with her. We rode together in the truck, and it was not just all right; it was fun. Of course I went to school and come home with her too. We was always glad to see each other and hated to say goodnight, and I guess we could have found our way to Ned Anderson's barn blindfolded. I was as contented as I knew how when I was with Nancy, but I kept thinking of her and the money I had to make, and I drove the clamming til it liked to kill me. It got so it was no use staying out late nights: I would fall asleep, or I would fall asleep in school the next day. So there was a week, after a while, when I only see Nancy daytimes and a couple of evenings.

Then there was the day I counted over my clam money, what I had left after going to dances, and I had enough to get the clothes I wanted. I had more than enough. I bought the money order that day during our nooning. I went clamming that afternoon, and when supper was over I sealed the order in an envelope and addressed it and went over to the post office to put it in the slot so the early mail the next day would get it.

Coming back from the office I took a short cut toward our part of the village. I was aiming to go to Nancy's. The short cut is a dirt road that is not used much, but there are usually a few tire marks on the snow in it. I was about halfway in, I guess, when I see this car pulled over to one side. Everybody knows everyone else's car to Oak Harbor, and I knew this was Lysol's.

I was about thirty feet from it, I guess, when I heard the voice and the laughing. I didn't stop walking. My muscles just went automatic. And I don't know why I looked, neither, when I got up to it, because I might as well see it written out in her own handwriting as hear her laugh. But I did look, and then ran.

I don't know if they ever see me or not, and it don't matter. I stopped running when I was out of sight. My mouth was open. I felt like the air was pressing in on me and going to crush me. I felt like something under my ribs was going to bust. And still I didn't feel angry. I knew Nancy had promised me nothing; she hadn't lied. I closed my mouth and grabbed my lower lip with my teeth, and walked back to my own house. In the shed was our clam hoes and burlap sacks and hods we used for clamming, and I recalled what the Old Man once said, that it takes a strong back and a weak mind to make a clam digger. "Well, I guess you qualify," I told myself.

I come into the kitchen and shoved my hands in my pockets. Corinne was the only one there. She was reading the paper on the kitchen table. "In early, ain't you?" she says.

"Yes," I said. I clenched my fists in my trouser pockets, trying to keep quiet. Corinne glanced up and took a good look and didn't say nothing. In my pocket I felt the money I had left over after sending the order. I pulled it out and laid it on the table.

"What's that for, Tommy?"

I didn't dare look at her. "You said you'd get a permanent if you had the money to spend, didn't you?"

Corinne stared at me for as much as half a minute. There wasn't no need for me to tell her nothing. She looked like she felt everything I did and wanted to help.

"Thank you, Tommy. I'll get it."

I almost run out of the kitchen and up to my room and lay face down on the bed. She knew all right, but I thought I wouldn't be able to stand it if she see me crying.

After that night I didn't care if I did nothing. I almost stopped clamming, and everything I used to do at school went all to pieces. I kept away from Nancy there, never looked at her, and I noticed she stayed clear of me as best she could.

It was about then I talked Elwood and Corinne into letting me quit.

VI

When I woke up it took some time to get squared around. First I had to get it through my head that I was aboard the *Icecap,* and not ashore somewhere where Mac and Phil and others would be nearby. Then I remembered Elwood was no doubt in the engine room, and Tarbox in the wheelhouse. I knew that because I could hear the others. I did not turn my head nor open my eyes much. I was remembering the cabin, where the bunks was placed and the lockers Wid and Jappie would be sitting on, the hinged table, the galley stove, and the hatch.

The *Icecap* was pitching now, more than she had been before. I could feel her prow pushing down into the seas and shoving me toward the head of my berth. Now and then she would slap hard into the seas with a heavy jolt, and I began to wonder how the timbers and planking could hang together.

I said I could hear the others, and I could. I recognized their voices right off, but the first of it I never noticed what they was saying. Then all of a sudden it began to get through to me. I lay there for a while, not turning over or nothing, just like I was asleep. The Icecap took an extra heavy plunge.

"Christ, what are we into?" Wid asked.

"I'll bet old Tarbox never nosed her into a worse northeaster than this," Jappie said.

"Just bracing its feet," Lysol told them.

"I'd hate to see one you thought meant business."

"Just wait."

"I don't care what you call it," Wid said. "There sure is one hell of a draft."

From the way he was speaking, I guessed he was kneeling on one of the bunks and staring out a port.

"Let's have another drink."

I almost believed I could hear the liquor gurgling down Wid's throat.

"Christ, you don't have to drink it all."

"I got another bottle," Lysol said.

Yes, you stinker, I thought, out from under my bunk where I had it hid.

"I got to dig enough clams to get me about a case of this stuff."

"You dig that much, mister, you'll have one hell of a sore back."

"Why can't they pay us a decent price?"

"They're paying a decent price — if you don't eat."

"Yeah."

"And Tarbox takes his cut for transportation."

"Well, he has to, don't he? What do you think, he'd go freighting for nothing?"

"No, but it all mounts up."

"There ain't much left, not after a man pays a bill or two."

"Who pays a bill?"

"Them factory sons-of-bitches! Why don't they allow a man enough to get by on?"

"They'd pick their mothers' gold teeth," Wid said. " 'Why should I pay eighty cents a bushel when I can get all I need for fifty-five?' Charlie Means heard him say it over the telephone to Boston."

"Some factory managers!"

"Greedy gutted bastards."

"Christ, they got to live."

"Yes, but by-Jesus, they don't have to live on me."

"How about another swallow? That last one felt good."

I wondered when they would ever reach the end of that bottle.

"Ben Jenkins is worse'n a bank anyway," Wid said.

"That ain't possible."

"The bank wants your right leg and half your soul for security. Prove you don't need it, they'll lend you the money."

"For Ben Jenkins anything's possible."

The *Icecap* took an extra heavy plunge and it sounded like one of the men must have pitched forward.

"Where the hell are you going?"

"Goddamned if I know."

"I won't dispute that any."

For a minute they was all quiet, except one of them let out a heavy gasp. "Mister, that stuff's high powered!"

"I drink that the same's water."

"Yes, I guess you do."

"You look it," Wid said.

"Gentlemen," Jappie said. "Gentlemen, I want to introduce to you this evening —"

"Christ, what now?"

"Lost his marbles."

"Gentlemen, gentlemen: I'd like to introduce to you tonight —"

"Sit down."

"Before you fall down."

"Please," Jappie said. "Don't you see all them people out there?"

"Wid can't see two feet," Lysol said.

"I can. I can see three — three foot six maybe."

"All them people," Jappie said, "waiting to hear a speech."

"Tell 'em to go home," Wid said.

"You really think I should ask them to go away?"

"It wouldn't hurt my feelings none."

"I don't know," Jappie said, "whether they'll go or not."

"Costs nothing to try," Wid said.

"Tell them to get the hell out. They're making me nervous."

"Can't stand crowds," Lysol said.

"Gentlemen," Jappie said. "Ladies and gentlemen —"

Lysol snorted.

"All you good people," Jappie said. "It gives me great pleasure to introduce to you this afternoon —"

"Give him another drink," Lysol said.

"What do you want to do, drowned him?"

"That would shut him up."

"Tell 'em to go home," Wid said.

"Gentlemen, please," Jappie said.

"He means us."

"Let us be polite. Let us have some manners."

"We've got 'em, God damn bad ones," Wid said.

"To introduce to you," Jappie said, "a man who — who — What in hell is your right name, Wid?"

"Who cares?"

"To hell with it."

"Give him another drink."

"But I can't remember your right name, Wid."

"Introduce Lysol."

"Lysol?"

"Sure. Let Lysol speak to 'em."

"Gentlemen," Jappie said, "to introduce to you a man who —"

"You said all that."

"I know, but I'm saying it again."

"Once is enough."

"Let him talk."

"Godsakes, I can't stop him."

"Just let him talk."

"A man," Jappie said, "who is well known as the father of more children than any other man to Oak Harbor."

"Le's have a drink on that," Wid said.

"'S a damned lie," Lysol said.

"It is not," Jappie told him. "Count 'em up."

"Count 'em yourself; you know so goddamned much."

"Well, there's Margaret Clement's girl," Jappie said.

"I never touched her but once in my life."

"Once is enough."

"You keep saying that."

"Supposing I do?"

"And Jean Andrews' kid."

"He's Ace Martin's," Lysol said. "You can see it all over him."

"Ace's, hell!"

"Well what about Corinne Mason?" Wid said. "You've had her knocked up tighter'n drum before now."

"Yes, God damn it, and I'd be getting more now if you hadn't talked me into this clamming junket."

"Sh-h-h, for Christ's sake!" Jappie said. "Her kid's right there in the bunk."

VII

All of a sudden everything went quiet. It wasn't really quiet, of course. The *Icecap*'s diesel was droning on just like the world stood still in the same place it had before. The wind howled through what little rigging the *Icecap* had on her stubby mast, and the seas pounded her bows like a brace of piledrivers. She tossed, and swung above a sea, and dropped like a hailstone.

I lay there like I was froze, like time had stopped, and the *Icecap* was falling away from me, and the ocean was, and the whole world even, leaving me floating there in space and darkness. A queer thing: a storm comes up (maybe it is just a squall, or then again maybe it is a tan-toasting hurricane) and a hand reaches up inside your brain somewhere, battens down the hatches and closes the ports. You see the breakers and feel the wind. You sense the pull of the tide maybe, but the idea that you're really on a lee shore don't get through to you, not the first of it. You are below decks and even the ventilators are closed, you think.

That was the way I was, my eyes closed, paralyzed, my brain a blank because I didn't dare let it think. I had yanked the cables right off the battery. Or that is, I thought I had. I thought I had everything battened down, but somehow a man's gear doesn't quite hold. Along comes a gale with a force to it you never imagined, or a sea hits you tougher and with more twist than any you've seen, and something gives. First there is just a little air leakage, sharp and keen like the cut of a razor, and then a hatch or a port is stove in and you catch the full blast.

Corinne. That's what I saw, as soon as I saw anything, lying there with my eyes shut. It is queer, the things a fellow will remember, or only half remember, at a time like that, and no sense to it. Like being back in the darkness in my bed, my mouth dry, my head burning, calling for Corinne, and seeing her leaning over me, warm, and finally bringing the water. Or crying, crying louder, trembling and shaking with fear in the nothingness of the night, and no Corinne, no Elwood, no anyone until at last I was sick, retching and beyond tears, the minutes stretching out into endlessness, and when there was a voice down there in the kitchen it was not the right one. She was a long time coming that time, and other times too. I began to remember all the days (was I four or five?) the days he was at the house, sometimes wanting to play with me, or bringing something, and how I hated his being there and was glad when Corinne give me a nickel and sent me to the store on an errand. She always did.

Well, was this bit of information I'd picked up anything new? Wasn't there a part of me somewhere that had had this locked up out of sight since God knows when, where I didn't have to look at it or think it? And now, because Jappie had opened his mouth and said half a dozen words so I could hear them, it wasn't like news; it was like recognizing something. Now I was taking it out, turning it over in my hands to look at it, saying slowly and quietly, "Yes, yes, I knew this always." But it was a queer breathless kind of quiet. I kept asking myself, "Are you surprised? This isn't a shock, is it? Nothing is changed. Everything is just like it was before."

But it wasn't. There ain't much that ever is. You can't get words unspoken; you can't unthink nothing. The little place in your brain has opened up; the doors are wide, and close them all you want, there is no forgetting what used to be inside. It's there now, and part of you.

I could feel my heart beating, and knew I was breathing in short little gasps. One hand was grasping the edge of the pipe berth like it was all there was between me and death. I kept trying to see Corinne, and believe it or not her face wasn't clear to me any more. That sounds crazy. I thought it was crazy too. It scared me. I could see the pattern on the apron she wore; I could see the way she walked, and hear her voice. In a minute maybe I wouldn't be able to do that. It wasn't right to feel like I did about Corinne. I don't know if I hated her. Maybe I did. But I could remember the way she said, "Thanks, Tommy," that night I give her the money for a permanent. It was like my heart was out on a skewer and turned on a fire. I was losing her and I wanted to howl. Damn damn, God damn. . . !

I clenched my teeth and tried to be fair. If Nancy'd been somebody else's, would I have stopped? Or would Nancy have stopped? That was easy. I'd never blamed Nancy, not really, not even when — so why Corinne?

But it was no use. It wasn't the same at all. I *was* Corinne's and it wasn't right. There was the Old Man, Elwood I mean. I thought of him aft in the engine room now. I thought of how he'd fished and clammed, bought stuff for me, for Corinne, and Muriel, give me lickings when I needed them. He must have known 'way back. All to once I see why he had not wanted me on the *Icecap* with him. He'd wanted me back home at the house near Corinne, that is, until he'd found Lysol wasn't going to be left behind in Oak Harbor. But then he hadn't wanted to go shipmates with Lysol neither, and no wonder. So here we was, the three of us, thanks to Tarbox.

I felt I wanted to see Elwood. I felt like I wanted to say, "Look, I owe you something. I owe you things I can never pay back. I —" But did I? And anyway, I knew I would never say it.

And Lysol? The rot-gutted son-of-a-bitch! The way I see it, he had took everything, give nothing, and cared for no one, not me, not Nancy, not Corinne even. And he had stole what I could never get back. The only one that mattered was Lysol, and to hell with us, where Elwood — but Elwood was different.

And Lysol was right there in the forecastle with me for all I knew, standing there, staring, with Jappie and Wid, waiting to see if I was awake, waiting to see if I'd heard what Jappie had said. My jaw snapped shut and the muscles of my arm tightened until it shook. If he was standing there now . . . If I'd had him before me that second, and any way to do it, I'd have crushed his skull in like a gull's egg.

I knew I mustn't hurry. I tried to listen, to hear them if they was there, but the only sounds was of the merciless, ungodly pounding of the *Icecap* into the seas, and the rattle of gear and pans below decks. Even then I kept my eyes shut for about a year, my teeth pressed together, my hand clutching the edge of the berth. I knew what I would do. I had everything thought out like it had already happened. I opened one eye. They was gone. They had gone topside as quiet as if they'd flew up the hatchway one by one and never touched nothing.

I lay there in the bunk, my feet braced against the lockers to keep from being thrown out on the floorboards, bracing myself with both hands. I went toward the hatchway, picking up a hammer from a locker beside the stove. The hatch was part way open. I mounted the ladder.

Snowflakes struck my face as I reached the deck. I saw it wasn't a thick snow yet, but they were fine flakes and it was going to last a while. The wind drove them across the deck in white streaks and lashed at my face. The *Icecap* pitched, and I hung onto the hatch coaming with my free hand. There was black and white mountains all around us, the foaming crests pitching sharp and biting into the troughs and snapping at the sides of the *Icecap* like the bared teeth of angry dogs.

I saw all that in the first second, but what my eyes fastened on was Lysol, back to, leaning against the wheelhouse, his feet braced against the low bulwark. I never figured anything. It was like it was all one motion from the time I left my bunk, my heart pounding, my hand clenched finally around the hammer handle, and my jaw and guts tense. He was three steps away from me. I took two of those steps, staggering a little on the pitching deck, and pulled the hammer back over my right shoulder.

All to once three things happened. There is no doubt about two of them because they was as true for others as they was for me. And the third one is true too, only I can't prove it. There is a moment there, a tenth of a second maybe, when the hammer in a man's grasp don't move. It has finished its swing back and it has not started forward. Just in that instant, I saw the cap on Lysol's head, I mean like I had not seen it before. I saw the fuzzy red fabric and a little of Lysol's hair sticking out underneath. Then it wasn't his cap or his head at all; it was mine, my own head I was about to strike, feeling the skull crush and the sudden blazing pain. In another second I'd have put my left hand up behind my ear to feel the place, and I'd never have brought that hammer forward, not like I'd meant to, not if I'd had five full minutes clear sailing. I could feel the sweat break out all over me, like at night sometimes.

Tarbox must have had the wheelhouse window open to speak to me or something. Anyway, I was right under it. His hand reached out there and gripped that hammer gale force. Out of the corner of my eye I saw his sleeve and knew just what was happening. If I'd had time, and wanted to, I couldn't have moved, not an inch. I'd just have watched him like I was half awake.

What I didn't see was the wave. Tarbox must have let go the wheel to stop me, and accordingly the *Icecap* fell off to leeward a bit and took the next sea broad on the bow. It was like about one-third of the Gulf of Maine had jumped right aboard of us. For a moment I didn't know but we was about to go under. There was a loud crash, like the splintering of wood, come with a roar. I was down, the seas foaming over me and washing the *Icecap*'s deck until it was out of sight.

I fetched up against the starboard bulwark, bruised in more places than I could count, and choking sea water out of my mouth. I was some seconds struggling and thrashing, trying to get halfway to my feet. It felt like an hour before I did. Tarbox had the *Icecap* back on course by then, and she was pitching into them seas not quite head-on. The punt he had lashed to the deck amidships had taken the heaviest part of the sea, and was ruined, good only for kindling wood. The dory on the engine-room trunk, aft, was still unhurt. I shuddered with the cold of the wet clothing, crouching on the deck like I didn't dare to stand again for fear Old Man Ocean would knock me flat. Then suddenly I realized what I should have seen right from the start: no Lysol.

Although I knew better, I looked to leeward. There was, of course, nothing but the sharp, jagged peaks of twisting seas, lurching and tossing. For a second I found myself thinking back and wondering if I'd hit him. Then I knew I hadn't. I got to my feet and jumped to the wheelhouse door. I swung it open. Tarbox stood there, legs braced wide apart to hold him from falling, fighting the wheel to keep the *Icecap* eased into the seas the best he could. He hardly turned his head toward me.

"Lysol! Lysol!" I shouted.

"What?"

"Overside."

Tarbox reached for the throttle and put her down to dead slow.

"Can't turn," I heard him say.

I knew he would be risking everything if he did swing the *Icecap* side-to in them seas now. And no use anyway. He would not likely find his man, and if he did, he'd have damned small chance of picking him up. Still, I knew he might try it.

"Can you see him?" Tarbox asked, then stood there silent with his mouth open as the *Icecap* dug her prow into an extra big one.

I clung to the door and the brass support on the wheelhouse and was surprised when the wind, the heave, and sea water didn't set me adrift. "Haven't tried," I shouted, but I couldn't tell whether he ever heard me.

"Get . . . others," Tarbox said.

I suppose I nodded. I remember slamming the door and looking for something else to grab hold of. There was a stay just aft. I took a grip on that and on the corner of the wheelhouse. In spite of the wet and cold, I felt like I was sweating. I kept thinking about Lysol. I hated him, and I was scared of losing him. I was all light and gut-empty, just as if I'd killed him myself. I thought about being out there in that cold water, the icy shock of it letting you breathe only in short little gasps, if that much, and fighting, straining to stay on the surface when you know damned well no one can pick you up in time. And then the choking on sea water until there is less and less consciousness, and finally only a slight twitching. And the fish . . .

Christ, I thought, I am going to be sick. But I knew I had to get aft. "Get aft, get aft," I told myself.

There was a high trunk over the engine room and a handrail on the trunk; I tried to grab that rail and work aft to the hatch. It was ungodly slow going, and when I got there, the hatch cover was closed tight. Down below, under that hatch, warm and dry, and alive, or so I supposed, was Elwood, and Wid, and Jappie.

VIII

Suddenly, while I was working my way aft, beyond the hatch I see something huddled around the after bitts, and while I am watching, it moves and gets up on its knees. I began to shout. I don't know what I was saying. I was just yelling. The wonder of it was that over the sound of the wind and the seas he could hear me at all. He hung onto the bitts, got up, and started toward the hatch. I had reached it by then and was trying to slide the cover back. I hung onto the edge with both hands and shouted to him. "Going below?"

Lysol shook his head like he was trying to clear it, and stared at me. His expression was odd. I didn't doubt he had been out for a few minutes, and then I remembered he was drunk too. "God damn him to hell!"

His voice was an ugly growl. I couldn't tell who he was damning, whether he thought someone had throwed him against the bitts or what. I pointed down at the hatch. At first I thought he didn't understand my motion. Then: "Hell no!"

I guessed he was thinking about Elwood's being down there and his refusing to bunk up forward. I pounded my fist on the hatch cover, and all to once it slid back. Wid stuck his head up. "What in hell are you celebrating?"

"Open up," I said.

"It's open. What more do you want?" Wid stepped back out of my path and I started down the ladder. Lysol was working his way along the weather side of the trunk toward the wheelhouse, pausing and hanging on, when the *Icecap* rolled far over and green water whipped about his boots. His lips was open, and his teeth shut tight. 'Tain't no goddamned use hiding liquor from me, son."

I didn't answer. I pulled my head down out of the wind and was in the engine room.

"For the love of Jesus, close that hatch," Wid said.

I did, and braced myself against the ladder and looked at them. A little light come in through the ports, and Elwood had on the twelve-watt bulbs, what there was of them. The air was thick with the stink of diesel fuel and the rummy breath out of Wid and Jappie. Elwood was crouched next to the engine. "Hi," he said.

I stared at him and opened my mouth to speak before I realized that now Lysol wasn't lost and I had nothing to tell them.

"What is it?" the Old Man asked.

I shook my head.

"Tarbox need a relief?"

"Yeah," I said.

"Christ, I should think so," Wid said and started for the hatch.

"What the hell happened to you?" Jappie asked. "Go overside?"

"If I had, you wouldn't be asking me nothing," I told him.

"Take them wet things off," Elwood said.

"A man don't go overside but once in this weather."

"Better take them off," Jappie said. "We'll get dry gear for you."

"Take them off," the Old Man said.

"All right."

For a wonder, he had extra clothes. They was old, and dirty, and full of holes, and they didn't fit, but they was dry.

Elwood jerked his head back to the diesel when she resumed speed. "What in hell Tarbox trying to do?" he asked.

"He thought Lysol was overboard," I said.

Elwood looked thoughtful and said nothing. Jappie took the last puff on a rolled butt, crushed it out under his boot, and went up the ladder and through the hatch.

"He was on the after deck."

"Hunh?"

"Laying against the bitts."

"That was a bad sea," Elwood said.

"I know."

"That the one got you?"

"Yeah."

Elwood shook his head. "We got no license being out here."

"You ain't lying."

"I wish to hell you had stayed home, like I said." Elwood was staring at me. "What the holy hell is the matter with you?"

"Nothing."

He grunted like he did not believe me and kept on staring. Then somebody opened the hatch again. Snow blasted its way through the opening and swirled into the engine room. Wid's scrawny face peered down at us. "Give us a hand with some lines up forward, will you?"

"Who?"

"Anyone."

I started to go, but Elwood put a hand on my neck. "What lines?" he said.

"Tarbox wants something to hang onto, forward. Lysol and Tommy was damned near overside already. He thinks he may have to anchor."

"My Jesus, you don't tell me!" Elwood said. "He's learning. No, I'll go. Watch the engine."

"Don't know nothing about it," I told him.

"Who does?" Elwood asked, and was gone.

I squatted there on a tool chest, staring at the diesel for a while, checking the oil pressure and r.p.m. gauge, just like I would know if they was right or not. The *Icecap*, rolling and pitching, nearly threw me on my head once or twice.

Over the scream of the wind, the thunder of them seas punching the *Icecap*'s hull, and the drumming of the diesel, I could hear the tools clanking against one another in that box. I pulled at the tops of my boots and chewed an unburned match. If them tools would just shut up!

Finally I climbed the hatchway ladder. I opened the hatch and pushed my head and shoulders above decks. The snow was driving in thicker now, a regular blizzard, and from our changed position in the wind I guessed that Tarbox was trying to work up into the lee of Conway Island, although God knows the shelter it makes is little enough. Leaning far over to starboard I could see past the wheelhouse and forward to the bow. There was Elwood. He had strung a half-inch line between a stanchion and stays and he was about to make it fast beyond the winch. Then I see Lysol.

I don't know why it was Lysol doing the work, and not Wid, except that Lysol always run of an idea that he knew how to do everything better. He had worked up the port side inch by inch the same way Elwood had the starboard, and now the two of them was together. I could tell Lysol wanted to make the lines fast one way, and Elwood another. I saw them chewing and jawing a minute up there on the rolling, pitching bow of the *Icecap*, first one swearing and then the other. At last Lysol snaps the line right out of Elwood's hands and makes them fast the way he wanted.

Elwood turned aft, bracing his feet, grabbing at the new line and anything steady he could get his hands on. Even at that distance the look on his face was not pretty. Lysol followed him a few seconds later on the same side, him too hanging onto the line they had just rigged. He went into the wheelhouse.

I dropped back into the engine room, and a few minutes later Elwood was on the ladder and closing the hatch above his head, using brusque, swift movements, and swearing, not at me, and not to me, but just cussing, repeating, over and over. He stood a few seconds, one hand still on the ladder, looking about the engine room. With his free arm he pushed the cap back from his forehead and scratched his scalp, then shoved his hands one at a time into his pockets for warmth. Part of the time I couldn't hear what he was saying, but his lips kept moving.

"Nice fellow," I said.

"Yeah."

"Got a skinful, ain't he?"

"Christ, that don't signify," Elwood said. "I been drunk too, now and then, but it didn't make me a complete son-of-a-bitch; or that is, I never supposed . . ."

"No."

"By God, I sure hate being shipmates with that thing."

"I don't love him none," I said.

"You don't?"

"No."

"What did he ever do to you?" Elwood asked.

I only half heard him. I was sitting on that tool box again, looking past Elwood and trying to remember all the times I had ever seen Lysol, trying to pile up evidence for what I'd heard. For a second I caught myself thinking it was a bad dream I'd had up in the fore peak, but then I knew better. I could see Lysol down around shore where it didn't matter, or in his car with Nancy where it mattered a lot, but the times he'd been around home, which mattered the most, weren't clear. I knew he had been there, and been there plenty; I just couldn't see him, not like I saw other things. Maybe my memory was losing Lysol. Not that I gave a God damn!

Corinne, and then Lysol! I wanted to remember Corinne's face. I tried. I wrinkled my brow and squeezed my eyes shut. I tried to remember Nancy and Nancy's voice, but there was no benefit to that. Lysol had everything. Nothing was no use. Christ, I thought, I am an orphan. And suddenly it seemed to me like the *Icecap* was the loneliest craft afloat, the loneliest, emptiest goddamned place there was anywhere. And then Elwood, who had been watching, was standing in front of me, his feet wide apart, balancing himself against the roll of the *Icecap,* and saying, "What has he done? What has the son of a whore done to you?"

I had forgotten Elwood. Them wrenches was still rattling around in the tool chest. I set out to ask Elwood why he didn't fasten them down. He was staring me right in the eye, almost like I was guilty of something, like I killed Lysol that time he went overside, or I thought he went overside.

"There's no need to look right through me," I told him. "I ain't done nothing. I only heard —"

"What?"

I didn't answer.

"What?" he asked. He had to raise his voice over the sound of the engine and wind and seas, but not that much.

"Nothing," I said.

"Has that jeezily goddamned fool told you . . ."

I looked away. Elwood's hand was into my shoulder. It hurt. I twisted and turned under it and jerked myself free. "He didn't tell me nothing," I said.

But Elwood had seen my eyes. He had been watching my face.

"All right," I said, "try having a sea knock you down in the scuppers and see how you like it."

"I know how I like it," he said. "That ain't bothering you none. You'd snap back from that like a steel spring. Look here!"

I had to look. I didn't want to; I just had to.

"What's Lysol told you? What's he said where you could hear it?"

I tried to look down. I tried to keep my mouth shut.

"Come on," Elwood said.

I wondered if maybe the *Icecap* would sink and drown all of us. Perhaps it would spring a plank. It might happen any time. It might happen this minute and the water would gush into the hull and I would never have to tell Elwood, nor think of Corinne, nor Nancy, nor see Lysol again, nor — I glanced down at the floorboards looking for water.

"Tommy." He wasn't ordering me that time, and he wasn't exactly pleading with me neither, but it was close to it. I looked him in the eye and he said it again. "Tommy —"

"He was drunk," I said. "And anyway, Jappie —"

I stopped, watching him change. He was standing there now, in the crazily pitching and bouncing engine room, muttering and swearing, his eyes big, clenching and unclenching his fists.

"It wasn't their fault," I said. "They was drunk. They thought I was asleep in the bunk. I don't doubt they'd forgot I was in there and —"

"And Corinne?" Elwood said. "Corinne?"

He must have seen the blood drain from my face. I wasn't going to be sick. I knew I wasn't. But I felt sick. I tried to ease back onto that tool box. I wanted to sit somewhere before the *Icecap* pitched me into the diesel.

"It don't matter," I said, and I knew my voice was breaking. "Christ, I don't care, I —"

"The Christless almighty bastards!" Elwood's fists was going up and down like the tappets on a gas engine. It made me mad seeing him. It made me mad seeing him get mad, although I thought he couldn't hate any more than I did. I don't know why it made me feel sick seeing him go like that, unless it was that he was the last thing, the last thing to grab hold of and hang onto, and now to have him run off his course like that . . .

He was calming down slowly. His hands still worked, but more now like he was mixing dough. He wasn't looking at me; he stared past me into the *Icecap*'s timbers like he was seeing every splinter and spike, and each one was one more bitter fact hitting him in the face.

Then I realized that what looked like calming down wasn't that at all maybe. I remembered what I'd felt like up forward in the cabin, like every move, every act was already settled. I hadn't even thought when I'd grabbed that hammer, and gone toward the hatch, and made my way across the deck to where Lysol was standing. It was more like I was just blinking my eyes or taking a breath. And now Elwood . . .

He turned suddenly and his hands grasped the hatchway ladder. Much as I hated Lysol, I knew I had to stop him. Better than I liked, I knew what errand he was bound on, and to have Elwood do that, like he was doing it for me, or like he was doing it because of me — God, not Elwood, I thought, not Elwood!

I could see his hands gripping the sides of the ladder, and I wanted to reach out and pull him off, but I couldn't move. I was paralyzed. It was like I was nailed down to the jeezily toolbox, like when in a dream you are on the railroad track, trying and straining to step out of the way, only you can never move fast enough, and the locomotive comes nearer, and nearer, and nearer . . .

But there was no locomotive here; there was just me and El-wood in the engine room of the *Icecap*, and Elwood going on deck blind crazy with anger.

The *Icecap* rolled worse than ever suddenly, and I was flying toward the workbench to port. Then she trembled like a leaf and pulled herself up. I was off balance, but I was standing, and able to move. I had to grab something to keep from falling, and the nearest and handiest thing was Elwood, still on the ladder.

He shook me off and I was on the floorboards, my knees bruised and stinging with the shock. When I looked up, I could see him opening the hatch. I sprang for him again, grabbing his belt with one hand and an arm with the other. He swore this time, but I was ready for him and he couldn't throw me off like he had before.

"Let go! God damn it to hell!" He didn't shout. His voice was quiet and terrible.

I swung my forearm over his shoulder and under his chin. For a second it was like the world was upside down, and I wondered if the *Icecap* had turned over. Then I knew it hadn't. We hit the floorboards together, Elwood on top, both of us thrashing, and me clutching to keep him from getting free. But there wasn't enough of me. Elwood was halfway up in a few seconds, his face red and angry. I don't know but he would have hit me. He was bent over me, his arm drawn back, when the diesel slowed.

Both of us stopped struggling.

IX

If you are on the water much, especially in winter, you know why. The engine is what gives you forward motion, and without forward motion you can do nothing, or close to it. A man might as well be out without a rudder. You cannot go home nor anywhere else, and it will be more than you can do probably to keep your craft headed into the seas. If you are on a lee shore, or in very bad weather, having the engine going may make the difference between saving and losing your boat, not saying anything about yourself, and perhaps others.

So when the rhythm of ours changed sudden, Elwood looked up, and best as I could, laying on the floorboards, I cocked my head toward it to listen. She speeded again, then dropped off to almost nothing. We knew that wasn't Tarbox playing with the throttle; he wouldn't behave like that.

Elwood jumped off me, swearing, and I got to my feet. By then he was fussing around the injector pump, changing the charge of fuel. I squatted beside him, watching. From the way the engine limped, I judged he was not improving things none. He was muttering something about the injector nozzles, and I went over to the toolbox to get a set of wrenches. When I held them out to him, Elwood pushed my arm away, shaking his head. "Hell, boy, as long as she's turning over at all, I don't want to stop her," he told me, "not in this sea."

He was bending over now, making an adjustment on the timing, once in a while upping the revolutions per minute for a few seconds, but presently they would drop off again. Then a new adjustment, a speeding up, slowing down. I set there watching the engine, tensing up every time it slowed, my hands itching to get at it, to change this or that or the other, to try to keep it going. But Elwood was already doing that, frigging around with everything in sight, and there was nothing for me except watching.

"Go up to the wheelhouse, Tommy, and tell Tarbox what we're up against. He'll think I've gone crazy down here."

He sounded like the old Elwood, and I was glad, glad the diesel had half broke down this way. I nodded to show I'd heard him, and started to mount the ladder to go topsides, but just as I was reaching above my head for the hatch cover, it slid open. A pair of boots swung into view and filled up the square of flying snow and gray daylight. I dropped to one side to keep from being stepped on, and Lysol come down the ladder.

"What the hell's wrong?"

"Dirty injectors, I guess," I said.

"Christ, yank 'em off and clean 'em out," Lysol said.

Elwood jumped like he had touched a hot wire. "Now you'd make quite a mess of things, wouldn't you?" His face muscles was drawn tight, scowling, and he turned right back to the engine like Lysol had never been there to begin with.

That didn't seem to make Lysol feel no better. He stood there bracing himself with one hand on the ladder, his clothes half froze, dusted over with snow, and wet through. I could see the outline of a bottle in one of his pockets, and his breath filled the engine room like a cloud of smoke. "No need to act like a goddamned old woman all on account of a little sea."

"Yeah?" Elwood mumbled.

"Take the bitch down and make her tick."

"Mind your own business."

"And drown for it, eh?"

"Who's drowning?"

"By-Jesus we all will, if you can't get more'n a couple three knots out of the old hooker."

"We got no license going much faster'n that in this dirt anyway," Elwood told him.

"Christ, let me at them tools and I'll show you something."

Quicker'n a mink, Elwood scooped a twelve-inch Stilson up off the floorboards and held it in his right hand, ready to swing. Lysol had let go his hold on the ladder and was coming toward the diesel.

"One more step and by God I'll let you have it right in the face!" Elwood's voice, thin and sharp, came from between his teeth.

Lysol stood still, swaying with the pitch, or maybe his drunkenness, and stared at Elwood like he couldn't believe his eyes. Then he crouched, or squatted, but he didn't advance. The two of them hung there, just glaring at each other, and beyond them the diesel spluttered and coughed, and the *Icecap* limped plunging into each sea.

"Tommy," Elwood said, "I told you to see Tarbox."

"Yeah," I said. I didn't move.

"Well, get at it."

I stared at him. I didn't want to leave, not while Lysol and him was balanced there like a couple of roosters.

"Get going."

I went that time. I tried to turn to windward as I came from the hatch, but a blast of snow drove me to leeward. I clung to the handrail and pulled myself forward. Every step or two the *Icecap* would slow, twisting into a sea, and I would brace myself against the rush and pull of the water around my boots.

It was a world of snow now, thicker and sharper than ever. The waves, each one a great black wall, loomed at us out of the whiteness, and curled, thundering and spitting, against our hull. I could see a length, maybe a length and a half, beyond the *Icecap*'s bow, but not too clearly, and all the seas out there looked the same. They all looked like surf. I knew they was not surf, or at least I hoped not, because if they was, we would not last ten minutes. Elwood was right: wherever we was, it was a hell of a place to be, and a damned poor time to be there.

When I reached the wheelhouse, I could see the deck amidships and forward. The cover of the cargo hatch had been slid over to windward against the bulwark, and was lashed down with a line.

This left the cargo hatch part open, of course, and every third or fourth sea was sloshing into it. Forward of the hatch, Wid was swinging the handle to our bilge pump, pouring a steady stream on to the deck and into the scuppers. I grabbed the handle to the wheelhouse door and jerked it open. Jappie was steering. He cut his eyes quick at me and then swung them back to the compass card and the water. The *Icecap* rose out of a trough and the wheelhouse door swung against me. I grabbed at it and hung on.

"Tarbox!" I shouted.

Jappie pointed out through the window and down toward the cargo hatch. He was too busy judging the slant and force of each new sea, and fighting the wheel, to speak to me or anyone else.

I took one step back, and a gust of wind shut the wheelhouse door for me, shattering the glass. I started forward, ducking my head to dodge wind and snow, and reaching for a hold on anything in sight, ringbolts, cleats, hatch coamings, anything. I felt like any minute I might be blown clear of the deck and lost in a swirl of snow before I hit the water, and I wondered how Wid could do it, grabbing nothing but the handle to that bilge pump and still hang on, working.

I pulled myself to the edge of the hatch and looked below. All there was was darkness and the old smell of fish. Then, finally I made out a figure, forward and to starboard, crouching down there near the turn of the bilge. That was Tarbox.

For a second or two I felt as if the *Icecap*'s decks was awash. Wid, working that pump, was knee deep in water. I pulled myself over the edge of the coaming and dropped heavily into the cargo hold. I thought down there maybe it would be drier. It wasn't, much. Bilge sloshed about my boots, and every so often a few buckets of sea water surged through the part-open hatch.

Beyond me Tarbox was down on his knees struggling with something. A mallet, chisels, saw, caulking iron, and some blocks of wood was laying around him. He glanced at me and nodded. I could see then he had cut away part of the sealing, and down between the timbers was a leaking seam, a badly leaking seam. Tarbox was struggling to patch it and not having much luck. It looked to me, even with Wid on the pump, like we was going to have to start bailing.

Tarbox looked back over his shoulder. "Get Elwood, will you?"

"We got trouble with the diesel," I said, but the sea climbed aboard just then and Tarbox never heard me.

"I can't check this damned thing," Tarbox said. "Elwood's better at it. We can't stop it, but maybe he can check it enough —"

"We got dirt in the injectors," I shouted.

Tarbox swung around slowly to stare at me.

"Dirt . . . injectors," I said.

"How do . . . know?"

"Elwood . . ."

"Still going?"

I nodded. "A little."

"Tell Elwood to come forward. Got to have him."

"Lysol," I started to say.

"No, Elwood."

"Lysol's down aft," I yelled.

"What of it?"

"Wants to clean injectors."

"Who?"

I shouted, but another sea washed our decks and seven eight bucketfuls slid through the hatch. I dodged over to the far side and because the *Icecap* was rolling, fell against the sealing. When I was righted, I said, "Who's going to stop him if you take Elwood?"

"I'll stop him, God damn him!" Tarbox yelled over the sound of the wind. "Tell him . . . said . . . leave . . . hell alone."

Still I didn't go. I wanted to ask what made him think my saying that would stop Lysol. But then, I didn't want to speak to Lysol at all if I could avoid it, and how would I explain that?

I climbed the ladder to the edge of the hatch and waited until the next big one had passed before I stepped on deck. At least I had the wind to my back, going aft, gripping the wheelhouse door, then a stay, another stay, and finally the handrail on the engineroom trunk. Before I reached the hatch, it opened, and Lysol lifted himself on deck. He clung to the handrail and stared forward for a moment. "Look!" he said.

All I could see was snow and waves.

"Godsakes, look," he shouted. "Can't you see it?"

I stared hard over the starboard bow again, blinking, trying to see through that blizzard. Suddenly it seemed to me like the snow thinned just enough so I could see waves breaking, not losing their crests in the wind but doubling over on a reef. My heart jumped about two feet.

"Over there," Lysol shouted. He was pointing to port this time. Dimly I could make out the shape of a line of spruces.

"Conway Island," I yelled.

"Goddamn right. Come on forward: we got to unship them anchors."

"Tarbox sent me for Elwood. I got to —"

"To hell with Elwood. Get going. You're in my way."

"We're leaking."

"We'll be worse'n that if we ain't fetched up on our ground tackle, time that engine fails."

"But —"

"Let her leak!" He commenced pushing me. I tried to explain it out to him, but it was no use. I had to move, and with him behind me there was only one way to go: forward. When we reached the wheelhouse, Lysol yelled through the broken window at Jappie, and Jappie nodded his head, showing he'd seen everything as quick as we had. At the cargo hatch, he leaned over to talk to Tarbox, and I got away from him and inched aft to the engine room.

Below decks, even with the diesel going, it seemed terribly quiet. It was peaceful, too, out of the snow and wind. Elwood looked up from where he was on his knees beside the diesel. "What now?"

"We got a leak amidships. Tarbox wants you to come up there and fix it."

"Who does he think I am, God Almighty?"

"From the inside," I said. "Just check it."

"Christ yes, I guess so," Elwood said. "Goddamn rotten butter-tub." He was wiping his hands on some cotton waste and getting ready to go topsides.

"We're up under Conway Island now," I said.

"Much good that'll do."

"Better'n nothing, ain't it?"

"Could be. Could be worse — if you're on the wrong side of it."

"We're on the right side."

"We are now," Elwood said, and he climbed the ladder and went on deck.

X

Seven eight minutes after Elwood left, the diesel coughed, fired, coughed again, and stopped. I had tried to do what I could, changing the charge and timing, to keep her going, and in the end probably I had stopped her instead. I figured that scarcely mattered: she would have stopped anyway soon enough.

I went over the adjustments once more, my face and hands down close to the hot metal reeking of grease and fuel. I checked the oil in the tanks. Then I turned her over with the starter. She groaned and growled and ground, but didn't testify. I was stopped. Perhaps if she had been a gas engine, if she had been something I knew the first jeezily thing about . . .

I was going to stick my head up through the hatch to see how many seconds we was from the finish (if this was it, I didn't intend to be cooped up below decks), but just then the hatch slid open and Wid started down, shouting as he came, and all excited.

"I'll handle the damned thing, Tommy. I'll make her talk. You get forward and help Lysol with that anchor."

I set out to say I'd help anyone but Lysol, but then figured this wasn't the time. Besides, I was low man on the *Icecap,* and an order was an order, especially when it sounded like that. So I climbed up on deck again. We was rolling like an empty barrell now, and side to it. I needed both hands to hang on with. I see Tarbox leaning out of the wheelhouse, yelling at me. Couldn't hear him at all, but I guessed that, like Wid, he was telling me to get forward to help Lysol. I grabbed a handrail and a stanchion, bracing my feet between the bulwark and the trunk. Every time my side rolled down I just hung on while the seas tore at my boots and strained to sweep me off the deck; on the up swing I strained to take a step or two.

When I had the wheelhouse broad on the beam, Tarbox stuck his head to the broken window. He was in there alone. Jappie was on the pump and Elwood was in the hold struggling to patch that leak. "Get going, Tommy. Lysol needs help getting that hook un-shipped."

"What the hell did you think I was doing?" I shouted, but he was back out of sight. I did not even see why he was in there. With no power on her, he could not do anything from the wheelhouse to help, not that I knew of, unless he was standing by for Wid to get her going. He was in for a hell of a long wait, to my mind.

As I worked my way past the cargo hatch, I caught a glimpse of Elwood down in the hold bent over that leak. A sea almost flattened me over the hatch cover, poured through the opening, and caught Elwood across the back. I could see him shudder, cringe, shake himself, and keep on working. I could make out perhaps a foot of sea water sloshing around in the bilge. Half the time Elwood had to work with his arms right in it.

Jappie was clinging to the pump just forward of the cargo hatch like he was handcuffed to it, and working it every second to boot. I inched past him, grabbing the stays, and then one of the lines Lysol and Elwood had rigged, but neither one of us tried to speak. Too busy.

I could see by then that Lysol was having troubles. He had unlashed the large anchor and levered the shank up onto the rail. The davit and winch was iced up to a fare-ye-well and no use to us. Only thing was to lever it up over the rail, using the winch handles. His hands must have been about numb working on all that heft of cold, galvanized metal in a snowstorm. Besides that, the bow rolled as bad as the rest, and pitched worse. I see right off that a man would do nothing with gloves on here, and I pulled mine off and stuffed them into a hip pocket. Then I reached down to give Lysol a hand.

"Christ, son, out of my way," he shouted.

"Don't 'son' me," I yelled.

"Get . . . anchor . . . unlashed . . . small one . . . one . . . hold her alone . . . wouldn't hold . . . canoe . . . this."

I knelt by the other anchor, hanging on with one hand and plucking at the lashings with the other. "You know so damned much," I growled. But if he heard me, he didn't show it. I did not care then if he never heard me, if he went overside with that anchor and I never laid eyes on him.

The lashings was crusted over and tight. I let go my hold on the line and used both hands, praying something would keep me glued to the *Icecap*'s deck. I stayed there, anyway, while I tore my nails and cut my fingertips on the icy knots. But getting the thing unlashed was just the beginning. Raising one end to the rail was a chore, but I done it.

Out of the corner of my eye I could see Lysol pulling and hauling to get his over the edge of the bulwark and heading for bottom, but I'd be damned if I'd help him, not if we went to hell for it. He managed finally, with a lot of grunting and gasping, and the heavy line run out through the hawse hole, Lysol all the time jumping to keep his boots clear of the loops. Then he took a few quick turns on the bitts and leaned over to help me.

I wanted to tell him to stay out of my way, like he had me, but I didn't. If we was to get the job done, he would have to do part of it. Without too much trouble we canted her up then, let her go, and paid out the rode. Lysol turned back to his own line and give it more scope until we had used up almost all there was. "Good enough, boy," he says, "make her fast." And we slapped more turns around the bitts with a hitch on top, then waited for the *Icecap* to fetch up, which she did with considerable of a jerk.

Lysol pulled himself back toward the wheelhouse to port, and I to starboard. He was there ahead of me, inside with Tarbox, and I wouldn't go in. I swung around to the lee of the wheelhouse, hooked my elbow around a stay and shoved my bare hands inside my jacket and under my arms. They ached and burned with the cold, and for a time the more I warmed them, the worse they ached.

I was getting my gloves back on when I see Elwood coming up through the cargo hatchway, shaking his head and growling and fuming. He made his way to the side of the wheelhouse where I stood and stayed there talking with Tarbox without going in. The *Icecap* was head to it, now, of course, and pitching wildly, but she was rolling less.

Tarbox wanted to know how the leak was, and Elwood tells him it's damn bad. They both had to raise their voices over the sea and wind, and at that sometimes half what a man said was carried away. "Sure . . . patched it . . . inside . . . best . . . could . . .call that . . . ?"

"Not so bad . . . was?"

" . . . don't suppose . . ."

I didn't doubt Elwood had cut the leak down eighty per cent, and Tarbox didn't either, I guess, because he asked no more questions and I never see him go to look for himself.

"Them anchors . . . dragging . . ." It was Lysol's voice. He was leaning past Tarbox and yelling in hopes Elwood could hear him.

" . . . don't think so," Tarbox told him.

"Watch . . . little spruce . . . tip . . . Conway . . . forward of stay . . . bit . . . bit . . ."

"Pitching . . . bad . . . can't tell . . . where," Tarbox said.

" . . . can . . . watch . . . long enough."

Tarbox looked anxious now, really keyed up in a way he had not been before. He left the wheelhouse to work his way forward, and left the door swinging like he expected Elwood to go in, but the Old Man shut it, leaving Lysol inside and him out. He moved over beside me. "Better if I stay away from that joker."

"Yeah," I said.

"One of these days . . . break . . . goddamn . . . neck."

I didn't answer.

"Tommy, better stay out of boats, stay off the water."

"If I ever live to get off it."

Now it was Elwood's turn not to answer.

"You think we're dragging?" I asked.

" . . . don't . . . but so."

We had both turned to watch Tarbox, who had made his way to the bow faster than I would have thought he could, his tall, lanky body slanted into the snow. He was leaning over, trying to feel the pull of them anchor rodes, which he should have known he couldn't, not with the vessel lurching and pulling like it was, but of course he was nervous. He shook his head and started back. When he reached us, Lysol opened the wheelhouse door.

"What . . . tell you?"

". . . dragging . . . afraid," Tarbox said. ". . . Wid . . . engine . . . don't know what . . ."

"Two . . . row . . . the dory . . . ashore . . . hitch line . . . big spruce . . . hold . . . hell snaps."

"More line . . . anchor rodes," Elwood said. ". . . hold . . . more . . . scope."

Tarbox jerked his head aft. "Ledges."

". . . can't . . . to drag more . . . safe," Lysol said.

". . . got . . . try it," Tarbox said.

Elwood shook his head. ". . . take . . . Jesus Christ . . . launch dory . . . today."

". . . call . . . Lord, then," Tarbox shouted. "Tommy . . . coils manila . . . below." He pointed toward the forecastle hatch.

I started on my way. When I got up by Jappie, he looked at me and shook his head without ever stopping pumping, as much as a man would say, "Boy, it is tough!"

The forecastle seemed almost warm and quiet after being on deck, and I wished I could stay there. I knew it wasn't safe, but it looked safe and felt safe, and I wanted to turn in and sleep. I wanted to cover my head with the blankets so I would see nothing and hear nothing, and pretty soon I would feel nothing nor remember nothing neither, and just go on sleeping and sleeping. Like a damned spruce tree or an alder. I wished to hell I was like a spruce.

I found the line stowed in a locker under one of the bunks. They was two coils and ungodly heavy, but I managed to get one of them up the ladder and through the hatchway. Tarbox met me there and took that one. ". . . back . . . other," he shouted.

Getting that second coil on deck and down aft was no party. I see Tarbox having plenty of trouble ahead of me, and I had worse. I went down once, sprawled against the wheelhouse, my knee bruised and my arm damned near broken, I thought. I come close to losing the coil overboard. Without doubt Elwood and Lysol would have helped me if they had seen, and if they could have, but they had been working on the lashings to that dory. She was small for a dory. They had her down off the engineroom trunk by the time I got there, and righted as well. There was two pair of oars, bailing dishes, fresh water, a painter, grappling, and such gear. They stowed that stuff on the deck in the lee of the bulwark, and the Old Man made the end of the painter fast to a stern cleat aboard the *Icecap*.

Then the four of us gaffled onto the dory. First we dragged it as far aft as we could. When Tarbox shouted, we lifted it up, two on a side, and shoved the stern out over the taff rail. Then we waited, watching the pitch of the *Icecap* and the way the seas was coming. Finally Tarbox see what he calls a good chance and yells, "Heave!"

We got her on the crest of a sea all right, but at that when she slid in, she took aboard a half barrel of water. She hung right aft of us, bouncing around like a toy balloon. The Old Man took in easy on the painter, bringing her as close as he could without shattering her against our stern. Lysol was standing by with a bailing dish in one hand, and when he see the right chance, he took a long step aboard. Elwood passed him a pair of oars and slacked off gradually on the painter so she would ride easier. Then Lysol begun bailing to beat hell.

All this time the snow was whipping us like flying birdshot. The *Icecap* was dragging little by little and there wasn't one of us, I'm sure, but had his mind on it. I thought Lysol would never get her bailed out enough, though I don't doubt he may have hit a new speed record.

Wid came up through the engine room hatchway, took a brisk look at what we was doing, and shouted something to Tarbox, who went below with him to the engineroom. I couldn't hear a word either one of them said. About that time Lysol threw the bailing dish down in the bottom of the dory and shouts, "Come on!" I set out to put my foot up on the rail, but Elwood shoved me back. I looked at him and see him shaking his head at Lysol.

" . . . trouble?" Lysol yelled.

I knew what it was all right, and maybe he did too. The Old Man was getting aboard no dories with Lysol, and not because he was afraid to neither. Lysol had one hand on each side of the dory, for balance, and was leaning toward us.

" . . . no more . . . good here . . . than . . . to home!"

Elwood was mad now. "Come aboard then. I'll go alone!"

"By-Jesus . . . don't need you," Lysol yelled. "Pass that line."

I was turning to the engineroom hatchway to call Tarbox, because I believed he could straighten out the argument, perhaps by going himself, when I heard a yell. It was not a word of any kind; it was just a shout or a scream, and I knew it come from Lysol. I jerked my head up and see what had happened: an extra heavy sea had put so much strain on the dory that her painter had snapped. I could see the torn, parted end dragging from the dory's bow. Lysol was struggling to get the thole pins in place and the oars between them so he could row, but already the dory had swung side-to. The crest of the next sea broke into it, knocking Lysol flat and washing one of the oars out of reach. The next sea filled it. I see Lysol throw his weight to the up-side for balance, but it was too much and over she went. When he came up, he struggled and strained to lay one hand on the gunwale of the dory, but one of them sharp, white-toothed crests carried it out of reach.

I knew then there was just one chance. There was a coil of three-eights inch line laying near the rail at the Old Man's feet. If one of us threw that . . . I plunged toward him and reached for that line. I had my fingers right around it when Elwood's boot come down on the back of my hand like a steel vise and stayed there.

XI

Over and over I say to myself even yet, "Are you sure you couldn't have thrown Elwood off? Are you really certain?" And I do not know the answer.

I see Lysol's face and eyes nights, sometimes, and I wake up sweating. I try to tell myself I did as much as I could, as much as anybody could in my place, but it don't make me feel much better, and it don't change nothing about Elwood, nor about Corinne.

The first of it, I thought the Old Man's foot was there by mistake, but when, swearing and yelling, I looked up at him, I knew different. His face wasn't turned my way, but I could see it. He was looking aft where the view, right at that moment, wasn't especially pleasant. My Jesus, and I thought I knew what it was to hate!

I threw the line. Oh, yes, I threw it all right, as soon as Elwood lifted his foot. By then, of course, it was too late, or the line was too short. Put it either way you want. A man's life in water like that, damned near freezing, and with a gale of wind besides, can pretty near be measured in seconds I guess, especially when the man's wearing the heaviest kind of boots and clothing. What was happening then, whether it lasted a few seconds or a few minutes, seemed to go on for an hour, while I squatted there, my hands clawing into the rail, helpless, and my gut empty and quaking.

The Old Man never said nothing. He turned away and pulled himself forward along the engineroom trunk until he was near the wheelhouse. He stood there, one hand on the wheelhouse, the other on a stay, bending over.

This time I really hollered for Tarbox, and something of what I felt must have been in my voice, because him and Wid made it on deck quicker'n I'd ever seen them jump. I couldn't make them believe nothing the first of it; there was so little to see, except the frayed end of the parted painter, and Elwood propping himself up there amidships. For a minute Tarbox done nothing except stand there muttering over and over to himself, "Jesus-Jesus-Jesus . . ."

Wid kept shouting questions at me, but they was all the same kind of questions and the same answers I'd already give.

Tarbox looked at me like he was puzzled. "You say the painter parted?"

"That's right."

"He didn't have no oars?"

"He lost one, next sea . . ."

" . . . never reached?" Tarbox was pointing at the line we had just pulled in over the stern.

"Nowhere near," I said.

Tarbox turned to stare at Elwood's back. The Old Man had not moved. Then he looked back at me and kind of grunted, but he never said nothing.

We worked our way forward to the wheelhouse. Tarbox opened it up and pulled Elwood in. Then the rest of us squeezed inside too, Jappie included. It seemed like the one thing all of us wanted right then was company; we couldn't have stood it being off anywheres alone, except the Old Man maybe. He slouched in a corner looking at the deck and wouldn't speak, wouldn't lift his head to glance out a window. To him, I guess, nothing made no difference yet, and just the sight of him made me feel miserable. I wanted to say something, to tell him — but what the hell could I say?

Jappie had to be told, of course, and he too done his share of God-damning and questioning. He had left the pump because it had commenced to suck dry and he figured he could afford a rest. He had battened the cover down on the cargo hatch now, and apparently the *Icecap* was leaking nowhere near so much as she had been.

There was a gale of wind coming in through the broken glass to the wheelhouse door, but nobody made no move to stop it.

"I knew Elwood would fix that leak good," Tarbox said.

"Ain't going to make much God damned difference whether he did or not," Wid said, "if she goes on dragging her hooks."

"We ain't even got no dory now."

"How's the engine?"

"I ain't got the injectors back yet."

"Well, suppose you get right down there and hop to it," Tarbox said.

"You got to have a college degree to get them things right."

"Never mind; try it anyway."

"Sure," Wid said.

"Well, let's go then," Tarbox said. Suddenly it was like we was all coming to life. "The rest of us will add that manila, double strength, to the anchor rodes and give her more scope."

"She ain't got much room to swing in."

"We got to take that chance," Tarbox said.

We all knew that. It looked like the only chance left. So out we went on deck again into snow and wind and no solid footing. Tarbox had us drag the ends of the lines up to the bow, one man staying aft on each side to make sure the coils didn't foul. Elwood and Jappie was getting to work at the hand-numbing job of hitching them lines in the cold and wet when I see Tarbox staring toward Conway Island again. The seas didn't seem to have moderated a mite, and the snow was still flying, but there was just a little less wind, and a man could keep a fairly steady view of the trees on the island if he kept his mind on it.

Suddenly Tarbox begun shouting to the other men to quit work account of he thought the anchors was holding. Right away all of us took bearings on one of the trees, and allowing for the yawing and pitching, we thought she was holding. For the time being maybe we could draw a breath and feel safe.

Tarbox asked the Old Man to go to the engineroom and see if he could help Wid make the diesel tick, and told me to build up the fire in the galley and heat some grub. Jappie come below with me, and Tarbox stayed in the wheelhouse to patch the broken door with a length of canvas and four five laths.

I split kindling and felt a little better when the stove begun to warm up. Jappie set on the edge of a bunk saying again and again, "By Jesus, I hate to think about it, hate to think about it."

"Maybe you think you're the only one?" I asked.

He didn't answer. I made coffee, boiled potatoes, cooked eggs, put canned milk, nut butter, jam, bread, and stale doughnuts on the table, and we ate. I was hungry all right, but everything I ate was about the same as so much fodder.

"Hell of a lot of clams we're getting this trip," Jappie growled.

"That's too goddamned bad," I said.

"We didn't come for fun."

"Good thing, ain't it?"

"It don't matter what happens, Tommy, you still got to have mouthbait."

"Yeah."

"And the damned stuff costs money."

"Let's go on the town," I said.

"Christ, we may, at that."

Jappie reached across the table and speared a piece of bread with his fork. He folded the bread and rubbed it around in the juicy egg yolk that was left on his plate until the plate looked like the cat had licked it. Then he stuffed the bread into his mouth, but the bread was too big, and streaks of yellow stained the stubble of his beard. "What's wrong with the engine?"

I shook my head. "Nobody knows."

"They can't find out?"

"They ain't," I said. "If Elwood don't none of them will."

"You think a lot of Elwood, eh Tommy?"

"Why not?"

"More coffee?"

"On the stove," I said.

Jappie poured his coffee, canned milk, and sugar in equal parts. When he had drunk that and smoked the end off a cigarette, he went aft to fetch Wid and relieve Tarbox. I was glad to see him go. I stoked the fire, made more coffee, and cleaned up the mess Jappie had left.

Tarbox ate without talking, and Wid talked to himself, mostly about the engine. "If it ain't the injectors, it must be . . ." It was like he was talking to Tarbox, only Tarbox never answered. You could not even tell if Tarbox was listening. After a while, Wid was just mumbling to himself.

I set on the edge of one of the bunks and every few minutes my eyes would shut, but that was no good because then I would begin seeing that white foam astern, and that dory, and . . . so I tried hard to keep my eyes open.

Wid acted nervous and ate fast. He got up to go aft to the engineroom.

"Lay down and catch a sleep," Tarbox told him.

"Don't need no sleep."

"Damned queer if you don't."

"Yeah."

"You stay away from that diesel," Tarbox said. "Company might have a little bit of it left."

"What the hell good is it if it don't go?"

"Did you read the directions about them injectors?"

"Sure I read them," Wid said.

"Did you know what you was reading?"

"What the hell you think I went through the ninth grade for?"

"I've often wondered."

Wid pulled his jacket on and went topsides.

Tarbox set there drinking coffee and puffing a cigarette. The coffee cup had been full and there was puddles of coffee around it on the table where it had spilled when the *Icecap* pitched badly. Tarbox didn't seem to notice them. He stared straight ahead. "Never should have left them," he said. "Should have been aboard there myself . . ." He went on mumbling, swearing to himself. He looked at me sometimes, but at first he wasn't talking to me and I didn't answer. Then he glanced up sudden, like he had just remembered something. "Tommy, what the hell did you think you was doing with that hammer?"

"What did it look like I was doing?" I asked.

"I'd hate to say what it looked like."

"I guess you'll think about what you've a mind to."

"I don't know what to think," Tarbox said. "Why in hell I ever let you get aboard . . ." He was staring at his boots.

"After all, I didn't hit him," I said.

"No . . ."

"And all I done was what I told you: I threw that line."

"I don't ask why," Tarbox said. "If you say you threw it, you threw it." His voice sounded like it was miles away.

"It ain't my fault," I said. "If that painter —"

"Christ Jesus!" Tarbox put his head down and rubbed his forehead with both hands.

I had forgot for a minute that weak painters aboard the *Icecap* was Tarbox's responsibility. For that matter, everything aboard was his responsibility. I tried to think of something to say, but there wasn't nothing. All I could do was stand there looking at him and feel lower than a mud eel.

Finally he straightened up. "I'll get Elwood," he said. "Give the Old Man a good meal, Tommy."

"What's he doing, listening to the radio?"

"Just on watch. Anyway, tube's gone. No reception."

He pushed his arms into his coat, pulled down the earflaps on his cap, shoved his hands into wool mittens, and climbed the ladder. When he pushed back the hatch cover, I could hear and feel the wind, but there was less of it, and less snow too. I was surprised it was dark out already; I had lost all count of time.

I cleared the table and cleaned up the coffee and put out plenty of grub for the Old Man. He come below a few minutes later, shedding his coat and cap and gloves, and hanging them near the galley range. He looked around for a second like he didn't know what to do next, and then set down to the table where I had put the food. He tried to eat, but it was no use. I see him shovel a few forkfuls in and bite into a slice of bread, but he chewed a lot and swallowed little. After a while he pushed the plate away.

"That food is all right," I told him.

"I know." He slid over onto one of the bunks and sat on the edge. The checkers Wid and Jappie had been playing with was laying on the blankets, and Elwood picked up seven eight of them checkers, passing them back and forth. I was doing the dishes. At last he said, "You going to talk to Mart Teele?"

"And what do I want to talk to Mart Teele for?"

"He's the man to see."

"I got nothing to say to no deputy sheriff."

"No . . . ?"

"They tell me the law don't do nothing to you for something you don't do," I said.

"I ain't so sure about that. Maybe I'll talk to him myself."

"All you will do is spread it around."

The Old Man shrugged.

I said, "Will you quit worrying about a no-good son-of-a-bitch?"

"I know you didn't like him . . ."

"Like him?" I said.

"But even then —"

"Christ, let's not go into that," I said. "Figure it up, what he done *for* me and what he done *to* me . . ."

Elwood stared at the bunk opposite with the look of a blind man.

"Stop thinking," I said.

"That's easy to say," Elwood told me.

As if I didn't know that!

XII

I was some glad to see Wid and Tarbox join us below decks. Tarbox reported the wind and seas both moderating, and Jappie had offered to stand watch. My turn was going to come next. Tarbox got out his pipe, and Wid had a cigarette, but we didn't talk. There wasn't much I could think of was fit for talk.

"Play you a game of checkers, Elwood," Wid said.

Elwood shook his head.

Tarbox stood up, says he is going to turn in, and switched off all the lights but one dim one. "Them batteries ain't going to last forever," he says, and crawled into his bunk all standing. The rest of us done the same.

I lay there wide awake, and besides going over everything else, thought about getting home. It looked, now, like we was going to get there somehow, some time. I tried to see myself living there again in the house with Corinne, with Elwood, and just a short ways from Nancy's, and I knew something would have to be done.

There was too many pictures in my mind that hadn't ought to be there. I would never be able to look at Corinne and not see Lysol, nor at Elwood and not see him neither. I thought of setting at the kitchen table, eating, Elwood to one side of me and Corinne to the other, pretending everything was the way it never had been, and I knew it was not going to work.

Mostly, I thought, it was Corinne. It seemed to me now like she was a stranger, like she was somebody I didn't even know and never had known. I didn't believe I even wanted to know her. I did not want to look her in the face and be reminded of all the things I once hadn't known. I twisted and tossed and turned in my bunk. The one thing I wanted was to make shore, to find something solid to hang onto. *Our Father which art in heaven* – if I could have said that and had it mean much, or even *Our father which art on earth,* and been sure of it . . . The time was when I would have been sure of Elwood. Not that I blamed Elwood exactly or that I held it against him. I knew somehow it was account of me probably he had done it, but that only seemed to make it worse. Nancy — Lysol. Corinne — Lysol. Elwood — Lysol. Lysol. Lysol. Lysol.

I would have said that I did not sleep at all, that I just lay there in the berth feeling alone, lonelier than anything in the goddamn world, the way I had felt suddenly again and again the last few hours, but I know I slept because finally Tarbox was shaking me by the arm. "Tommy! It's your watch, Tommy."

I sat up quick and struck my head on a deck beam.

"Easy, Tommy, easy," Tarbox said.

"I'll be right there," I told him.

I blinked my eyes and peered around the cabin in the dim light. I could hear Wid snoring, but Elwood was wide awake. He moved a little so his face was outside the shadow of the upper berth, and even in that light I could tell he had the look of a man who ain't slept. His eyes was not looking at me or Tarbox; they was just staring up at the deck.

I put on my cap, mittens, and heavy jacket and went topsides. Behind me, in the forecastle, Tarbox was putting wood in the stove. When I came through the hatchway the wind tore at me like a snapped whip. I pulled the hatchcover closed behind me, and in darkness, both hands on a line Tarbox had rigged during the night, felt my way across the pitching deck to the wheelhouse. I put one hand on the knob.

"Come in; you're out," Jappie says.

"That's what I'm doing." The wheelhouse was warm and snug, and Jappie had pushed down one of the windows and was squatting on a stool, his feet twisted around the legs, holding his head out in the wind to stay awake.

"God, boy, it's a good thing you come or I'd have dropped right off.

"No wonder," I said. "How are we riding?"

"Eight bells and all's well, wind northeast, blowing like hell," Jappie said singsong.

"That's what *you* say."

"All right, so it ain't. But it sounds good."

"They ain't no doubt about the wind part of it," I said.

"And that ain't what it was: it's already backing into the north."

"How can you tell?"

"I can feel it."

"What's the radio say?"

"How would I know. A tube's shot."

"Oh, yeah," I said, remembering.

A gust of wind filled the wheelhouse as he opened the door to leave. Then the door slammed and I was alone. The first of it, I closed the window he had rolled down, but like Jappie I found the wheelhouse became so close and warm with the heat piped in from the galley stove that already I was half asleep. I opened the window and took up his old stand. I was surprised to find it less like a gale than before. I thought maybe the thing was blowing itself out and that by daylight we might have considerably calmer water.

I craned my neck this way and that, but the darkness looked all the same in every direction, and I told myself I was a mighty poor thing to leave on watch: I could not tell if the anchors was dragging, if there was breakers astern or if there wasn't. And besides, the way things had gone, I scarcely give a damn. For all the good I was doing, I might as well have been below and asleep, might better, for that matter, because up there on deck I kept thinking and remembering . . .

Then suddenly I found I was beginning to see a little. It might have been an hour later. I could make out the bulwarks, the cargo hatch, and the mast. I looked up and see there was a break in the clouds and some starlight was coming through to us. I watched them clouds and it seemed to me that if we was hanging the same direction we had been. the clouds was rolling off the wrong way. I switched on the binnacle light for a second to have a look at the compass card. It made me jump like I'd had an electric shock. I had another look at the compass and right away I knew we was in for more trouble. I must have dozed off for sure.

That wind was northerly. It was sweeping down across Canada, over two hundred miles of Maine, and several miles of bay water, and hitting us with express-train force. It made Conway Island a threatening shore instead of a poor shelter. It was putting a strain on our anchors from a new direction, and if they dragged this time . . .

I got out of that wheelhouse and worked my way to the forecastle hatch, pushed back the cover and called Tarbox. I didn't have to speak twice. Within a second or two he was beside me, his feet on the ladder and his hands on the hatch coaming. I explained what had happened.

"Go back to the wheelhouse, Tommy; I'll be right up."

He dodged below for his cap, mittens, and jacket, and by the time I reached the wheelhouse, he was behind me. He had felt the wind, and from the stars he knew I was right, but he switched on the light for a moment and looked at the compass anyway. I see him suck in on his under lip. The binnacle light lit up his face in an odd way, all ghostly and shadowy. He pushed the switch and we was back again in darkness. "The hell of it is, Tommy," he said quietly, "there ain't much we can do."

"No?"

"That diesel needs a better mechanic than any of us."

"You've tried it?" I asked.

"No use. If Wid can't make it run, I'm sure I can't."

"I suppose."

"We can't shift no anchors farther to windward; we got nothing to shift them in. If they hold, and if the rodes ain't got too much scope, we might possibly be all right. We could take in on them a little, but they'll be more likely to drag if we do."

I didn't say anything. I guessed he was just thinking it out loud to himself. I closed the wheelhouse window part way to shut out some of the northerly. It was working up a considerable chop now against the seas from outside. This shore wind was going to flatten out the ocean, but doing it it would raise an unmerciful chop across the bay with sharp seas four five feet from crest to trough maybe.

Then Tarbox said, "We're dragging all right." He stared through the wheelhouse windows. I heard him draw a deep breath. Then for a minute he was quiet, and there was just the wind, the seas slapping against us, and the monotonous rattle of gear. After a while he said, "Tommy, you'd better rouse out the rest of the crew. This might be a poor time for a man to be in his bunk."

I went forward to the hatchway, faster this time because I was getting used to the road, and went below. There was no need for me to go below, but I wanted to get in the lee for a minute. "All hands!" I shouted.

Elwood rolled out of his bunk right off.

"What for?" Wid asked.

"Tarbox says to rouse all hands, I rouse 'em."

"Tarbox can go to hell."

"He will, and so will you, you don't drag your ass on deck in a hurry."

"What's the trouble?" Jappie asked.

"Wind's northerly, a goddamned tantoaster," I told him.

"Let her shift," Wid said.

"Besides that, our anchors is dragging."

"Well, why didn't you say so?"

Elwood was on the ladder and going through the hatchway, and Wid and Jappie was on their feet.

"I don't see what we can do," Wid said.

"You can get up there and have a good look, can't you?" Jappie asked him.

We all climbed on deck and made our way to the wheelhouse. There didn't seem to be much to say. "This time it looks like she was all talked over," Jappie said.

"I mistrust it is," Tarbox says. "Maybe some of us ought to be on the stern deck."

Nobody moved the first of it. Then Jap went out and Wid and I followed him. The handrail on the engineroom trunk was beginning to ice up now the temperature had dropped some, and the wind was whipping spray port and starboard. We hung onto the rail just the same; it was the only thing to hang onto, and the *Icecap*'s new motion, shorter and jerkier, wasn't no pleasanter than the old one had been. Once aft, we tried to find shelter in the lee of the engineroom trunk, what there was of it, or to crouch next to the bulwarks and look out over the stern.

What we was watching for, of course, was surf or rocks or both. Every sea had a broken crest on it that flashed white in the starlight, and sometimes them whitecaps is big enough so you can't tell them from the first of a breaker. Every minute or two I thought we was into the surf, but each time we wasn't.

I kept trying to think what them rocks was like on the shore of Conway, whether they was smooth and sloping, or rough and jagged and standing up. I mistrusted they was perpendicular and pretty uneven, since that was what most rocks was around home, the kind you wouldn't choose to get banged up against by a few tons of sea water. Looked at the best way we could, our chances wasn't too good. From the after deck, the three of us would see what was coming and might possibly have slim luck, jumping, but just the same, I commenced to wish I was in the wheelhouse again where there was warmth.

I was about to go forward when I see Wid reach across and punch Jappie in the muscle to get his attention, and point out over the stern. I couldn't see nothing new, but a second later I felt it, a hard, rock-bottomed blow that shook the *Icecap* from end to end. I shuddered and cringed. We all knew it was coming, but if there is one thing a man on the water hates and despises more than another, it's to have his boat touch land when he don't intend it. A cracked plank or frame is like a broken bone in a man's body, and I don't doubt Tarbox would rather have broke his bones than the *Icecap*'s timbers.

After that first one, we was right into it, the surf boiling up around our after deck, the rudder splintering under our stern, and the keel crushing and grinding into the shore. Every blow made the *Icecap* shake and tremble, and I clung there, gritting my teeth and hating it, hating it because I had to give up hope for the *Icecap* now she was no longer afloat.

Wid and Jappie was half standing, and I knew this was the time a man was supposed to jump if he was going to, but nobody who wanted to live would be so foolish as to jump into the mess around us. Tarbox and Elwood had stuck their heads out the wheelhouse doors and was watching. I don't know how long we held on there; it felt like hours, but I know it wasn't because the dawn didn't come then. The *Icecap* kept pounding and groaning, and I begun to wish if she was going to break up she would do it quick and get it over with.

Then I see that Wid and Jappie was shouting back and forth into each other's ears and looking out over the stern like there was something special there. Then I see what it was: the place the *Icecap* was going ashore wasn't rocky; it was a pebbly beach, and with not too steep a slope. That meant that although the *Icecap* was going to be badly damaged, probably beyond repair, she was not going to be cracked up into kindling wood in the next twenty minutes, and it give all of us a chance not to be hurt.

Wid and Jappie went right back to the wheelhouse, and I followed them. "Almost the peak of the flood tide," Jappie said.

"Good thing, ain't it?"

"Sure is."

While we stood in the wheelhouse, hanging on and and waiting, feeling the slow, miserable destruction of the hull under us, Tarbox would go look first into one hatch and then another. He reported plenty water in the hold. Planks was badly sprung on one side all right. The *Icecap* had listed over to port, but the drag of the two anchors held her bow more or less off the beach and kept her from climbing in on her beams' ends.

Soon we could see that the waves was not coming so far up the beach as they had been, nor was they foaming and boiling up so high around the *Icecap*'s quarters. We had gone in on the high tide and wouldn't be molested no more by the damned seas for a little over twelve hours. If we was lucky, by that time, the wind would have moderated. Already, because she was firmer on the beach and less under the pull and strain of the water, the *Icecap* was pounding and groaning a good deal less, and we knew that in a short time she would be cocked up there on the shore as solid as Noah's ark after the flood.

It wasn't long before Tarbox sent me below to build up the fire in the galley stove, that is, providing our bunks and gear wasn't too badly damaged for use. They wasn't. There was plenty of salt water over the floorboards toward the bow, but that wasn't bad, and within a half hour it disappeared. The lights still worked about half strength; there was a good draft through the stove pipe, and twenty minutes later I had her reasonably warm down there again. There was a blast of air making in through a gap in the planking some- wheres but that could no more be helped than her listing to port.

Soon the others come below decks and made themselves as comfortable as they could. I turned in but couldn't sleep, just lay there and rested. And Jappie and Wid, who never do nothing else, got out the checkers. There ain't neither one of them would refuse if you asked him to play checkers to his mother's funeral.

XIII

When the *Clara Ann,* the company's other smack, slid up to the factory wharf to Oak Harbor two days later, we was standing on the deck amidships. The crew made the bow and stern lines fast, and we stared at five six of the fishermen and clamdiggers was hanging around the factory wharf, and they stared back.

It seemed like a damned queer way to come home. Most of the time aboard the *Icecap,* or what was left of her, on Conway, we had stayed below decks or up in the wheelhouse. In daylight, on the low water, we had gone out and walked all around her on the beach, getting a look at the damage, which was plenty. Her wheel and rudder had been mangled; there was four five good-sized holes in the planking, and without doubt timbers cracked beyond them.

None of us went up onto the island no distance. We could not see tramping around in nine ten inches of snow on a place where there wasn't nothing but gulls' nests even in summer. Another twelve hours and we'd have had to go up there scratching for dry wood for the *Icecap*'s stove, but we never come to that, and was all just as well satisfied we didn't.

It was still blowing northerly, only not so hard as before, when the *Clara Ann* found us and sent two men in a dory to take us and a little of our gear out aboard. That was just dumb luck because as yet, of course, no one had missed us.

I tried to stay away from both crews on the trip home, because very quickly I got tired answering questions, and because I had something else to think about: how was I going to tell Elwood? and when was I going to tell him? I know I had lots of time to decide that aboard the *Icecap,* laying there on the beach at Conway, and I had tried to too, but I guess all the time there was didn't help. Elwood had laid in his bunk almost all that time, not talking, his eyes open, and he had not looked toward me or spoke to me.

So by the time the *Clara Ann* lay to her berth in Oak Harbor, I was not furthered any. As I said, nothing seemed real. It was like everything was happening in some kind of motion picture and in a few minutes the lights would come on and I would go out the door into the town at night. Instead I was tossing my gear up on the wharf along with the rest. We had not had no chance to bring our clam hoes, hods, or that stuff when they took us off Conway, so they was still aboard the *Icecap.* The wharf was all tamped-down snow and quite slippery and dirty. Wid and Jappie commenced talking all excited to the fellows that was standing around, but Tarbox made right for the company office in the factory. Elwood and I struck out for the town road in silence.

I knew in a few minutes I would have to speak, because there was a fork up ahead and it was the one that counted. I was feeling as frantic as a hooked mackerel. I hadn't been able to figure out even how to begin. I put my gear down in the snow and said, "Wait a minute."

"Hunh?"

"I guess I'm going to go this way."

He stared at me for ten twelve seconds. "What for?"

"I just want to."

"It's a hell of a long way around to the house."

"You don't understand," I said. "I ain't coming back."

It took some time for that to get to him. It was like I had struck him in the face. He give me one long look that wasn't hate, and wasn't scorn, and wasn't friendly neither, just a look, and then he turns and starts on his way.

I stood there while he took a few steps, and then I knew I couldn't let him go off like that. "Hey!" I shouted. Elwood kept right on moving. I run after him and grabbed his arm. "Listen," I said, "I don't want you thinking . . ."

He stared at me the same as if he was saying, "Well, thinking what?" And I stood there, one hand clutching the sleeve to his mackinaw, wishing to hell there was some words to use, some way to say what was rolling around in my guts and spinning in my brain.

"It ain't on account of you," I told him. "Not on account of what — well, what happened out there . . ." I couldn't finish.

"I know better than that," Elwood said.

"Look. I hated him like hell, see? Once out there I, myself, I had a hammer pulled right back over my shoulder, only —"

"Yeah?"

"Well, Tarbox and a sea hit me all to once, and after that — There ain't nobody never done so much for me as you done." With the toe of my boot I kicked the snow in the road.

"How about Corinne?" Elwood asked. "And that little bitch lives up the road?"

"She don't matter much," I lied.

"Which one?"

"Nancy,"

"And Corinne?"

I looked away from him, feeling the breeze blow around my head, watching the snow lifted gently and drifting up over a clump of bushes. "Maybe *you* can go back," I says, "I can see that, but I ain't going to."

"You don't want to go by nothing concerning them two," Elwood told me.

"No?" That was easy for him to say, but it looked to me like a high average.

"You'd better come on home with me."

I thought about it, not that I hadn't been thinking about it for hours and hours, about seeing her, and talking to her, and being in the same house day after day, and in a way there was nothing I wanted more. I wanted that so bad I felt hollow and empty, and yet it was like there was two *me* s, and the other me couldn't stand it, could hardly bear thinking about it and wasn't going to put up with it. I stared at the drifted snow, at the houses and sheds and light poles there to the center of Oak Harbor, and I had never seen them look so ugly and desolate and lonely. I shook my head.

"All right, Tommy. I know I can't tell you nothing." Elwood was not saying it in a nasty way. He sounded decent. "I always want you to get by. You know that."

"Yeah."

"All right, then, I guess I'll be on my way," he said, and he turned real quick and walked up the road.

I stood there in the breeze watching him — I knew he would never turn around once he had started — until he was over the brow of the hill, and there was just the sheds and backhouses, the blank homes and bare, leafless maples of that bit of Oak Harbor before me. The wind snipped at the snow, spinning it sharp and biting around my face and shoulders, and in the telephone wires above my head it moaned. I kind of shuddered, and turning the other way, struck out towards Bangor.

XIV

So here I am, up country, in what anybody in his right mind would call a good berth. I have clean, dry quarters, all the food I can eat, work I like, and a boss who is an easy man to get on with. The pay is not too high, but what do I need money for? Anyway, Arch Lockey and his wife both like me, and I can go so far as to say Helen likes me. It might even be — well, it is something a fellow can't help thinking about, can he, especially where I know Arch would do all that he properly could for me if I wanted a start somehow on my own?

Anyone would think I had swung up into Aroostook and fell into a butter tub, but I am here to say the butter tub ain't made that wouldn't turn rancid with me in it. It is hard for me to believe so much has happened in just one winter, that is it only three and a half four months since I went clamming with Elwood and Phil and Mac, that Nancy was just back there in December, and that a few weeks ago Lysol was still alive and I thought of Corinne as, well, the way I always had thought about her. It has been the longest winter I've known, all right, the one that has made me older than any other and made me wish to hell I was about six again.

Soon everything will be coming to life around here: Arch will cut seed and take the tractor out plowing. The new earth is going to lie cool under the fresh sun and there will be such a thing again as robins and red-winged blackbirds, or so I suppose. But never mind all that.

Right now I am setting on the edge of the bed in my room to the top of Arch Lockey's house, thinking how it is just tonight — I suppose I should say "last night" now because it is near dawn — how it was just last night Helen and I talked, or anyway I talked, in front of the stove-fireplace they've got downstairs. Arch and his wife was out and stayed late — they come in only an hour or two ago — and Helen and I found ourselves left alone there by the fire.

I was squatting on a bench just to one side of it and Helen was on the couch right in front. There were not many lights on, just the one at her end of the couch. I put a couple fresh sticks into the firebox. We could hear a howling gale of wind outside and it made us feel all the more warm and comfortable there next to the fire. Helen asked me a question or two, and first thing I know, I am talking. I must have talked a long time.

Arch Lockey was right: he said that when I come to tell anybody, it would be to a woman. Helen may be young, but she is, as the fellow says, old enough. You might think I would feel like a fool to set there telling her about Nancy, and about Corinne, Elwood, Lysol, and the *Icecap*, but I didn't. She made it easy for me somehow. She listened like she meant to, and I guess she did.

It was late when I come to the end, and I realized that some time or other Helen had switched off the light at the end of the couch. There was just the dim orange light and the nervous shadows from the firebox splashing about the room. She was setting forward on the edge of that couch. Sometimes she would look at the fire, and some of the time she was looking at me, and the *Icecap* was right there in the room with us, and Conway Island, and all them fellows. There wasn't nothing left to say, and I just squatted there, looking into the coals, asking myself why I spilled all that stuff to Helen, why I should want to get her all stirred up, and why it was I felt calm, and better.

"Tommy," she said softly. "I'm sorry. I'm so terribly sorry."

I had never heard her voice like that before, and it went through me sudden and sharp as if my hand, hovering over an engine, had touched the hot end of the ignition system. And then there was that glow, like sometimes when Arch was kidding me and I would feel it all the way through. It was like setting down to food when you hadn't eaten since God knows when, or after hours of miserable, sweating labor in the hot sun, you took the first swallow of cool, fresh water. It was what I was yearning for all right.

I knew then that I could move over onto that couch and Helen would not push me away, that I could lay my head in her lap and feel the warm touch of her fingers through my hair and across my face. and that was all I wanted, all. It seemed like I wanted that more than anything in my life.

I sat there looking at her and I got to admit I did not see her too clearly, because I was surprised that she felt the way she did. I told myself, "Come on, now, get up, get up and go over there." But right while I was saying it to myself in the half-darkness, it wasn't Helen I was seeing; it was Nancy, in spite of they was so different, and I remembered how Nancy could be, tender and soft.

Or was it Corinne? Suddenly, like it was something I had never thought of since, I remembered running to her, the center of the world, the center of all warmth and protection from terror, from hunger, from anger, running to her, my head slashed and burning from a blow on a rock, and being lifted in strong arms, being held close to her softness and warmth. And yet, Corinne . . . ?

The Old Man had said, "Don't go by nothing concerning them two." That's easy to say, Elwood, but what else was there for me to go by? I like the heat of a hot stove, but I ain't put my hand on one since I was four, and it would be quite a chore to get me to do it now.

I couldn't move. I couldn't go to Helen because she didn't stay Helen, and even when she did, I kept seeing them cars that called at the Lockeys' house evenings, almost all evenings. This was the first night in two weeks she hadn't been out. Sometimes they was old Chevvies, but once in a while they was an Oldsmobile or a Buick. All them fellows, just finishing school, or going on to school, or maybe in pretty good jobs even now. And Helen . . .

All to once she got up and was standing beside me. I could have trembled. She put her hand on my head.

"You mustn't mind," she said. "Please don't mind."

My elbows was on my knees and my face right down into my hands. All night I had talked and talked, but now I could not speak. If I could have moved! If I could have made myself touch her! Or if Helen had been a little bit older . . .

She run her hand through my hair once, and held it there for a few seconds. Then she said "Goodnight, Tommy."

I looked up at her and she smiled. Christ, this was enough to break the heart of a stone statue. I couldn't even smile back, and she went quietly across the room and went upstairs.

I set there by the fire until there was not a sound in the house, but the things I thought and the things I see in the coals of the fire was nothing new; they was just over and over again . . . Finally I come up here to my room. I have folded the blankets across the foot of the bed, the sheets and pillowcases. I have picked up all my own stuff and put some of it in the wastebasket and the rest in my canvas bag. I have set on the edge of the mattress, waiting for Arch and his wife to come in and get to sleep, and now I am still waiting, waiting until nearly dawn, because it is no sense starting before that.

In a few minutes now, I will pick up that bag and leave. I will walk down the road to the main highway, and pray that the first truck or car will be driven by someone who doesn't know me or Arch Lockey neither. And it won't make no difference whether it is going north or south, because there is towns in both directions, and for me one of them is going to be just as good or bad as another.